Visit us at

E-discovery: Creating and Managing an Enterprisewide Program

A Technical Guide to Digital Investigation and Litigation Support

Karen Schuler
Cathleen P. Peterson and Eva Vincze Technical Editors

David Benton
Paige Cole
Nicole Donnelly
Heather Evans
Eric Feistel

Art Gilliland
Jack Halprin
Jonathan Hassell
Greg Jordan
Liz Kofsky

Unique Passcode

94824976

PUBLISHED BY
Syngress Publishing, Inc.
Elsevier, Inc.
30 Corporate Drive
Burlington, MA 01803

E-discovery: Creating and Managing an Enterprisewide Program
A Technical Guide to Digital Investigation and Litigation Support

Printed and bound in the United Kingdom
Transferred to Digital Printing, 2010

ISBN 13: 978-1-59749-296-6

Publisher: Laura Colantoni   Page Layout and Art: SPI
Technical Editors: Cathleen Peterson   Copy Editors: Audrey Doyle, Mike McGee, and Chris Stuart
and Eva Vincze   Indexer: SPI
Cover Designer: Michael Kavish   Development Editor: Gary Byrne

For information on rights, translations, and bulk sales, contact Matt Pedersen, Sales Manager, Global Corporate Sales, at Syngress Publishing; e-mail m.pedersen@elsevier.com.

Library of Congress Cataloging-in-Publication Data
Application Submitted

Lead Author

Karen Schuler is a forensic, electronic discovery, and technology professional with more than 18 years' consulting to legal, government, and corporate entities. She's a testifying expert on the field of e-discovery, as well as a frequent speaker and author on preservation, collections, e-discovery, and document review. She regularly advises her clients on their data preservation and collection, analytical, and enterprise discovery strategies. Ms. Schuler has both national and international experience advising on issues such as defensible and admissible data preservation and collection methodologies, electronic discovery processing, document review, and data mining and analysis. As a former forensic examiner for the U.S. Securities and Exchange Commission, founder of one of the first forensic technology companies on the east coast of the U.S., and a consultant, she focuses her practice on mitigating litigation risks associated with preservation and collections throughout the electronic discovery process.

Technical Editors

Cathleen P. Peterson is a counsel at WilmerHale, one of the country's leading law firms. She is a member of the firm's Litigation and Controversy Department, specializing in large case management, e-discovery, and the intersection of law and technology. Ms. Peterson serves on the firm's Large Case Management Advisory Group and E-discovery Committee. She played a central role in developing the firm's best practices for managing, staffing, and coordinating complex matters. She also specializes in optimizing technology for large-scale litigation and investigations. Ms. Peterson has extensive experience in developing strategies for preserving, collecting, and managing electronic data. She regularly provides counsel on selecting and deploying analytical tools that can be used to enhance legal review, generate efficiencies, mitigate risk, and leverage technology to facilitate rapid case assessment. Ms. Peterson's practice includes multimillion-dollar SEC investigations, complex litigation, and internal investigations. She also provides counseling on regulatory compliance and data retention policies. Ms. Peterson serves on advisory councils for a number of vendors in the e-discovery space. Prior to developing her focus on electronic discovery, Ms. Peterson spent more than a dozen years representing U.S. and foreign airlines, online travel service providers, shippers, and other businesses in their commercial activities and dealings with the U.S. government, with a focus on regulatory compliance and administrative litigation.

Eva Vincze, PhD, directs the Master's of Forensic Sciences programs in security management and high-technology crime investigations at The George Washington University, in Washington, D.C. She designed, developed, and implemented one of the first graduate-level programs in digital forensics as well as several innovative training programs for international and national government and law enforcement groups. Dr. Vincze has presented and taught at a variety of forensic science seminars and workshops across the United States, Europe, and the Middle East. She is a member of the International High Technology Crime Investigation Association (HTCIA), the American Society of Training and Development (ASTD), and the Federal Bureau of Investigation's Citizen's Academy. She is a board member for the Mid-Atlantic High Technology Crime Investigations Association. She has actively participated on a number of digital forensics certification and accreditation committees. Her present research activity is focused on the use of technology and gaming to enhance education in the forensic sciences, including the design of simulations and virtual crime scenes.

Contributing Authors

David Benton served his country as a counterintelligence special agent. He was deployed into numerous theaters of operation, and his unit was awarded the Meritorious Unit Citation by the director of central intelligence, John Deutch. After five years in the military and traveling extensively, he was honorably discharged. He joined the Georgia Bureau of Investigation as a forensic computer specialist. He was eventually promoted to a supervisor's position in the bureau's Internet Crimes Against Children Task Force. He has conducted computer forensic examinations on several high-profile investigations, including the Dewin Brown investigation, computer intrusions at a major educational institution, and numerous other cases. He has testified as an expert witness in more than a dozen trials. David is an associate editor of *The Journal of Applied Digital Forensics & eDiscovery* and the coauthor of *A Practical Guide to Computer Forensics*. David holds his CFCE, EnCE, and CISSP certifications.

Paige Cole is a legal specialist and discovery compliance specialist for The Williams Companies, a Fortune 500 energy company headquartered in Tulsa, OK. Ms. Cole has more than 10 years of litigation experience in the areas of complex commercial litigation, securities, labor and employment, and ERISA litigation. For the past three years, Ms. Cole has been focused on e-discovery, including the creation and implementation of her company's discovery response team, which was formed in 2007.

Nicole Donnelly is a director in the Electronic Evidence Consulting group of FTI's Technology practice and is based in Washington, D.C. Ms. Donnelly's areas of expertise include computer forensics, data extraction and analysis, and computer technology. Ms. Donnelly gained 10 years of expertise in computer forensics with the federal government in issues ranging from national security objectives to securities fraud. In her 12 years of work in computer forensics, Ms. Donnelly has accumulated extensive experience providing life-cycle support for computer forensic requirements and data extraction. Ms. Donnelly has acquired several hundred computer images from a variety of computer media and has performed numerous examinations with a variety of commercially available and proprietary forensic software packages. She has applied this experience to electronic discovery in order to provide full client support in data identification, collection, analysis, format and file system conversions, online hosting, and production. She has worked extensively with Windows and Macintosh computers, Windows-based server environments, and tape data. Prior to joining FTI, Ms. Donnelly was a contractor to the U.S. Securities and Exchange Commission and a computer forensic analyst with Safe Harbor Systems. She also spent 12 years with the Central Intelligence Agency traveling extensively in support of the Directorate of Science and Technology and the Directorate of Operations. Ms. Donnelly holds B.A. degrees in computer science and art history from Rutgers College, Rutgers University. She also studied at the University of Reading, England. Her postgraduate education includes specialized government training, EnCase and Access Data forensic training, Macintosh forensic training, and participation in technical seminars. She is a Certified Computer Examiner (CCE), an EnCase Certified Examiner (EnCE), a Global Information Assurance Certification Certified Forensics Analyst (GCFA), and a member of the Mid-Atlantic High Technology Crime Investigation Association.

Heather Evans is senior counsel and director of discovery for The Williams Companies, a Fortune 500 energy company headquartered in Tulsa, OK. Ms. Evans has 15 years of litigation experience working as outside counsel and corporate counsel in the areas of complex commercial litigation, securities, insurance defense, and ERISA litigation. Additionally, Ms. Evans authored the Antitrust Section update in the State Antitrust Practices and Statutes in 2000. In the past three years, Ms. Evans' focus has been on e-discovery. She is a speaker at conferences on various e-discovery topics and heads up her company's Discovery Response Team, which she formed in 2007.

Eric Feistel is a marketing and public relations professional and writer with more than 12 years' experience in the high-tech and litigation support industries, including the fields of electronic discovery, information security and compliance, backup and disaster recovery, and computer networking. Over the years, Mr. Feistel has authored or contributed to numerous IT- and legal-focused articles, white papers, Web seminars, case studies, and reference guides regarding leading technologies and best practices for information management. He is currently the product marketing manager at ONSITE[3,] where he manages marketing programs for the company's full range of electronic evidence solutions. In this role, he provides a number of online educational resources on electronic discovery and frequently provides content for detailed responses to RFI/RFP requests from leading law firms and Fortune 500 corporations. Before joining ONSITE[3], Mr. Feistel served at RenewData, where he managed continuing legal education courses about electronic discovery and managed marketing programs for the company's ActiveVault evidence management solutions.

Art Gilliland is the vice president of product management for the Symantec Information Foundation and Compliance teams. His teams are responsible for product strategy and market development. His teams also define the product road maps through close interaction with customers and partners. Mr. Gilliland joined Symantec through the acquisition of IMlogic, the industry leader for instant messaging security and management. One of the original IMlogic team members in 2002, Gilliland served as the vice president of products and marketing. In this role, he led product management, strategic alliances, and marketing demand generation. Mr. Gilliland is the author of several key patents for instant messaging security. He earned a B.A. in economics from Carleton College and an MBA from the Harvard Business School.

Veeral Gosalia is a managing director in the Electronic Evidence Consulting group of FTI's Forensic and Litigation Consulting practice and is based in London. Mr. Gosalia's areas of expertise include data extraction, data analysis, computer forensics, and e-discovery. He has assisted attorneys and corporations in understanding the issues surrounding electronic evidence, including the acquisition, analysis, and production of data. His industry experience includes the health care, consumer and industrial goods, entertainment, biotech, food retail and service, hospitality, and insurance sectors. Mr. Gosalia has extensive computer forensics experience. He has assisted on matters related to the forensic acquisition and examination of computer systems, e-mail, and various types of computer media. He has acquired several hundred computer images and coordinated seizure efforts across the world. He has experience dealing with EU data privacy issues in regards to performing computer acquisitions and tape restorations. He has served as an expert witness and provided expert reports in matters related to evidence destruction and theft, spoliation, and chain-of-custody issues. Mr. Gosalia has extensive data extraction and analysis experience. In this capacity, he specializes in the extraction of data from a variety of database systems and accounting packages to provide rapid access for analysis. He has built databases and developed processes to detect fraud in insurance claim filings, accounting data, and financial transactions. He has developed automated procedures to identify preference payments in relation to bankruptcies. Experience in this area includes the analysis of 1.6 million electronic medical claims for insurance abuse.

Jack Halprin is the director of e-discovery for Autonomy. He manages the product line strategy for Autonomy's Legal Hold and Early Case Assessment solutions, speaking frequently on enterprise legal risk management and e-discovery at industry events and seminars. Mr. Halprin is actively involved in the Electronic Discovery Reference Model (EDRM) forum, currently leading the EDRM Metrics 3 working group. With a B.A. in chemistry from Yale University, a J.D. from the University of California-Los Angeles, and certifications from the California, Connecticut, Virginia, and Patent Bars, Jack has varied expertise that lends itself well to both the legal and technical aspects of electronic discovery collection and preservation. Prior to joining Autonomy, Mr. Halprin was with Guidance Software as senior product marketing manager/product manager for e-discovery, where he developed business partnerships, drove product development, conducted research, and created integrated marketing efforts for EnCase eDiscovery. While at LexisNexis Applied Discovery, Mr. Halprin served as Corporate Electronic Discovery Specialist, increasing company knowledge of e-discovery-related topics and delivering continuing legal education sessions for corporate legal departments. Prior to working in the e-discovery field, Mr. Halprin worked for BAR/BRI Bar Review, where he created and launched a Patent Bar Review program and delivered lectures for both the patent bar exam and state bar exams. He also was a litigation associate at Santa Monica's Haight, Brown & Bonesteel.

Jonathan Hassell is an author, consultant, and speaker residing in Charlotte, NC. Jonathan's previous published works include *RADIUS* and *Learning Windows Server 2003* for O'Reilly Media and *Hardening Windows* for Apress. His work is seen regularly in popular periodicals, such as Microsoft's *TechNet* magazine, *PC Pro*, *SecurityFocus*, and *Windows IT Pro* magazine. He speaks around the world on topics such as networking, security, and Windows administration.

Greg Jordan is the director of litigation support for Arnold & Porter, LLP. Mr. Jordan consults with legal teams regarding the use of technology to manage document-intensive litigation matters from discovery through trial. With 20 years of experience in the field of litigation support, Mr. Jordan brings a wealth of knowledge and unique perspective to his position. Prior to this, role Mr. Jordan was a senior project manager at Howrey & Simon, where he served as liaison between legal teams and litigation support staff. At Howrey, he conducted design meetings and monitored technology-related activities to ensure cost-effective, client-oriented outcomes. Mr. Jordan received his B.A. in international studies from George Mason University.

Liz Kofsky is a program manager with worldwide responsibility for Open Text's Content Lifecycle Management and Records Management solutions, including business planning, go-to-market execution, and product strategy. Ms. Kofsky holds a bachelor of commerce from McGill University and an MBA from the University of Ottawa. She has spent 15 years in information technology, specializing in records management.

Cheryl McKinnon is responsible for go-to-market strategies for the flagship Livelink ECM Collaborative Content Management product suite at Open Text™ Corporation (NASDAQ: OTEX, TSX: OTC), the largest independent provider of enterprise content management (ECM) software and solutions. Open Text supports approximately 46,000 customers and millions of users in many of the world's largest companies, government agencies, and professional service firms. Open Text's Livelink ECM® solutions unite people, processes, and information, helping organizations improve productivity, automate processes, and manage large volumes of documents, e-mail, and other content. Cheryl has a special interest in the challenges facing the information worker in the increasingly electronic work environment. She works closely with marketing, sales, and product specialists to research current and emerging challenges in information management and to expand market awareness of enterprise content management technologies and strategies. Cheryl brings more than 14 years of experience in the content management area with Open Text, previously Hummingbird and PC DOCS. She has several years of market and requirements research in addition to experience in consulting and training. She is actively involved with key industry associations such as AIIM and ARMA. Ms. McKinnon holds a B.A (honors) from the University of Winnipeg and a master of arts from Carleton University. She also has completed required coursework for a PhD at the University of Ottawa.

Contents

Foreword

Have you wondered what it takes to implement or expand a corporate e-discovery program? Consider this point: if you understand where your electronically stored information (ESI) resides, the format in which it is stored, the amount of ESI your organization actually has, how accessible it is, your ability to search and extract it from enterprise systems (as well as local hard drives), and how to deliver that data to a vendor or to process it yourself internally, then you're probably well ahead of the curve. But if that's not you, you're really not alone in wondering what to do next. Over the last couple of years, corporations have taken a leading interest in electronic discovery (e-discovery) by mandating their preferred vendors for processing and review, internalizing their preservation and collection methodologies, and attempting to limit the overall scope of the document review process. With this new trend for internal proliferation, enterprise e-discovery technologies are becoming more widely available and accepted. However, the advancements in these technologies have not really caught up with the needs. Although there are very good technologies available for enterprise preservation, search, and identification, no one "silver bullet" technology currently provides the complete package from preservation to review and production. This is not to say that there are not some good vendors out there that can effectively span the spectrum with an extensive range of offerings, but again, no one technology platform has yet been offered that can single-handedly cope with all possible scenarios for e-discovery. Therefore, one of the goals of this book is to provide an objective toolkit for corporate teams to be able understand today's available e-discovery methods and technologies.

Another area of consideration is that the e-discovery landscape has changed significantly over the last 10 years. With cases such as *Zubulake v UBS Warburg* and *Coleman v. Morgan Stanley*, the courts have identified that spoliation will not be tolerated and that e-discovery responsiveness and due diligence are requirements. As professionals in this industry, we take this very seriously in order to ensure that our clients or our own companies submit admissible and defensible evidence. Complicating matters is that the e-discovery field is currently undergoing rapid growth with a plethora of new vendors, technologies, and new "experts" appearing on the scene. Care must be taken in selecting the right solutions you need, as some of the new choices available today are from organizations with only limited experience in the e-discovery field. For companies that are starting an e-discovery program, the task will be to identify those professionals who are truly familiar with this industry as well as the types of pitfalls that must be navigated. But because the demand for expertise seems to be exceeding the supply, we bring you the introduction of this book, which was created to enable legal and technology professionals to gain a working knowledge of the necessary components for initiating or expanding their e-discovery programs and learn how to obtain tools to manage their collections, document review processes, and productions.

Ten years ago, it was common to forensically acquire hard drives that on average held about 10 gigabytes of electronic documents. As the years went by and ESI became a larger issue (primarily due to the growth of electronically transmitted documents and communications), the requirements for collecting and preserving ESI have expanded considerably. For example, today an average hard drive can hold approximately 60 to 80 gigabytes of electronic documents, which includes many more e-mail messages than we would have seen 10 years ago. According to research conducted by The Radicati Group for one of its recent studies, in 2003 users spent about 17% of their day managing e-mail; in 2006 that number grew to 26%, and it is projected that by 2009 users will spend approximately 41% of their day managing e-mail. Radicati further estimated that in all of 2006, approximately 183 billion e-mail messages were sent, and with an increase expected every year in the amount of e-mail being sent, our need to find new e-discovery solutions, technologies, and methodologies has also dramatically increased. With every e-mail message, there is a storage requirement, and depending on your company's infrastructure and policies, you might need to consider searching for e-mail not only on the e-mail server itself but also on hard drives, files servers (both home and common directories), loose media, backup tapes, and perhaps a home computer from time to time. But e-mail is really only part of the equation you must consider. With e-mail comes attachments, and with attachments, you must consider numerous file types, databases, encryption, and password protection.

To facilitate your quest to come to grips with e-discovery, we have assembled a team of experts for the topics covered in this book. The contributors include corporate legal team experts on creating e-discovery programs, outside counsel with years of experience assisting clients on e-discovery struggles, expert litigation support professionals who know how to get productions done right the first time, forensic experts, and also consultants and strategists who work with some of the largest organizations in the world. This team will for a short time become your advisers and strategists by providing insight into the various e-discovery tools and techniques. Part of the reason this team of astounding professionals were gathered in order to create this book was to be able to share information that is not routinely disseminated throughout our industry. With that, our goal is to provide you with enough information to answer the questions you may have about your e-discovery program and to help you to possibly identify new methods and technologies that can assist in your decision-making process.

The following are just some of the important topics addressed within the pages of this book.

- New trends throughout the e-discovery industry
- Information management tools and techniques
- Ways to bridge the gaps between information management and e-discovery
- Methods in creating a discovery response team

- Checklists, forms, and tools that can be utilized for preservation and collections management

- Tactics for defensibly collecting evidence

- Systems and methods used to identify and search electronically stored information (ESI) residing on enterprise systems

- Early case assessment tools to reduce the overall population of ESI

- Considerations for selecting a document review platform

- Production considerations and ideas

With this book in hand, your team will have a valuable resource in order to take those next steps for your e-discovery program. But we should also preface that this industry is in a state of rapid change and, as new technologies become available, updates to the content of this book will be a necessity. For the time being, the book should help you to better understand some of the cutting-edge technologies available today from a range of companies, such as Autonomy, CaseLogistix, Clearwell Systems, Deep Dive Technologies, Guidance Software, FTI Consulting, Index Engines, IndyGo, LexisNexis, MetaLINCS (Seagate's E-Discovery Solutions Division), ONSITE³, Open Text, PSS-Systems, Symantec, and WorkProducts. We thank all of these organizations—although certainly this is not an exhaustive list—for providing additional insight and content for this book and for their thought leadership within this growing industry.

— *Karen Schuler*

Chapter 1

Trends in Enterprise E-discovery from the Corporate Perspective

Solutions in this chapter:

- **The Focus on Litigation Preparedness**
- **The Emergence of Better Enterprise Search**
- **The Threat of Discovery Trolls**
- **Centralization of E-discovery Efforts**
- **Folksonomies**
- **Enterprise Software and Litigation Support Platforms**
- **Insourcing the E-discovery Process**
- **Automated E-discovery Review**
- **Records Retention and Accessibility**
- **The Market and Profession Overall**

- ☑ **Summary**
- ☑ **Solutions Fast Track**
- ☑ **Frequently Asked Questions**

Introduction

E-discovery is such a broad and encompassing topic that enhancements, improvements, and other changes in corporate best practices are emerging on a near daily basis. Major areas where corporations are looking at e-discovery and changes to its landscape include:

- Focusing on litigation preparedness

- The emergence of better enterprise searches

- Complications from "e-discovery trolls"

- Centralization of e-discovery activities and actions

- The emergence of folksonomies in corporate e-discovery

- The merging and mashing up of enterprise applications and litigation support applications

- Insourcing the e-discovery review process

- Completing reviews in automated ways

- Examining record accessibility and retention policies

- Taking other steps to cut e-discovery costs

Litigation is not something to take lightly, of course, and e-discovery is one of the central pieces of the puzzle. Mistakes should be as few and far between as possible. "As notable cases such as *Qualcomm v. Broadcom* and *AMD v. Intel* have shown, under the revised Federal Rules of Civil Procedure, the ramifications from e-discovery mistakes can be far-reaching," said Craig Carpenter, VP of E-discovery Solutions and General Counsel for Recommind.

As the vast amount of information in corporate databases, messaging systems, and file servers only continues to increase, that proverbial needle in the haystack is even harder to find.

In this chapter, we'll talk about how things should get easier in the next few years to come.

The Focus on Litigation Preparedness

In corporations worldwide, but especially in the United States, there is an increased focus on being prepared to respond to and vigorously defend matters surrounding pending litigation. Particularly with regard to the recently amended Federal Rules of Civil Procedure and the new requirements in e-discovery, you will find counsel and companies paying new attention to both how to avoid and how to respond to lawsuits. The FRCP, to which all companies transacting business within the United States are subject, allows that either party in a civil lawsuit may ask for the other party to produce documents or electronically stored information, or ESI, that may support its claim in the lawsuit or the defense against such a claim in a lawsuit.

Indeed, consider the following statistics on the threat of litigation looming on the horizon. The litigation threat is a large and growing problem for enterprises. Here are few indicators of the scope of the problem, based on an annual survey by the law firm Fulbright & Jaworski LLP.

- One-third of U.S. corporations are facing at least 25 lawsuits.

- 18 percent of companies are defending themselves against more than 100 lawsuits in the United States alone.

- 48 percent of companies reported they faced new regulatory proceedings within the past year.

- 40 percent of companies have been hit with at least one lawsuit in the past year with more than $20 million at stake.

Part of being prepared in this litigious age, at least from the corporate perspective, is the confidence that your colleagues can produce accurate records that the FRCP can demand at any point in time. In order to do so, rigid policies, simple and well-defined processes, and intelligent content management solutions must all operate within an overall e-discovery program. You will see companies looking to outside counsel for consultation on creating and developing these plans in order to be better prepared for any litigation that might arise. While creating this plan is a formidable challenge, there really are no alternatives, and companies are beginning to realize that sobering fact.

The Emergence of Better Enterprise Search

It has been said that there are many millionaires to be made and companies to be started in the area of enterprise search. When you consider the fact that much of our economy is based on knowledge product and not on manufacturing tangible goods and services, it is apparent that the immense amounts of information generated within businesses in this country is staggering. What's even more crippling is the thought of having to find a specific reference or narrowly relevant documents in that giant morass.

At times, it seems that user-friendly computer searching is something only Google has been able to do with any competence and simplicity. When was the last time you tried to find that key e-mail and failed? Do you remember a phrase that appeared in some document you read within the last six months but are at a loss as to where to find it? Do you even know where you would start?

The same problem faces e-discovery professionals, who often know much less than a document's owner about the content and context in which it can be found. Now software developers and computer companies are beginning to realize that search is a monster that can be tackled from a variety of different approaches. As co-workers need the ability to find information generated by their colleagues, even those located on another continent or in another time zone, or documents written in a different language, litigation support professionals also need the ability to sift through these vast piles of data with ease, accuracy, and not just a basic set of keywords.

The good news is that new enterprise search platform features are emerging to integrate with litigation support software to help corporations get their arms around their data. These platforms are starting to offer the following advances, among others:

- **Conceptual search** It is onerous to transform thoughts into computer language in order to get search results. Such an approach not only leads to frustration, but incompleteness and inaccuracy as well. Natural language search tools are emerging that actually allow professionals to query the software in a way that feels normal and comfortable to them, resulting in a better quality result set with fewer missing items and fewer false positives.

- **Automatic categorization** Imagine receiving a search result set that was automatically categorized into easy-to-read lists based on where they were found, how often they occurred, what type of result hit they are, what project they relate to, and any other "sortable" information in the metadata of the file itself? By having automatic categorization in your platform, you can easily include—or just as easily exclude—large groups of results that have relevance (or not) to your case.

- **Advanced algorithms** The very kernel of search tools—the algorithm through which the index of terms and items is created—is improving as well, making individual computers more powerful and less complex. Better search software will find more information, index it better, and return more useful result sets.

Ultimately, enterprises will be able to benefit from the legal and productivity benefits that come from merging the features of search and information management tools.

For more information on how enterprise search software itself is transforming and maturing, consider the book *Making Search Work – Implementing Web, Intranet, and Enterprise Search*, by Martin White (2007, ISBN 978-1-85604-502-2).

Tools & Traps...

Desktop Search

One wrinkle in this fabric is the emergence of desktop search products. As the popular blog Lifehacker points out, "In a world where a search box puts the entire Internet at your fingertips, it seems more pointless and inefficient than ever to drill down through your file structure when you're looking for a specific file on your hard drive. In the past few years, we've seen myriad desktop search applications designed to fill this need. But which is best? And if users see search become more and more effective, they may be more prone to:

- Organize information less and less, and
- Keep more and more information

Obviously, a lack of organization is problematic for e-discovery efforts since it promotes a certain lack of completeness to the result set. However, keeping more information than ever also runs counter to the advice of counsel in many cases. Records retention programs are important. We'll touch on them later in this chapter, but be aware that desktop search and enterprise search are not the same and may cause divergent outcomes in some situations.

The Threat of Discovery Trolls

Perhaps you know of the "patent troll" movement. According to Wikipedia, "[a] patent troll is a pejorative term used for a person or company that enforces its patents against one or more alleged infringers in a manner considered unduly aggressive or opportunistic. A related, less pejorative expression is non-practicing entity (NPE) which describes a patent owner who does not manufacture or use the patented invention."

Patent trolls work a lot like any other company that is involved in defending and monetizing a patent portfolio. However, their main objective is gaining revenue from licensing patent deals, sometimes under the threat of litigation, on existing technology—not on developing new technology that ultimately is patentable. This is accomplished in a number of ways:

- They monitor the market and watch for potentially infringing technologies.

- They examine published patent applications for signals that other firms are manufacturing potentially infringing technology.

Once they've identified a target, they start the war. First they may sue a vulnerable company that has much at stake, or limited resources for defense, mainly to establish a precedent to convince other players in the industry to enter into licensing agreements. Or, they may invoke the "shock and awe" offense and litter an industry with suits.

Now, the United States Supreme Court has recently ruled that injunctions must have a standard test of reasonableness applied rather than be granted automatically, a significant blow dealt to the legions of patent trolls. Indeed, Jessica Holzer in *Forbes* concluded, "The high court's decision deals a blow to patent trolls, which are notorious for using the threat of permanent injunction to extort hefty fees in licensing negotiations as well as huge settlements from companies they have accused of infringing. Often, those settlements can be far greater than the value of the infringing technology: Recall the $612.5 million that Canada's Research in Motion forked over to patent-holding company NTP to avoid the shutting down of its popular BlackBerry service." However, there is clearly money to be made by patent trolls.

Similarly, e-discovery trolls are emerging from the woodwork and making up a newly significant threat to firms. As e-discovery costs mount and gain attention from media outlets and news channels, there will likely be an increase in these "troll" types of lawsuits. This really hinges on the emergence of the new Federal Rules of Civil Procedure code as it pertains to e-discovery. Lexbe LC (www.lexbe.com) offers the following rundown of the new rules' significance to e-discovery:

- *Rule 26 Automatic Disclosure of ESI:* Parties in litigation must provide a copy (or description by category and location) of ESI that will support that party's claims and/or defenses.

- *Rule 26 Enhanced Meet and Confer Requirements:* Parties must meet and confer at the outset of the case to discuss their plans and proposals regarding the conduct of the litigation, including any issues relating to preservation, disclosure, or discovery of ESI, including the form in which ESI should be produced and claims of privilege, or protection as trial-preparation material.

- *Rule 26 Inadvertent Production of Privileged Information:* If discovery information is subject to a claim of privilege, or protection as privileged trial-preparation material, the party making the claim may notify any party that received the information of the claim and the basis for it. After being notified, a party is required to promptly return, sequester, or destroy the specified information and any copies it has, and is not permitted to use or disclose the information until the claim is resolved.

- *Rule 26 Production of Information "Not Reasonably Accessible":* A party need not provide discovery of ESI from sources that the party identifies as "not reasonably accessible because of undue burden or cost." The party being asked to produce ESI bears the burden of demonstrating that the information is not reasonably accessible because of undue burden or cost. Even if that showing is made, the court may nonetheless order discovery from that party if the requesting party shows good cause.

- *Rule 33 Production of ESI in Response to Interrogatories:* Rule 33 provides the option to respond to an interrogatory by specifying and producing the business records, including ESI, that contain the answer.

- *Rule 34 Production of ESI in Response to Requests for Production of Documents:* Rule 34 provides the option to respond to an interrogatory by specifying and producing the business records, including ESI, that contain the answer.

- *Rule 37 – The "Safe Harbor" Provision:* Rule 37 pertains to remedies for a party's failure to respond to, or cooperate in, discovery. Amended Rule 37 provides that, absent exceptional circumstances, a court may not impose Rule 37 sanctions on a party for failing to provide ESI lost as a result of the "routine, good faith operation of an electronic information system."

As these rules percolate through the community, some malcontents, deserving of the troll title, will take advantage of this opportunity and know that many firms cannot meet these new e-discovery requirements or would rather enter into a settlement than a costly litigation sequence. This poses a significant challenge to companies.

Centralization of E-discovery Efforts

You know that a legal hold—the notice received from counsel to an organization that suspends any regular schedule of processing data, like tape recycling—is the start of a long process. A legal hold means current or anticipated litigation, a forthcoming audit, an upcoming government investigation, or even other matters. These legal holds can affect normal business procedures that deal with active data and deserve careful attention.

With offices now being better connected and operating systems making it simpler for administrators to manage computers all around the world from a single pane of glass, law firms and in-house legal departments are beginning to realize that "remote" legal holds are a great way to ensure that potential evidence isn't spoiled, opening up the firm to a huge potential liability. These remote holds have the ability to collect and preserve "epaper" or other electronically stored information (ESI) remotely, without incurring costly travel expenses from sending people out into the field to make an image of each data custodian's computer drives, sometimes with surgical precision. With powerful software to support the process, litigation holds are easier to roll out, administer, and manage from a central location.

Some platforms are focused on delivery and acknowledgment of the preservation hold notice itself, and period reminders. As these platforms evolve, they are moving from the preservation phase into the collection phase of e-discovery as well.

Look at the e-discovery hold notice response plan shown in Figure 1.1 that the Office of Financial Management for the State of Washington is working on (retrieved from www.ofm.wa.gov/rmd/publications/ediscovresponsepln.pdf; look for a zoomed-in version and other clever insights into the hold response process):

Figure 1.1 An Example of an E-discovery Hold Notice Response Plan

Step	Responsible	Action	Task	Outcome
1	OFM and AGO Legal Team	Establish the preliminary scope and subject matter for hold notice.	1) Collect list of names involved in case (Data Custodians) 2) Establish preliminary subjects for data identification and instructions for named data custodians	Preliminary scope of the hold notice is established.
2	OFM Legal Team and OFM IsD Assistant Director	Inform OFM IsD of the Hold Notice and data subjects	Meeting of OFM Legal Team and IsD management to: 1) Review/assign roles and responsibilities for implementing the IT Hold Notice Response Process 2) Review standard data preservation plan to see if any adjustments are necessary - including standard list of potential data sources and the questionnaire used to interview each named data custodian	Clear marching orders for OFM IsD management to implement the IT Hold Notice Response Procedures
3	OFM Legal Team	Issue formal Hold Notice to the Agency involved parties.	Send message to involved parties to refrain from adherence to destruction policies for broad definition of data to preserve.	Moment the process begins
4	OFM IsD Assistant Director	Assign OFM IsD management level person to be in the role of "Electronic Data Collection Coordinator" for the case.	Provide the assigned Electronic Data Collection Coordinator the details of the case and give them clear marching orders to implement the IT Hold Notice Response Procedures	Someone is responsible for the planning preservation and collection efforts and work begins.
5	OFM IsD Electronic Data Collection Coordinator	Ensure secure storage areas for applicable electronic data are established for the case	1) Plan and, if appropriate, build case folder structure following accepted general guidelines and Checklist Template for holding unstructured electronic documents 2) Establish a voice mail hold area 3) Establish a Email hold area 4) Develop instrctions on how to use these areas for people involved in the case	1) Case electronic records storage areas are setup 2) Logging data collection efforts begins
6	OFM and AGO Legal Team	Strategically refine scope of records and means of preservation and production.	1) Revise subject areas and records to preserve based upon current knowledge and legal input. 2) Collaborate towards legal and practical decisions about measures for preservation and gathering of records given the needs of the case at hand.	Strategically refined search terms and measures for preservation and assembly of records.
7	OFM Legal Team	Follow up on initial hold notice to affected individuals. Identifying specific steps to take for preservation.	Send message to involved parties. 1) Include instructions for using the electronic record storage areas 2) Message should include overview of key process steps 3) Message should identify who is in the role of Electronic Data Collection Coordinator	Begin collection of data with the benefit of strategic decisions to refine preliminary hold.
8	OFM Legal Team and Electronic Data Collection Coordinator	Review the instructions for use of the areas setup for collecting electronic data related to the case	1) Meeting to review and document decision to proceed with Data Collection Interview 2) Draft message to Agency involved parties	Consensus on structure of data hold areas and instructions to be given to the Agency involved parties
9	Electronic Data Collection Coordinator	Complete the Data Collection Interview with all named staff as soon as possible	For each person named in the scope of the case: 1) Schedule an interview to complete the checklist 2) Document the findings 3) Communicate exactly what we will be doing with this persons data and answer any questions they may have.	1) Completed interview notes 2) Data collection underway 3) Data collection log entries completed
10	Electronic Data Collection Coordinator	Develop preliminary data collection plan	Draft plan document and electronic review with OFM Legal Team and IsD Management	Preliminary data collection plan completed
11	Electronic Data Collection Coordinator & OFM Legal Team and AGO	Analize results of the interviews	Meeting to adjust scope and/or data collection plan if necessary	Data collection plan completed and clear direction to the Electronic Data Collection Coordinator to proceed with data collection
12	Electronic Data Collection Coordinator and IT support staff	Collect electronic data sources following the data collection plan	1) Copy snap-shot of each persons personal Folder (I Drive, Local Drive) or pertinent portions of that drive, Inbox, and shared Work Area TECHNOLOGY To Use: Local Drive = Ghost Network storage = RoBo Copy Inbox = ExMerge 2) Inform OFM Legal Team upon completion	1) Snap-shot data collection completed. 2) Disaster Recovery backup of the data collection has been made. 3) Data is on-line and on backup tape at this point. 4) Snap-shot process is complete
13	Electronic Data Collection Coordinator & OFM Legal Team	Develop on-going data collection plan	Draft plan document and electronic review with OFM Legal Team and IsD Management	Monitoring Plan completed
14	OFM Legal Team and Electronic Data Collection Coordinator	Monitor on-going data collection efforts performed by involved parties	Involved parties are using the copy areas identified in the hold notice.	Tracking as needed.

Wouldn't it be simpler if this plan and the respective action steps within it could be carried out from a central location, all on managed computers? That's definitely the way legal holds are trending in the coming years. For instance, products like Desktop Legal Hold, that are already on the market, try to solve this need. Desktop Legal Hold allows companies to lock down electronic documents and files that reside on remote laptops and desktops, but not on corporate network file shares or other "bins" of information.

Folksonomies

Folksonomy sounds like a strange word, but it is indeed a growing phenomenon that is rising against stingy crusty machine categorization. Folksonomy, which is also known as collaborative tagging, social classification, social indexing, and social tagging, involves a community of users collectively creating and managing tags that are assigned to certain content for the purposes of categorization and organization. Unlike machines, where traditionally material is indexed by subject and accessed by keywords that attempt to match up content with a query string, folksonomic tagging allows users to create their own tags, which are freely chosen and not part of a strictly controlled vocabulary. The idea is simply that if the ultimate users of the content can categorize the content themselves when a document is created or stored, such tags will make searches more accurate and generate many efficiencies.

A bit of history… Along with the Web 2.0 phenomenon spearheaded by Internet visionary Tim O'Reilly, folksonomies began becoming popular in 2004. The biggest example is the social bookmarking site del.icio.us, which allows users to save bookmarks of interesting Internet and Web sites they find in their surfing and associate tags with them. Other del.icio.us users can then search on tags or specific users they are interested in and in the resulting response find Web sites that are probably more relevant than the results a general Web search would likely provide. Tagging in this sense is simple and not very burdensome and results in a new way to consume information for end users. The site is shown in Figure 1.2.

Figure 1.2 The Delicious.com Web Site

In addition, tag clouds can be used to visually augment a tag presentation and show the most used tags in any given period. A tag cloud is shown in Figure 1.3.

Figure 1.3 A Tag Cloud

Programmes of study Museum award for RCMG co-ordinated cultural exhibition Continuing 40th Anniversary Scholarships MA/PGDip in Learning and Visitor Studies in Museums & galleries Update 1 (pdf 700Kb) Professional Development Museum Studies Home UNIVERSITY HOME online form bildersuche Research Museological Review Jobs Desk MAINTAINER PhD Studentships Staff List Rethinking Disability Representation. UNIVERSITY SEARCH RCMG staff pages £1.7million research grant shared by Museum Studies Lecturer Bookshop Museum & Society Departments Funding Opportunities webpage UNIVERSITY INDEX A-Z Leicester Study Series for Professional Development. UNIVERSITY HELP Masters Study Update 2 (pdf 1.65MB Representing and Interpreting Culture: World Arts/Museum Ethnography Material Worlds : a conference in honour of Prof Susan Pearce; 15-17 Dec 2008. Research webpages New Publications Museum & Society AHRC Masters PhD students RCMG, the Research Centre for Museums and Galleries PhD studies New MA/PGDip in Digital Heritage: Contact us

The following are two advantages of folksonomies:

- Users can discover who created a tag, and see the other tags this person created. In this way, users often find another user's tag set in line with their own interests, work, or habits, and then follow that user's tagging approach. This increases the accuracy and usefulness of the overall tag set.

- Enterprise users will increasingly look to incorporate peer feedback, also possible with tagging, and usage habits to determine the relevancy of information. Folksonomic tagging provides a way for these methods to be incorporated into enterprise search and e-discovery support platforms.

This type of social tagging is sure to make e-discovery search and review efforts easier.

Enterprise Software and Litigation Support Platforms

Many e-discovery experts predict that enterprise applications, including line-of-business applications and corporate business support systems, as well as litigation support platforms will become better at "working together." Since businesses use so many disparate applications, knowledge and work product is everywhere—and communication is everywhere, too. Expect software that allows for more aspects of litigation support, and e-discovery controls to be configured and managed directly from that software. Also expect more litigation support software to integrate with other applications and be able to support data retrieval and review from that software.

Insourcing the E-discovery Process

The spiraling costs of e-discovery are prompting more corporate legal teams—the in-house counsel— to do more e-discovery work in-house, as opposed to outsourcing that type of work to outside firms. In addition, the market for e-discovery specialists, including lawyers and managers, will increase as firms bring this work under their own roof, especially litigation with smaller, more manageable collections during the discovery process. Corporations are increasingly turning to outside firms in consulting roles, helping to identify best practices and procedures surrounding the almost inevitable process of responding to a suit. Exceptions to this type of movement include larger, more invasive suits that require larger collections or bring greater risk.

In-sourcing this type of work has also been made easier by the entrance of Web-based software platforms that allow discovery tasks to be performed from a variety of locations, even using teams in different geographical locations. In addition, knowledge management portals like Microsoft Office SharePoint Server and others are being installed in corporations worldwide, making this synthesis a bit easier to manage and perform.

Choosing an e-discovery review platform is increasingly important as well, and is a topic we touch on later in this book. A number of market entrants, such as Clearwell Systems, have helped define a data map so teams can easily find where data is located and introduce it into the result set.

Automated E-discovery Review

Another trend for e-discovery in the coming few years is automated review. If you have ever stepped through the review process, you know it is typically the most expensive phase of the discovery process. This type of review can be automated in such a way that, in some scenarios, it is more accurate and many times faster than a manual human-based review.

You will see outside firms offering services to create, develop, test, and document procedures that automated review systems will follow, a necessary step if your firm must prove the efficacy of any automated reviews you use.

Of course, while automated systems may ultimately be able to assign relevancy with accuracy equivalent to, or better than, sentient counsel, a firm must still budget for, and prepare for, an appropriate privilege review. Recall that the FRCP modifications allow for clawback agreements, but there is still a great disadvantage for a party to produce responsive, but otherwise privileged, data.

Records Retention and Accessibility

As more cases play themselves out in the court system, and companies and their employees encounter negative consequences for communicating in certain ways, enterprises are starting to realize that the value of retaining information drops like a rock when compared to the threat of that information being used against the firm. In addition, retained data is expensive to manage and costly to store, given rising energy prices.

Of course, e-mail messages are generally the most damning records in question during a suit, and this is especially true in heavily regulated industries like financial services and energy. (Remember Enron? Or the auction-rate securities suits?) Over the coming years, you will see technology teams and in-house legal affairs teams working together to decide the best way to archive and otherwise retain messages to balance business need and productivity concerns with potential exposure to costly litigation. Specifically, many corporations may make choices between archiving e-mails—storing them after they are sent or received—or journaling e-mails in real-time as they are received or sent.

We mentioned earlier in the chapter the problem of keeping information in a disorganized fashion. This type of behavior is at odds with best practices in records retention and content management, and as businesswide solutions like Microsoft Office SharePoint Server continue to mature and become simpler to use, you will see corporations looking to them to address the problem of free-form unstructured data that resides in many, sometimes even hidden, places in the business. Retention management is also made easier when:

- Retention policies are clear, simple, and easy to execute. They are not littered with complex nested logic.

- Data that is covered by those retention policies is stored in locations that are simple to find and well known. This results in a confidence that you have a complete view of your core knowledge set.

- Software is acquired that assists you in taking a proactive approach to records management and retention. Such software, from companies like Exterro and Orchestria, is available now.

NOTE

If you are interested in how users of Microsoft Office SharePoint Server can manage retention policies, see the downloadable book available from Microsoft's Web site at http://technet.microsoft.com/en-us/library/cc262578.aspx.

You will also see a focus on contractors, vendors, and other outside firms expiring potentially sensitive corporate data after their work is complete.

Corporations are also looking into potential exposure in their backup and archiving programs. It has been argued by some that backup tapes are still accessible under the new FRCP rules. Companies will turn to outside firms to help them restore data on legacy media that is not easily readable to a more accessible medium, and then catalog the contents and expire the content as necessary.

Overall, many businesses are determining that it makes more sense to invest in litigation readiness and records retention consultants than to engage in costly settlements or expansive suits. This is a challenging and expensive area, but the alternatives are uncertain and almost definitely more expensive.

The Market and Profession Overall

E-discovery is absolutely on every firm's radar, be it through their consultants or through discovery teams assigned in-house. For evidence of this, examine the following trends and statistics outlined in a whitepaper titled "A Conversation with Corporate Counsel: E-discovery Trends and Perspectives," by Ari Kaplan:

- 39 percent of respondents indicated that their general counsel has little to no involvement in the management of e-discovery.

- 75 percent of respondents ranked their organizations at a 7 or higher (out of 10) in terms of how well their legal holds are enforced, documented, re-issued, and monitored.

- Legal cost drivers are fairly evenly divided between patent/IP (28.6 percent), products liability/ class action (25 percent), and regulatory investigation/compliance (28.6 percent) matters.

- 89 percent of respondents work in legal departments that have an e-discovery response team in place.

- A majority of respondents (61 percent) did not feel that their organizations were particularly impacted by the amendments to the Federal Rules of Civil Procedure (ranking the impact at 5 [out of 10] or below).

- The relationship between legal and IT is improving dramatically. 79 percent of the respondents reported working "very close" with IT, and 61 percent noted that legal is "often" consulted when IT adopts new technology.

- 61 percent of companies have completed a litigation readiness assessment, most with the assistance of an outside source.

- 43 percent of the respondents admitted they did not know how much the company is spending in its entirety on e-discovery.

- 46 percent of the respondents do not have a long-term agreement in place with a preferred e-discovery services provider.

- Only 14 percent of the respondents engage national e-discovery counsel. The others use outside counsel for each specific case.

Corporations are also taking the following measures in order to get their arms around e-discovery costs:

- Establishing a standing data pool or e-mail archive for frequently recurring litigation;

- Hiring in-house e-discovery counsel and/or paralegal project managers to help oversee the discovery process and ensure that outside firms are operating in an efficient manner;

- Creating a corporate e-discovery steering board, including corporate legal, IT, and HR representatives to craft a holistic and well-integrated response to litigation;

- Establishing preferred vendor relationships with a short list of e-discovery vendors, contract attorney agencies, and law firms to control costs;

- Considering the use of off-shore attorneys for simple review or engaging firms that offer an "all-in" cost per page for routine attorney review;

- Engaging companies that bring together linguists, database specialists, and attorneys to cull data pools before preproduction attorney review begins;

- Adopting e-billing systems so they can better analyze vendor and law firm expenses for e-discovery tasks;

- Commissioning a survey of legal retention requirements to hone the types of documents and data that are subject to long retention;

- Drastically reducing the length of time that backup tapes are retained;

- Engaging consultants to assess their litigation preparedness and integrate their litigation and records management processes to reduce the volume of data sent outside for processing and review.

Summary

E-discovery is such a broad and encompassing topic that there are enhancements, improvements, and other changes in corporate best practices emerging on a nearly daily basis. Particularly with regard to the recently amended Federal Rules of Civil Procedure and the new requirements in e-discovery, you will find counsel and companies paying new attention to both how to avoid and how to respond to lawsuits. The FRCP, to which all companies transacting business within the United States are subject, allows that either party in a civil lawsuit may ask for the other party to produce documents or electronically stored information (ESI) that may support its claim in the lawsuit or the defense against such a claim in a lawsuit.

With all of these requirements, we looked in this chapter at the major areas where corporations are looking at e-discovery and changes to its landscape from their perspective. Specifically, we discussed:

- Litigation preparedness
- The emergence of better enterprise search
- Complications from "e-discovery trolls"
- Centralization of e-discovery activities and actions
- The emergence of folksonomies in corporate e-discovery
- The merging and mashing up of enterprise applications and litigation support applications
- The insourcing of the e-discovery review process
- The completion of reviews in automated ways
- The examination of record accessibility and retention policies
- Other steps to take to cut e-discovery costs

Litigation is not something to take lightly, of course, and because discovery is one of the central pieces of the puzzle, mistakes should be as few and far between as possible. Of course, that task is made more difficult by the vast amount of information in corporate databases, messaging systems, and file servers; that amount only continues to increase, making that proverbial needle in the haystack even harder to find.

Solutions Fast Track

The Focus on Litigation Preparedness

☑ Part of being prepared in this litigious age, at least from the corporate perspective, is the confidence that your colleagues can produce accurate records that the FRCP can demand at any point in time.

☑ In order to do so, rigid policies, simple and well-defined processes, and intelligent content management solutions must all operate within an overall e-discovery program.

☑ You will see companies looking to outside counsel for consultation on creating and developing these plans in order to be better prepared for any litigation that might arise.

The Emergence of Better Enterprise Search

☑ New enterprise search platform features are emerging to integrate with litigation support software to help corporations get their arms around their data.

☑ These platforms are starting to offer the following advances, among others: conceptual search, automatic categorization, and advanced search algorithms.

The Threat of Discovery Trolls

☑ E-discovery trolls are emerging from the woodwork and making up a newly significant threat to firms.

☑ As e-discovery costs mount and gain attention from media outlets and news channels, there will likely be an increase in these "troll" types of lawsuits.

Centralization of E-discovery Efforts

☑ With offices now being better connected and operating systems making it simpler for administrators to manage computers all around the world from a single pane of glass, law firms and in-house legal departments are beginning to realize that "remote" legal holds are a great way to ensure that potential evidence isn't spoiled, opening up the firm to a huge potential liability.

☑ These remote holds have the ability to collect and preserve "e-paper" or other ESI remotely, without incurring costly travel expenses from sending people out into the field to make an image of each data custodian's computer drives, sometimes with surgical precision.

☑ With powerful software to support the process, litigation holds are easier to roll out, administer, and manage from a central location.

Folksonomies

☑ Folksonomy sounds like a strange word, but it is indeed a growing phenomenon that is rising against stingy, crusty machine categorization.

☑ Folksonomy, which is also known as collaborative tagging, social classification, social indexing, and social tagging, involves a community of users collectively creating and managing tags that are assigned to certain content for the purposes of categorization and organization.

☑ This type of social tagging is sure to make e-discovery search and review efforts easier.

Enterprise Software and Litigation Support Platforms

☑ Many e-discovery experts predict that enterprise applications, including line of business applications and corporate business support systems, and litigation support platforms will become better at "working together."

☑ Because businesses use so many disparate applications, knowledge and work product are everywhere—and communication is everywhere, too.

☑ Expect software that allows for more aspects of litigation support and e-discovery controls to be configured and managed directly from that software.

Insourcing the E-discovery Process

☑ The spiraling costs of e-discovery are prompting more corporate legal teams—the in-house counsel—to do more e-discovery work in-house, as opposed to outsourcing that type of work to outside firms.

☑ In addition, the market for e-discovery specialists, including lawyers and managers, will increase as firms bring this work under their own roof, especially litigation with smaller, more manageable collections during the discovery process.

Automated E-discovery Review

☑ Another trend for e-discovery in the coming few years is automated review.

☑ If you have ever stepped through the review process, you know it is typically the most expensive phase of the discovery process.

☑ This type of review can be automated in such a way that, in some scenarios, it is more accurate and many times faster than a manual, human-based review.

Records Retention and Accessibility

☑ Over the coming years, you will see technology teams and in-house legal affairs teams working together to decide the best way to archive and otherwise retain messages to balance business need and productivity concerns with potential exposure to costly litigation.

☑ As businesswide solutions like Microsoft Office SharePoint Server continue to mature and become simpler to use, you will see corporations looking to them to address the problem of free-form, unstructured data that resides in many, sometimes even hidden, places in the business.

Frequently Asked Questions

Q: What can enterprise search applications bring to an e-discovery platform?

A: These platforms are starting to offer the following advances, among others:

- Conceptual search. Natural language search tools are emerging that actually allow professionals to query the software in a way that feels normal and comfortable to them, resulting in a better quality result set with fewer missing items and fewer false positives.

- Automatic categorization. By having automatic categorization in your platform, you can easily include—or just as easily exclude—large groups of results that have relevance (or not) to your case.

- Advanced algorithms. Better search software will find more information, index it better, and return more useful result sets.

Q: I've heard about the term "folksonomy" in the context of Web 2.0. What exactly is it?

A: Folksonomy, which is also known as collaborative tagging, social classification, social indexing, and social tagging, involves a community of users collectively creating and managing tags that are assigned to certain content for the purposes of categorization and organization. Folksonomic tagging allows users to create their own tags that are freely chosen and not part of a strictly controlled vocabulary. The idea is simply that if the ultimate users of the content can categorize the content themselves when a document is created or stored, such tags will make searches more accurate and generate many efficiencies.

Q: What about regular productivity applications— is anything there to make e-discovery, and particularly review, a bit easier?

A: Expect software that allows for more aspects of litigation support and e-discovery controls to be configured and managed directly from that software. Also expect more litigation support software to integrate with other applications and be able to support data retrieval and review from that software.

Q: E-mail messages are problematic in discovery. What is coming down the pike in terms of managing this exposure?

A: Of course, e-mail messages are generally the most damning records in question during a suit, and this is especially true in heavily regulated industries like financial services and energy. (Remember Enron? Or the auction-rate securities suits?) Over the coming years, you will see technology teams and in-house legal affairs teams working together to decide the best way to archive and otherwise retain messages to balance business need and productivity concerns with potential exposure to costly litigation. Specifically, many corporations may make choices between archiving e-mail messages—storing them after they are sent or received—or journaling e-mail messages in real time as they are received or sent.

Q: Do you see e-discovery becoming a more in-house procedure or will much of it continue to be outsourced?

A: The spiraling costs of e-discovery are prompting more corporate legal teams—the in-house counsel—to do more e-discovery work in-house, as opposed to outsourcing that type of work to outside firms. In addition, the market for e-discovery specialists, including lawyers and managers, will increase as firms bring this work under their own roofs, especially litigation with smaller, more manageable collections during the discovery process.

Chapter 2

Managing Information and Records in An Enterprise

Solutions in this chapter:

- Historical Evolution of ECM
- The Age of Compliance: Using ECM for Information Governance
- The Technology Components of ECM

☑ Summary

☑ Solutions Fast Track

☑ Frequently Asked Questions

Introduction: What Is Enterprise Content Management?

Enterprise content management (ECM) is a recent term created by software vendors looking to describe the value of an integrated approach to capturing and managing unstructured business content. The term was adopted more formally as an accepted technology category circa 2004, largely shaped by the publication of a market and vendor survey by analysts at Gartner.[1] Since 2004, the term has become widely accepted by software vendors, research analysts across the globe, and private and public sector enterprises. ECM is an integrated set of technologies and best practices intended to help business protect, manage, preserve and dispose of its physical and electronic intellectual corporate content. Leading ECM vendors are able to extend this management and control to a wide range of unstructured content types – paper files, word-processing or spreadsheet documents, graphics and images, e-mail, or Web site content – any of the day to day content created by information workers as part of typical business activities.

The Historical Evolution of ECM

Prior to the adoption of ECM as a broad category for integrated content management tools, most software vendors specialized in one or more technology components of what would evolve into the comprehensive definition of ECM: imaging, document management, records management, workflow, Web content management or search. The roots of these specialized components go back nearly three decades. As the personal computer became mainstream in the 1980s, many businesses invested in desktop systems equipped with word-processing, spreadsheet, data entry and simple graphics applications for office administration and support staff[2]. Though content could now be easily generated electronically, the final document was often printed for signature and filing purposes, with this physical output recognized as the record of a business transaction for corporate archives and legal purposes. The rise in popularity of desktops, however, ushered in the era of computer-enabled personal productivity gains – the ability to copy documents for reuse, templating, the ability to save to disk and make content portable and sharable, and the democratization of content creation allowing anyone with basic keyboarding skills to generate information for distribution and reuse.

As paper output of digitally created content rose, and as the nirvana of a "paperless office" became an objective in business, the conversion of paper documents to electronic format became mainstream. Imaging applications – hardware and software systems designed to create electronic snapshots of paper documents – became more mainstream for applications such as forms processing, claims intake, and other high volume routine intake applications. The emergence of standards is critical to mainstream adoption of technology, and in the mid-80s "Tagged Image File Format" – TIFF – became widely adopted by many vendors as the file format specification of choice for scanned image electronic output. With a portable, application-neutral format now supported by a wide range of scanning and imaging vendors, IT managers could now make safe investments, with confidence that the digitized content would remain retrievable and viewable even as software systems were retired and replaced. TIFF remains one of the most universally accepted and preferred image formats by many jurisdictions in the USA and Europe for legal admissibility and state/national archive accession of electronic records.[3]

In the early 1990s, the desktop PC proliferation continued its natural evolution, enabled by hardware and software vendors such as IBM, Intel and Microsoft, thanks to increasingly graphical user interfaces and mouse-driven office automation programs. Useful productivity tools continued to be delivered into the hands of an ever-wider base of office and information workers. The evolution of networked PCs—Local Area Networks (LAN) and Wide Area Networks (WAN) revealed the next wave of personal productivity—and introduced the concept of group or team productivity software suites to mainstream business. Electronic documents could now be created on desktop PCs, but rather than printing and faxing or physically distributing the content to other information workers, the files could now be saved into shared locations, allowing retrieval electronically with shared PC folder locations.

Networks became more prevalent in commercial enterprise and the value of shared transactional information—financial, planning, or inventory data—allowed organizations to get a single picture of true operational status in nearly real time. ERP applications and electronic accounting systems were key applications in the 1990s. Technology had demonstrated the value of streamlining data collection, order processing, inventory control. Imaging applications often fed the paper evidence of business into ERP or financial databases. System-generated customer numbers, purchase order numbers, and tracking numbers could now be used as validation or as single point of retrieval for all aspects of a transaction.

Networks also enabled the explosive adoption of e-mail during this time. Initially viewed as casual intra-office messaging systems, e-mail by 2000 had become the dominant channel of business communication. As e-mail applications evolved, applications such as Microsoft Exchange, Groupwise, and Lotus Notes also became used for team collaboration—shared public workspaces for document storage and retrieval, with basic foldering, permissions and search to help business workers manage shared content.

The 1990s proliferation of the LAN and WAN also saw the rise of what became the core point solution at the foundation of ECM—Document Management and Records Management. Emerging vendors such as Open Text, PC DOCS, and SoftSolutions were the early pioneers in this space—delivering workgroup productivity tools specifically designed to manage the version integrity, audit trails, security and metadata categorization of electronic documents. Leading vendors in this era typically specialized in serving the needs of specific industry verticals such as manufacturing, legal, government, and engineering.

Records Management vendors in the 1990s were typically small-to-medium sized firms and addressed two market needs. First, delivering electronic database-driven tracking and management tools to help organize and locate the large volumes of paper records, physical files and boxes typically held by government, corporate legal or other enterprise records centers. Barcodes, retention rules, storage instructions, location metadata were key functional components. Second, many of these niche vendors recognized the rapidly growing trend towards electronic content creation, and began to evolve their products to allow capture of electronic records in addition to physical records tracking. The ability to apply retention schedules, legal holds, records-specific metadata, and apply the same kind of preservation rules to digital content as with paper, introduced the needed technology that had been missing in those early years of desktop digital content creation. Strategic alliances and partnerships between Document Management and Records Management vendors became common, with commercial enterprise benefiting.

By 1998–99, the first wave of vendor consolidation struck the Document Management and Records Management industry. Many of the Document Management vendors moved specifically to acquire the Records Management vendors with whom they had established partnerships, fully recognizing the needs of their commercial and public sector customers to extend retention, legal compliance and corporate memory retention requirements more consistently to electronically generated content. Integrated

Document and Records Management, extended by imaging, workflow and full text search remain today the cornerstone components of an ECM integrated offering. Version control, content search, metadata categorization, group, user or role level access and security controls supplemented by the disposal and preservation rules from the Records Management extension form the basis for corporate electronic discovery initiatives today.

The year 2001 was a watershed in the evolution of records management as a profession. Threats to commercial enterprise emerged from two very different and distinct forces: the threat of disruption to the political and economic stability of the U.S. with the tragedy of September 11, as well as the wave of corporate governance scandals that shook the confidence of investors and financial analysts. The protection, authentication, preservation, and business continuity responsibilities of the records management profession were put front and centre—often making front page news as scandal after scandal revealed inappropriate handling of information, destruction, or falsification practices.

The regulatory and legislative compliance pressures that accelerated post-2001 have changed how many organizations think about business content—how they capture, retain, and ultimately dispose of that content. Corporations must evolve into an entity able to thrive in an era of litigation and new electronic evidentiary rules. Rooted in an era of mistrust and uncertainty, the wave of 21st century legislative and regulatory pressures has expanded the role of the records management professional. Technology solutions designed to address particular capture, storage, and disposition requirements abound, yet content-centric problems continue to plague the modern knowledge-economy enterprise. This post-2001 business context accelerated the evolution of individual point solutions into the idea of the comprehensive Enterprise Content Management suite. Software vendors that delivered only piece-meal components—standalone Records Management, Workflow engines, Portals, Web Content Management, Content Archiving—increasingly came under pressure to integrate into more mainstream applications or face marginalization or ultimately acquisition by a larger vendor looking to build a full-content management suite offering.

The immediate precursor to today's Enterprise Content Management definition was established by research analyst Gartner as the "Smart Enterprise Suite." This category ranked software vendors on their integrated offerings with emphasis on portals, collaboration, and content management capabilities. Smart Enterprise Suite was not widely adopted in the technology market and 2004 had essentially been superseded by the current vision of Enterprise Content Management. Missing from the definition of Smart Enterprise Suite were many of the technology offerings needed to meet the governance and compliance needs of modern commerce—records management, archiving, workflow and Web content management. The short-lived Smart Enterprise Suite concept, however, did have the positive influence of alerting businesses and technology vendors to the value of integration, of the importance of end-to-end content control and management systems. The 2002–2006 era was a turning point in the consolidation of vendor technologies as small- and medium-sized point solution providers merged with larger mainstream vendors in order to serve the needs of enterprise with specific and often onerous content management compliance challenges in those early days of electronic discovery and changes in evidentiary rules. Sarbanes Oxley in the USA, PIPEDA in Canada, Freedom of Information in the UK: these early years of the 21st century brought electronic content and records management to the forefront as businesses and government needed to assess internal practices to meet evolving legal and regulatory pressures.

The Age of Compliance: Using ECM to Establish An Information Governance Strategy

Business today relies on three fundamental elements: people, process, and content. Ultimately people are the most crucial of the three. Without human language, curiosity, and desire to improve material and social circumstances there would be no need for process and no content produced. This is not a new observation. That humans are uniquely furnished with the faculty of language and are thus compelled to form social, commercial and political associations can be traced back thousands of years.[4] Language and words are tools used to create common goals, bonds, and to forge relationships to improve our existence.

The social, commercial, and political associations that have emerged to serve people's needs require content and process to stay agile, relevant and to exist inside a framework of rules and acceptable practices. It no longer matters if these communities are physical or virtual—it is the environment in which we live and work. The capture, distribution, consumption, and protection of information across a broad range of physical and digital forms have become requirements to stay in business.

Information Governance has emerged as a term to describe "the collection of decision rights, processes, standards, policies and technologies required to manage, maintain and exploit information as an enterprise resource."[5] In the knowledge economy, businesses that rely on innovation, technology development, patents, regulated products, and creative arts must protect their core assets just as more traditional companies would protect their plants and property. Engineering and scientific expertise, synthesized and reusable best practices, and innovative market strategies are direct contributors to top-line revenue. Organizations that explore a corporate information governance strategy are seeking to guide how managers make decisions about content stewardship. They understand the need to align organizational technology and business objectives and articulate this vision to employees, key partners, and external stakeholders.

Content-centric best practices to help meet compliance and risk mitigation mandates imposed by law, regulators, or internal quality standards are complemented by a keen focus on developing ways to capitalize on the kinds of productivity and efficiency gains that grow out of an asset-management approach to corporate content. Enterprise Content Management solutions can help companies deliver a compliance program to deal with corporate information and the laws and rules that govern the preservation, discovery and disposal rules, while balancing the needs of the consumers and creators of that content, in the context of real business processes. The actions required to become ready for e-discovery can also have the added benefit of reducing IT costs and avoiding unnecessary re-creation of content. Preparing internal inventories of electronic content; of understanding the sources of content creation and consumption; of instituting programs to capture business records and proactively eliminate duplications, unimportant transitory or temporary content, of streamlining content flow through structured workflow stages—these actions can benefit both bottom line compliance mandates as well as top-line productivity pressures.

Corporations and public sector organizations look to deploy Enterprise Content Management solutions to establish an information governance strategy for their critical content. But companies often ask—where do we start? How do we articulate and execute a strategy for our own enterprise content? How can we address the fundamentals? How do we balance regulatory compliance pressures with a need to improve productivity? How can we make the right technology and change management investments to demonstrate both tangible cost savings as well as softer returns?

ECM software vendors have developed specific solution offerings designed to meet these essential needs—user productivity, business agility, cost, and risk mitigations—that are common to the enterprise. ECM offerings bring together the key elements needed to put an organization on the right path to governance strategy.

Senior management necessarily scrutinizes technology investments. Software acquisition at the enterprise level can no longer be done purely by IT. Nor can it be driven by requirements of only one department or business unit. Technology investments are increasingly required to serve three fundamental needs: to control costs and risks, to enable business agility, and to empower the business users. An ECM solution portfolio ought to meet all three of these corporate requirements.

The challenges surrounding effective content management strategies are abundant. Ever-increasing volumes of information, fractured systems that have been adopted over time, merger and acquisition activities resulting in disparate and disconnected IT systems are the challenges facing most enterprise today. These issues are now viewed against the backdrop of complex electronic discovery, regulatory, and legislative mandates that influence how organizations view and manage business content.

Companies are subject to regulations that require the protection and preservation of content. They must also show adherence to approved retention policies, as well as privacy and data protection regulations driven by the industry and jurisdiction in which they do business. Failure to meet these external obligations exposes the organization to possible financial penalty, loss of reputation and legal liabilities that affect business operations.

And the way that information workers use and access content continues to change: they are more mobile than ever and work with content across a variety of systems and devices. Ensuring secure access to accurate content on demand is critical to achieving corporate goals of productivity and efficiency improvement. As we approach the second decade of the 21st century, the public sector and many businesses across the G8 nations are seeing demographic shifts. This impending Baby Boomer retirement wave could result in a brain drain and loss of corporate memory. Best practices, corporate culture, years of accumulated implicit knowledge and experiences are at risk. Preserving intellectual capital and expertise as a competitive advantage is vital in today's dynamic and competitive business climate.

Critical to the success of an ECM deployment is engaging people as they use the content that is created and received as part of a business process. Understanding how content flows through an organization—who needs it, what applications are used, what are the stages of its evolution or approval, where does it go when finished, who cares about its preservation or destruction—these questions need to be part of an ECM deployment. User engagement and participation in the process is critical to success.

The Technology Components of ECM

All businesses, regardless of size, location, or market, require and use content—the material that constitutes documents, publications, and other information—from many sources in their day-to-day operations. As the volume and complexity of this content increases, so does the need to understand and manage it. Enterprise Content Management solutions provide the necessary foundation for an enterprise-wide strategy for information governance.

ECM solutions must support five key stages of the life of content: Creation and Capture, Collaboration and Review, Integration and Optimization, and Experience and Consumption— underpinned by Records Retention and Archiving to meet electronic discovery and preservation requirements.

The fundamental building blocks of an ECM strategy are document management, records management, document-centric workflow, content archiving, imaging, and application integration to many mainstream content authoring applications. These integrated components allow an organization to implement end-to-end content capture and management practices addressing the three universal requirements for success measurements: end user empowerment, business agility, and cost-and-risk reduction.

Organizations with particular needs to extend these core components can often make use of integrated ECM extensions to support enhanced collaboration and Web content management, digital and rich media management, reporting and analytics, ERP solutions, portal integration, as well as the rich application integration layers often delivered by a Services Oriented Architecture technology stack.

Empower Information Workers with Document Management

Document management and records management form the cornerstone of Enterprise Content Management. Designed to offer a secure and centrally managed repository for both work-in-progress and final output content. The fundamental tools include full text and metadata search, security, retrieval, version control, taxonomy, metadata categorization, and team and personal workspaces.

Organizations benefit from document management particularly when the requirements are driven by user empowerment and business agility needs. Document management also provides the framework upon which businesses can introduce the next layer of control and risk mitigation with fully integrated records management. As evolving evidentiary and disclosure laws broaden the scope of what is discoverable to all electronically stored information—not only business-declared final records—a document management underpinning for drafts, versions, and other forms of work-in-progress content is essential to managing risk and reducing cost of electronic discovery.

The document management component of ECM provides a secure repository for content of all types and formats—office applications, e-mail, graphics, CAD drawings, images and renditions, and an increasing range of new object types as organizations adopt more Web 2.0 collaborative tools inside the enterprise. Check-in/check-out, version control for simple and compound documents, audit trails, metadata categorization, comprehensive search, user, group, and role based access controls are all elements of the document management core offering, delivered through Web browser, common office applications, or Windows Explorer interfaces to meet a range of user preferences.

Users and administrators can create metadata, folder structures and taxonomies to meet both personal and enterprise organizational needs. Easy to understand toolbars, search capabilities, navigation panes, and document-centric function menus deliver rich and intuitive search and navigation features to both casual document consumers and more demanding content creators and reviewers.

Tools & Traps...

Can Your Business Benefit from Document Management?

A business can benefit from document management if the answer is yes to any of these questions:

- Is there confusion over which document is the latest or approved version?
- Are excessive duplications eating into available network storage capacity and causing bottlenecks during the electronic discovery process?
- Are business decisions made with incomplete or inaccurate information because it takes too long to locate the right content?
- Are employees frustrated or spending too much time searching multiple file shares or other storage locations?
- Do employees recreate or feel compelled to redo work because it is difficult to find? Are employees even aware of previous work done by colleagues or other business units?
- Are delays in information access and efficient content distribution causing bottlenecks and slowing completion of projects?

Deliver Results with Search

Most information workers are familiar with search technologies through use of Web search engines to find content. Search technology began to hit the mainstream of the technology world in the late 1970s often used in research and case management databases powered by mainframes and mini-computers.[6] By the late 1980s, search applications were targeted at early Internet and World Wide Web content, becoming widely used by public and businesses alike by the mid-1990s.

ECM suites generally contain sophisticated search engines and have fully integrated and permissioned indexing and retrieval as part of the core document and records management functionality. Users can typically use a range of search operators and techniques to get the right set of corporate content returned in a result set. Boolean operators are the most basic ways to filter and exclude content: AND, OR, NOT allow end users to apply simple conditions to the content that the system retrieves.

Where ECM search tools differentiate from more general purpose search engines is an ability to respect the security and access controls placed on the content managed in the ECM repository. Users, because of their group or role who are not allowed to see certain sensitive content, will not be allowed to retrieve it because the search results returned will restrict or block the content by authenticating against a document permissions list. When this search is used to meet electronic discovery requirements, organizations must ensure that the user performing the search can be safely and appropriately granted broader access rights to query against the complete repository.

Retrieval aids built into ECM search engines can help guide users on the content that is of most interest. Relevancy ranking is a concept that indicates how well a document meets the executed search criteria. Factors which typically contribute to a relevancy ranking are numbers of hits of the keyword in the document, value of linked content, and other forms of statistics. Relevancy rankings are typically displayed to users with meaningful visual guides such as ratings, percentages, or color codes.

Improve Business Process with Workflow

Document management also facilitates collaborative work, allowing information workers to rate, recommend, subscribe to notifications and share links to key content with their colleagues. A core feature of many document management offerings is a content-centric workflow tool, which allows both structured and ad-hoc routing of documents for a variety of approval, review and feedback processes. Using simple graphical tools to map out the process flow, authorized users and administrators can automate routine activities, streamline the movement of content across teams, show measurable cost and time savings by eliminating redundant stages, automate escalations, relieve the burden of using e-mail to transport duplicated attachments, and provide insight and transparency into process bottlenecks and missed deadlines. Structured content-centric transactions moved through stages with workflow also provide a high degree of logging and auditing into who has altered, removed, approved, or viewed content that may be subject to discovery at some future date. Fully traceable monitor lists and activity histories can assist in providing context around business decisions should dispute arise. Process intensive or highly regulated businesses can also benefit from electronic forms support for workflow applications. The ability to create and manage forms—to standardize data capture screens or to automate workflow initiation based on the data that is entered—allows routine transactional business processes to be automated, reduce turnaround times, and fully track or audit the decision tree and approvals.

Organizations with strictly enforced procedures for sign off, or who require authentication and non-repudiation, can deploy electronic signatures to mission-critical workflow scenarios. An electronic signature provides secure verification of a user's identity during a stage approval process and provides an increasingly accepted form of non-repudiation when reviewing electronic transactions during the discovery phase of online content. E-Signature technologies vary according to ECM platform, but they do require enhanced user authentication—often an additional password layer to verify that they are the approver of a task or workflow stage. Slightly more sophisticated is a Digital Signature which typically builds upon a corporate PKI (public key infrastructure) and includes encryption technology to verify against the users own private key as part of the signing process.

Tools & Traps...

Can Your Business Benefit from Workflow?

■ Productivity improvements can be achieved by streamlining routine tasks with assigned steps, instructions, structured approvals for parallel or serial workflows for either users or groups.

■ Complex procedures can dynamically spawn new workflows or tasks based on specified conditional rules.

■ Compliance or best practices requirements need to preserve previous versions of workflows—including audit trails and permissions.

■ Corporate management or operations need to be proactively notified if deadlines are missed or when tasks are completed.

Reduce Risk with Records Management

Records management is the next logical extension to document management and a critical component of an ECM offering. Records Management functionality enriches the metadata on content, enhances security, extends the corporate repository to physical objects and storage space management, and allows scheduled archiving, movement or destruction of content based on corporately approved retention rules and event triggers.

Some organizations may choose to deploy a records management module first as part of an ECM strategy, particularly if the largest source of pain for the enterprise is risk and cost management of legacy paper content. Highly regulated industries with rigid external compliance mandates, public sector, or paper-intensive processes can quickly benefit from the implementation of a records management offering as part of a governance strategy. In these cases, extending these capture, control and preservation requirements to a broader range of electronic work-in-progress content is what then drives subsequent adoption of a document management offering.

Records Management applications and the Enterprise Content Management systems into which they integrate are among the most consistently tested software tools in corporate environments. Because of the critical nature of electronic records, a variety of government-sanctioned standards, specifications and testing bodies have evolved globally. In the US, the most widely accepted compliance standard for Records Management applications is the DoD 5015.2 specification. Though designed primarily for US Federal Government needs, this standard has emerged as a benchmark for commercial enterprises seeking RM tools meeting a well-documented set of functional requirements.[7] Similar standards exist for the UK with The National Archives specification,[8] Australia's VERS,[9] and the European Commission MoReq II.[10] ECM vendors may choose to certify their records management functionality against any of these standards in order to meet their market needs, but most leading technology analyst surveys expect that at least one certification is met for the vendor to be officially recognized in the category of Enterprise Content Management.

Successful deployment of a records management initiative must include strong direction from internal business managers and corporate legal. Thinking about records management as purely a technology problem is unlikely to address the real business risks that could result from inappropriate destruction or retention policies. It is the business managers inside the enterprise that must face the legal compliance demands from external parties, and it is business users that generate the content that needs to be managed as a record. The deployments that are most successful are those that bring a cross functional team into the planning stages: business users, legal, IT, records or knowledge managers backed up with executive sponsorship and ongoing project funding for deployment and ongoing employee education programs.[11]

Tools & Traps...

Can Your Business Benefit from Records Management?

Organizations will benefit from a formal program to manage corporate records if the enterprise:

- Is a publicly-traded organization, in public sector, or subject to external health, safety, financial or environmental disclosure regulations.

- Operates in a jurisdiction or industry sector that is litigious.

- Needs to apply litigation or Freedom of Information holds to corporate content.

- Owns high-value intellectual property, digital assets, patents, designs, blueprints, scientific or other research contributing to the valuation or revenue of the business.

- Currently has no program to capture corporate memory, best practices or organizational knowledge strategic to keeping the business running smoothly during periods of staff turnover, retirement, elections, or mergers and acquisitions.

- Has paper, boxes or other physical artifacts that require preservation, easy retrieval or specific storage rules.

Reduce Costs with Intelligent Storage Management and Content Archiving

Successfully deployed document and records management systems will quickly demonstrate return on investment with improvements in user productivity—search, retrieval, reduction in discovery time and costs—in addition to offsetting network traffic and e-mail inbox overload. Providing users with the opportunity to collaborate in shared workspaces means avoiding incessant duplication of documents across folders, shared and local drives.

Another source of cost and risk reduction is an integrated and policy-driven content archiving strategy. As the document and records repository grows, or as IT management assesses storage costs across the enterprise, an intelligent archiving component brings solid cost-saving opportunities to the table. As content ages or changes status, it is typically used and retrieved less frequently, yet few organizations have solid insights into how often content is used, or what proportion of content is still viewed after six months. Intelligent storage management technology such as archiving can be deployed as an integrated component of ECM to give IT management the flexibility to move and store infrequently used or less critical content to more economical storage devices. By defining storage and archiving policies and rules, IT professionals can make the most cost-effective use of their hardware storage investments. High value and frequently used content can be directed to premium storage devices for high accessibility and rapid retrieval. (see Figure 2.1)

Stored content has a cost—the hardware devices, regular backup, tape circulation, and administration overhead. Policy-driven content archiving gives IT management an opportunity to reduce the cost and burden of content storage as its value or usefulness decreases. The ability to synchronize content value with vendor-agnostic storage virtualization opens the door to new ways to manage IT costs. Content archiving allows a liberal mix of storage technologies from a diverse group of storage vendors to be combined into one or more logical enterprise archive repositories. The storage of inactive or infrequently used content can be directly tied to records management storage rules, and item movement can be triggered by metadata or other key life-cycle events (see Figure 2.2).

Figure 2.1 Content on Tier-One Storage Carries a Persistently High Cost, Even As Its Usefulness Declines over Its Life Cycle

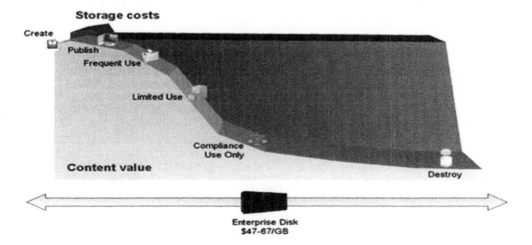

Figure 2.2 Rules-Driven Storage Management Ensures Content Is Moved to Less Expensive Devices As the Content Usefulness Declines over Its Life Cycle

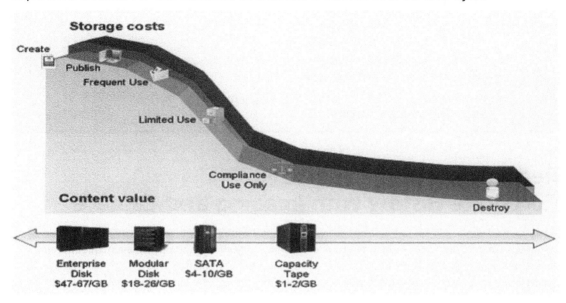

Electronic discovery requirements can be aligned with the business and retention rules designed to govern this content storage and long term migration and preservation. Documentation of applicable retention rules and storage policies of different content types is a necessary component of an information governance strategy. Such strategies must have demonstrable consistency, rules mapped to legal or regulatory citations and communication to employees to ensure full transparency and awareness to be accepted and enforceable.

Tools & Traps...

Can Your Business Benefit from Intelligent Storage Management and Archiving?

Organizations can benefit from measurable cost savings with content archiving if:

■ Existing in-house storage is approaching the terabyte level.

■ Current tier one storage holds content that is infrequently retrieved, or coming close its approved destruction date.

Continued

- IT management is not able to meaningfully exploit less expensive tape or disk storage devices.

- Business needs, electronic discovery requirements or external regulations demand that content has long term availability and readability requirements.

- Critical information needs enhanced protection with auditing, controlled deletions, encryption and access controls.

- Disaster recovery and business continuity planning must extend to electronic corporate content.

Reduce Cost and Preserve Corporate History with Imaging and Capture

The paperless office will be just a dream for most organizations. Many business-critical processes still rely at least in part on paper—accounts payable, contracts negotiation, order management, inbound correspondence, expense claim reimbursements, among others. While paper has a tangible quality that makes it attractive for on-the-road portability and reading, the effectiveness of relying on physical forms, letters and receipts is not ideal. Employees can fall into a habit of duplicating paper content, wasting resources and time, and creating the opportunity for information loss through improper storage, disposal or handling habits. Accidental disclosure of personnel or proprietary content or privacy-protected data by misplaced or stolen paper files is a risk to any organization.

Enterprise Content Management suites include integrated imaging applications to support a range of document capture scenarios for both high- and low-volume business needs. Typically integrated with a workflow module, organizations can use barcodes, Optical Character Recognition (OCR), and automated metadata collection and categorization to streamline the capture process and ensure valuable content is properly stored and organized in context with other related electronic case or project content.

Converting paper documents into industry-standard electronic image formats such as TIFF or PDF/A[12] can reduce costs, as the need to store non-essential paper or copies of convenience is eliminated. High-value paper records with evidentiary or historical value can be scanned and carefully preserved, allowing the electronic copies to be more widely viewed by a larger group of users safely and securely. Imaging applications also allow finance and accounting departments to easily match scanned invoicing or shipping records with related information created electronically in any number of applications—ERP applications such as SAP and Oracle—associated with meaningful metadata such as case or customer number, thereby reducing the risk of mishandling transactional content and missing deadlines or incurring contractual disputes. Familiar actions done on paper, such as sticky-note comments, annotations, redlining, and other markups are available electronically in most imaging applications.

Tools & Traps...

Can Your Business Benefit from Imaging and Capture?

Business can benefit from Imaging as part of Enterprise Content Management if:

- Warehouse or file room costs are high or rising due to storage of paper-based records.
- Retrieval of paper-based records is labor-intensive or slows down business processes by creating bottlenecks in the flow of work.
- Discovery orders require production of all relevant data regardless of media type or physical form.
- Historically valuable physical records are at risk by handling or movement.
- Business continuity or disaster recovery planning dictates that paper cannot be a single point of failure.
- Paper records contain sensitive personal, financial, medical or commercial proprietary information that requires specialized storage, structured disposal, processing or destruction methods.
- Information is needed across a geographically dispersed or cross-functional team and traditional fax, courier or mail methods are slow, inefficient and costly.

Ensuring User Adoption with Application Integration

ECM becomes adopted more rapidly by end users when using application integration functionality to extend content capture and consumption in the context of common business processes.

ERP applications are the framework for process-intensive business transactions. SAP, for example, has allowed organizations to streamline processes and consolidate cost centers and procedures. Bridging the gap between ERP transactional applications and the unstructured document-centric content that these applications rely on can be a key point of integration for ECM. Document access and linking tools provide single point of access for users to the business content they need, across information sources, and without requiring them to perform multiple searches or resort to paper procedures.

A strong integration with common office authoring applications eases adoption and minimizes retraining when the document management capture features are deployed to information workers. Users often spend a large proportion of the work day inside their e-mail applications. Integrations use familiar and intuitive e-mail notifications and connect the inbox and common document management objects such as folders, projects, and compound documents. Integration between mainstream office suites and document management functions mean users can open and save documents directly from the repository. Using familiar application such as Windows Explorer, users who can drag and drop documents and folders between their desktop and the repository with minimal retraining will be more likely to use the tools more regularly. Users who frequently travel or take their laptops home evenings and weekends will need to be equipped with offline support ensures work done away from the corporate network is synchronized with the repository to ensure documents are up-to-date and correctly versioned, and ultimately protected and preserved in a corporate repository—not on an uncontrolled laptop drive.

Get Ready for the Generation Y Workforce with Web 2.0 in the Enterprise

The workforce is on the brink of change. The Baby Boom generation, defined as those born between 1946 and 1964, is approaching the end of their dominance of the employment ranks, with recent US research noting that "members of the highly educated baby-boom generation have already begun to retire, and those retirements are expected to pick up sharply in 2011 when the first wave of boomers reaches age 65. By 2029, 44 percent of today's workforce, or 62 million working baby boomers, will have reached retirement age."[13] As the Boomer generation leaves positions of power, new managers and experts will take their place, often with very different expectations and assumptions about the workplace. As the twenty-somethings work their way up the corporate ladder, organizations should expect their technology envelopes to be pushed. Demand for rapid and intuitive search, online access to corporate content, collaborative chats, use of blogs and instant messaging, Web or video conferencing will be normal channels of business communication. The incoming generation is more wired, more mobile and more demanding of technology for personal productivity and networking. With these new demands for content access, search and collaborative work, companies can recognize a new window of opportunity to take control of their electronic knowledge assets by dealing with this new online generation who are less dependent on paper processes.

Businesses depend on effective and timely communication with customers, suppliers, and among employees. For companies with specific user productivity and knowledge sharing requirements, or those trying to attract a new generation of workers to their management ranks, a key component of Enterprise Content Management is Collaboration. Connecting people in a real-time, project- or team-based workspace, to circulate ideas, experiences, content, and best practices is an effective use of collaborative technologies. Whether driven by the geographic distribution of teams, by knowledge management practices, or because increasingly technically savvy business users prefer the ease of use offered by Web 2.0-inspired tools, organizations wanting to explore these new content sharing and creation tools need to review their use in the context of the same regulatory compliance and electronic discovery requirements as any other authoring tool. New online content sharing and creation tools must be viewed as electronically stored information and subject to any of the retention, security and preservation practices as e-mail or other more traditional office applications.

As organizations begin to explore and adopt more of collaborative Web-based tools inspired by personal use—wikis, blogs, discussion forums, real-time chat— they must look at ECM offerings that have stepped ahead in order to deliver the same risk and cost mitigation offerings that are used with more traditional content and communication types. Once again, the envelope of content types that can be defined as electronically stored information for discovery or legal hold purposes is broadened. Records management-friendly blogs and wikis, team collaboration sites, real-time project chat rooms, and other Web 2.0-inspired tools should all be deployed safely and securely, with integration back to the underlying ECM governance foundation. As adoption of Web 2.0 inspired tools become adopted in the corporate mainstream, appropriate use policies and capture and control policies in line with other forms of unstructured electronically stored information will become critical for corporate legal and records management professionals as governance strategies extend and adapt to new content types.

Other forms of rich media are increasingly being used by business to communicate with customers and prospects—podcasts, streaming video, rich graphics and animations—all of this new interactive content must also be reviewed as part of an inventory of electronically stored information. As product announcements, customer programs, or online advertisements are launched and consumed via corporate Web sites, the promises or commitments made in these emerging communication vehicles could also be subject to discovery orders. Engaging new business owners inside the enterprise—brand managers, Chief Marketing Officers—will be essential to keeping an information governance strategy complete and current. Many ECM solutions include tools and platforms to manage the special metadata, format support and compression requirements of rich digital media.

Control Corporate Identity and Communication with Web Content Management

Presenting approved and vetted content to both internal and external audiences is a strategic use of Enterprise Content Management in order to minimize risk of miscommunication or incur legal action due to inaccurate data. Using a managed repository delivered by an ECM deployment to populate public facing Web sites and intranets and extranets is a logical component of an overall corporate information governance strategy. Trusted content—the latest approved data sheet, the updated agenda, the legally approved terms and conditions agreement—can be safely delivered through an increasingly preferred channel of consumption, the Web.

Web Content Management is a component of most Enterprise Content Management suites, making it easy for business users to ensure that content is accurate, approved, and ready for broad publication. The enterprise can be proactive, using workflow, staging sites and subject matter experts to get content ready for public eyes. Feeding the right content to public or internal Web sites is part of the risk mitigation possibility WCM delivers by extending the controls expected an ECM system beyond the firewall and into customer and public facing sites.

As more business is transacted on the Web, and as public-facing Web sites become sales and e-commerce channels, accuracy of pricing data, transactional details, terms and conditions, and the capture of these business records is essential to meeting corporate governance, financial reporting, and litigation avoidance initiatives.

Content delivered via the Web can also be personalized, tailored to consumers by role, team, interest, or by preferred form factor, opening the door to content delivery and business transactions over a broader range of devices. Full compliance with accessibility standards, such as US Section 508, can be mandated to ensure the widest possible consumption of web sites and content by users regardless of visual or physical ability.

Accelerate Decision Making with Analytics and Reporting

Content that is managed, secured and tagged with corporate or user-driven metadata can reveal new perspectives on how information is contributed, used and collected during business activities. Fully integrated reporting on content usage patterns, auditing of revisions or inappropriate access is an essential tool to get metrics on Enterprise Content Management performance and adoption rates.

System administrators, information workers, and business analysts can all benefit from typical intelligent reporting features, such as ad-hoc queries, systematic scheduled reports, and easy reformatting of report data and layouts. Many Enterprise Content Management vendors provide integrated and secure reporting and analysis of all managed content, including metrics on system load and capacity, analysis of content types and consumption, dashboard views of workflow status, completion rates, and bottlenecks. Configurable data navigation maps allow business analysts to research and communicate structured or ad-hoc analysis capabilities to the users who need it—all while respecting the access controls and content security delivered by the Enterprise Content Management solution. Typical reporting and business intelligence offerings also provide full integration to many database applications, and can provide powerful views into metadata for reporting and analytical purposes across applications. Connecting records metadata with customer databases to get a full comprehensive view of all client communication, or consolidate contract expiry data into one view by bridging the contracts held in the document repository with milestones in a structured ERP application. These query and reporting applications can assist in the rapid retrieval and analysis as part of electronic discovery of unstructured content.

Control the Biggest Source of Electronic Risk with E-mail Management

E-mail becomes a particular source of pain for public and private sector organizations when the obligation of legal discovery or freedom of information disclosure arises primarily due to sheer volume levels. Having evolved into the primary means of business communication over the years, e-mail is a significant content management challenge due to massive quantity of messages, difficulty in separating junk from business value, and the ad-hoc deletion, storage or filing habits practiced by most users. E-mail also contains valuable content needed for ongoing business—attachments, approvals, management directives and announcements. Capturing these electronic conversations in context with other business artifacts is essential to understanding how decisions were made or transactions executed.

Organizations operating in litigious jurisdictions or verticals are often compelled to adopt Enterprise Content Management led by e-mail management as the key driver to make the business case for deployment. Getting control over e-mail capture, categorization and retention is the first step towards modern litigation readiness. Rapid and accurate search, retrieval and collection of e-mail, along with the other electronic content that requires review for discovery purposes, is essential to relieving the burdens faced by legal counsel, corporate compliance or records officers and the IT professionals managing the underlying systems. Successful records management initiatives must extend to e-mail repositories and outline the appropriate preservation, storage and disposal rules in accordance with internal business needs and external regulation requirements.

E-mail can be considered semi-structured content. While typical messages contain unstructured text in the body, e-mail headers provide structured metadata—to, from, cc, date sent, date received—that make automated capture and filing a reality. Depending on the needs of the enterprise, and of business users, automation of capture and application of records retention and metadata categorization can be done with individual messages by filing into managed folders created in the Document or Records Management component of ECM.

Each organization ultimately must assess which e-mails are worthy of records management protection and categorization as part of an ECM deployment. The jurisdiction in which the business operates, the vertical industry they identify with, and the types of products and services produced all help determine the laws, regulations and quality standards that will affect their compliance obligations.

E-mails are complex content types; there is more than just the body of the message. Additional information is often contained in an e-mail beyond the actual message. E-mail metadata typically contains transmission information including the date and time it was sent and received, who sent it, who received it (including CC), attachments, return receipts, and more. All of this information is generally considered a part of the e-mail record, and often must be captured and managed accordingly.

Tools & Traps...

When Should E-mail Be Considered a Corporate Record?

When should e-mails be treated as business records? Some key considerations to consider when determining compliance and retention practices for your business:

- Does it document a business-related event or activity?
- Is there demonstration of a specific business transaction?
- Are there supporting facts of a business-related event, activity or transaction?
- Does it provide information needed for other legal, accounting, business or compliance reasons?
- Does it show which individuals participated in a business activity?

Manage the Risk and Cost of Litigation

"The best offense is a good defense." These words are especially true for companies that are frequently faced with legal discovery orders. Many jurisdictions are updating and reviewing the laws, and case law is evolving regarding the requests, collection and disclosure of electronic information. The US amendment of the Federal Rules of Civil Procedure in 2006, in particular, has had a substantial effect on how records and compliance programs are instituted inside corporations.

Business needs to view litigation readiness in the context of an overall corporate strategy for information governance—not as purely an IT or General Counsel concern. Each corporate stakeholder has different needs, and sometimes these diverse needs compete with those of another group. For instance, while IT would like to reduce the online storage of e-mails, as system usage accelerates the legal and records management departments demand the preservation of more information, and for a longer period of time. It is important that each corporate stakeholder to understand one business needs of the other. Otherwise IT may implement user inbox storage quotas, which results in users deleting e-mails or offloading them to volatile and unmanaged personal archive files. Discovery motions affect the CIO as well—often, legal counsel simply doesn't have the access permissions or technical expertise to execute complex searches across the enterprise. The Legal department, alternatively, is faced with very different challenges, such as the skyrocketing costs of discovery and litigation support, having to respond to discovery requests in very short timeframes, and covering the cost of having to produce the a wide range of physical and electronic content for an adversary's discovery request. Finally, the Compliance department and records managers are burdened, as they have been struggling for years to emphasize the importance of managing business records appropriately, and often are significantly behind in managing new and emerging electronic content types. But now that content can be distributed by pressing the send button on an e-mail, many traditional approaches to records management must be revisited. The scope of what constitutes a business record has been significantly expanded as the definition of electronically stored information subject to discovery has expanded.

The concept of a Data Map—essentially an inventory guide of the electronic content and data stores inside the enterprise—has emerged as a best practice for proactive businesses wanting to ensure preparedness to meet post-2006 FRCP requirements and requests. The audience for this data map is not IT management, but general counsel, compliance, and records officers who will need to act if and when a hold order is issued on in-house electronic content. Five fundamental points, characterizing an ideal program, have emerged as guiding principles:

- Defensible record classification and retention policies: companies must map e-mail and other electronic content retention to applicable regulations and legislation to determine length of storage and any privacy issues that determine destruction or handling.

- *Built on a comprehensive content lifecycle management framework*: automated, secure and formally approved processes for retaining, storing and preserving records.

- *Extended to the entire enterprise*: centralized authority and access to manage all corporate content, including e-mail servers and team collaboration sites.

- *Providing seamless integration with discovery and litigation support systems*: to accelerate the collection, preservation, review and production of corporate records as evidence regardless of format or location.

- *Common intelligent storage for all corporate records*: using the inherent archiving capabilities of Enterprise Content Management to ensure cost-effective physical storage of content according to their categorization, ensuring integrity and admissibility.

Organizations with heavy e-discovery and repeated disclosure burdens can look to using Enterprise Content Management technology to automate and streamline more of the litigation readiness and realize cost savings by "in-sourcing" the early stages of search, categorization and collection. Once a collection set has been retrieved and reviewed, it can be used again to meet similar future discovery orders, thus delivering immediate cost and time savings. The inherent search, taxonomy, categorization and rule-based disposition abilities of ECM solutions can form the ideal foundation to meet the rigorous requirements of evolving electronic discovery and disclosure rules.

Summary

Enterprise content and information are essential to any organization and its management is just as important. Historically, imaging, document management, records management, workflow management, and Web content management were considered individual components. However, through the evolution of this industry came the introduction of enterprise content management (ECM) as a collective means. Today, ECM is a widely understood concept that allows organizations to employ suites of tools to better management their information and records.

Business, process, and content are the three fundamental considerations throughout business. ECM is no different as it takes a strong team or professionals, sound processes, and knowledge (or content) to manage businesses. Although the people component is still considered the most important element, technology components within the ECM stratosphere are ultimately what makes this industry tick. Because all businesses require and use content, the ability to technologically manage it is critical.

ECM tools have the ability to empower information workers, ensuring that confusion does not exist over the last version of a document or record, duplicates are removed, information is easily identified and accessed, employees are not frustrated with poor organization of information, and documents are not routinely recreated. Essentially, these tools strive to provide reduced risks, costs, and better information management. Additionally, and through better storage management technologies, businesses are able to better manage content archiving when they are approaching terabyte levels of information, need to reduce costs, better manage infrequently used content, or have a need to extend their COOP practices to electronic corporate content.

Solutions Fast Track

The Historical Evolution of ECM

- ☑ The years 1998–99 were the first years to see document management and records management industry consolidation.

- ☑ The year 2001 demonstrated threats to our political and economic stability, resulting in a greater need for protection, authentication, preservation and business continuity responsibilities for businesses.

- ☑ Post-2001 accelerated how businesses thought about how to manage business content due to regulatory and legislative compliance pressures.

The Age of Compliance: Using ECM for Information Governance

- ☑ The most fundamental elements to business are people, process, and content.

- ☑ Content-centric best practices help companies meet compliance and risk management requirements imposed by the courts, regulators, and internal quality control departments.

☑ Corporations and public sector organizations are more interested today in deploying ECM solutions to address information governance for their critical content.

The Technology Components of ECM

☑ As the volume of content increases, there is a greater need to understand it and manage it.

☑ Document and records management form the cornerstone of ECM.

☑ Smart storage management technologies and solutions provide more value to organizations through cost and risk reduction.

Frequently Asked Questions

Q: When should e-mail be considered a corporate record?

A: E-mail should be considered a corporate record when any of the following apply: (1) the e-mail documents a business-related event or activity; (2) there is a proof of a business transaction within it; (3) supporting facts of a business-related event or activity reside within the e-mail; (4) it provides legal, accounting, or business or compliance reasons, or (5) it indicates individuals who participated in a related business activity.

Q: What are the five fundamental points to manage the risks and costs associated with litigation?

A: Although there are many methods in managing the risks and costs associated with litigation, the points relating to this chapter include: (1) create defensible record classification and retention policies, (2) build a comprehensive content life cycle management framework; (3) extend this program to the entire enterprise; (4) integrate ECM with discovery and litigation support systems; and (5) select common intelligent storage for corporate records.

Q: What benefits are gleaned by businesses when having a formidable imaging and capture program?

A: Businesses can benefit from having imaging and capture technologies by reducing their warehouse or file room costs, improving retrieval times when needing to access these records, or simply by having the ability to geographically distribute this information that might have been otherwise unavailable to disparate offices or locations.

Q: How does rules-driven storage management ensure that content is moved to less expensive devices as the content's usefulness declines over time?

A: With a rules-driven storage management environment, companies have the ability to migrate their content from enterprise disks (ranging from $47–67/GB) to tapes (costing $1–2/GB). By understanding where information resides within this continuum, costs will naturally be reduced.

Q: How do ECM search capabilities differ from general search engines?

A: ECM search capabilities offer more security and access controls placed on the content managed within the ECM repository.

Q: How can a business benefit from workflow systems?

A: Workflow can improve productivity by streamlining tasks, complex procedures can spawn new workflows based on conditional rules, compliance or best practices can be established, or corporate management could be better informed.

Notes

1. *Magic Quadrant for Enterprise Content Management, 2007.* http://gartner.com/DisplayDocument? doc_cd=150426.

2. Forquer, Bill, Peter Jelinski, and Tom Jenkins. *Enterprise Content Management: Solutions—What You Need To Know.* Waterloo, Canada: Open Text Corporation, Third Printing 2006, p. 17.

3. "Sustainability of Digital Formats." www.digitalpreservation.gov/formats/fdd/fdd000022.shtml.

4. Aristotle, *Politics.*

5. Newman, David and Debra Logan. "Governance is an Essential Building Block for Enterprise Information Management." Gartner Research Note, May 18, 2006, p. 3.

6. Jenkins, Tom. *Enterprise Content Management: Technology—What You Need to Know.* Waterloo, Canada: Open Text Corporation, Fifth Printing, 2006, p. 59.

7. The full specification and list of vendors who have successfully passed the testing can be found at http://jitc.fhu.disa.mil/recmgt.

8. The National Archives Site, www.nationalarchives.gov.uk/electronicrecords/default.htm.

9. Province of Victoria Public Records Office: www.prov.vic.gov.au/vers/vers/default.htm.

10. European Commission Archival Policy site: http://ec.europa.eu/transparency/archival_policy/moreq/index_en.htm.

11. Useful guidelines, standards and best practices have been published by organizations such as ARMA. www.arma.org/standards/index.cfm.

12. "Sustainability of Digital Formats." www.digitalpreservation.gov/formats/fdd/fdd000125.shtml.

13. www.solutionsforourfuture.org/site/DocServer/08.Knowledge-Economy.pdf?docID=103.

Chapter 3

Bridging the Gaps between Information Management and E-discovery

Solutions in this chapter:

- **Understanding Archiving Technology**

- **Exploring Enterprise Content Management Technology**

- **Reviewing Information Retention Processes and Technologies**

- **Considering Technologies to Facilitate E-discovery**

- **Examining Backup, Recovery, and Security Technologies**

- ☑ **Summary**

- ☑ **Solutions Fast Track**

- ☑ **Frequently Asked Questions**

Introduction

We live and work in an information-driven world where the creation of digital information is a simple matter of convenience. Information is the lifeblood not only of modern business but of modern life.

And there's a lot of it. In fact, organizations are now dealing with petabytes of data, and the amount is growing every year. The number of bytes of data generated by computers and other devices may rival the grains of sand on all of the beaches of the world, according to one industry analyst.

Information is as distributed and mobile as today's workforce, and the uninterrupted flow of data is central to success. Employees, partners, outsourcers, consultants, and suppliers must be able to share and access information anytime and anywhere. And with high bandwidth Internet connections and Web e-mail now ubiquitous, and thumb drives and other small devices able to store volumes of data, creating and sharing information has never been more convenient, nor presented so many challenges.

It is truly a wide open world in which information lives. Needless to say, managing information is a critical yet tough job. It requires information to be secure, available, and accessible to the right people—from the CEO to legal counsel—at the right time.

Less than ten years ago, discovery was a labor-intensive process that involved the manual collection and review of hundreds or thousands of company records. Pretrial discovery conjured up images of attorneys working late into the night as part of an "eyeballs on" review of relevant documents and records.

Today that process seems antiquated. Attorneys now must collect, review, and preserve not just structured data such as company records and contracts but also unstructured data like e-mails, instant messages, and other electronic files related to the case. While formal records such as contracts, forms, and claims are an essential part of the discovery process, it is this unstructured data that can overwhelm the traditional discovery process. It is also unstructured information that often contains the smoking gun.

NOTE

Structured data is data stored in a structured format, such as databases or data sets. Unstructured data refers to masses of data that either do not have a data structure or have a data structure not easily readable by machine. Examples of unstructured data may include audio, video, and unstructured text such as the body of an e-mail or word processing document. (Source: The Sedona Conference)

Information management technology such as content archiving and enterprise content management systems can address these challenges by enabling organizations to store, manage, and discover electronically stored information (ESI). What is ESI? Information that is stored electronically, regardless of the media or whether it is in the original format in which it was created.

Understanding Archiving Technology

The archiving market began to take shape in the late 1990s. A number of software startups entered this market to address compliance and storage management issues related to Microsoft Exchange and Lotus Domino e-mail systems. KVS Software (now Symantec Corporation) and Educom (now Autonomy Corporation) were two of the early entrants in the market that continue to offer archiving solutions under the banner of larger public software companies.

In 1997, Enterprise Vault software was developed as an archiving solution for Microsoft Exchange by Digital Equipment Corporation's U.K.-based ALL-IN-1 engineering team, which was under the technical direction of Nigel Dutt. According to Dutt, the software went through several name changes, including Information Warehouse and Information Vault, before the team agreed on its current name—"enterprise" to represent the fact it could archive an entire company's Microsoft Exchange e-mail store, and "vault" to represent the secure repository outside Exchange to which the data is transferred. This notion of moving data from a primary messaging or file environment into a secure repository forms the basis of content archiving technology today.

Figure 3.1 is an example of the interface of an archiving solution. In this example, the archiving targets are listed on the left side of the management console. This instance is set up to archive data from Microsoft Exchange, IBM Lotus Domino, network file servers, Microsoft SharePoint, and Personal Store Files (PSTs). Granular retention categories can be created and applied to specific applications, users, and content (see Figure 3.1).

Figure 3.1 A View into the Archiving Solution

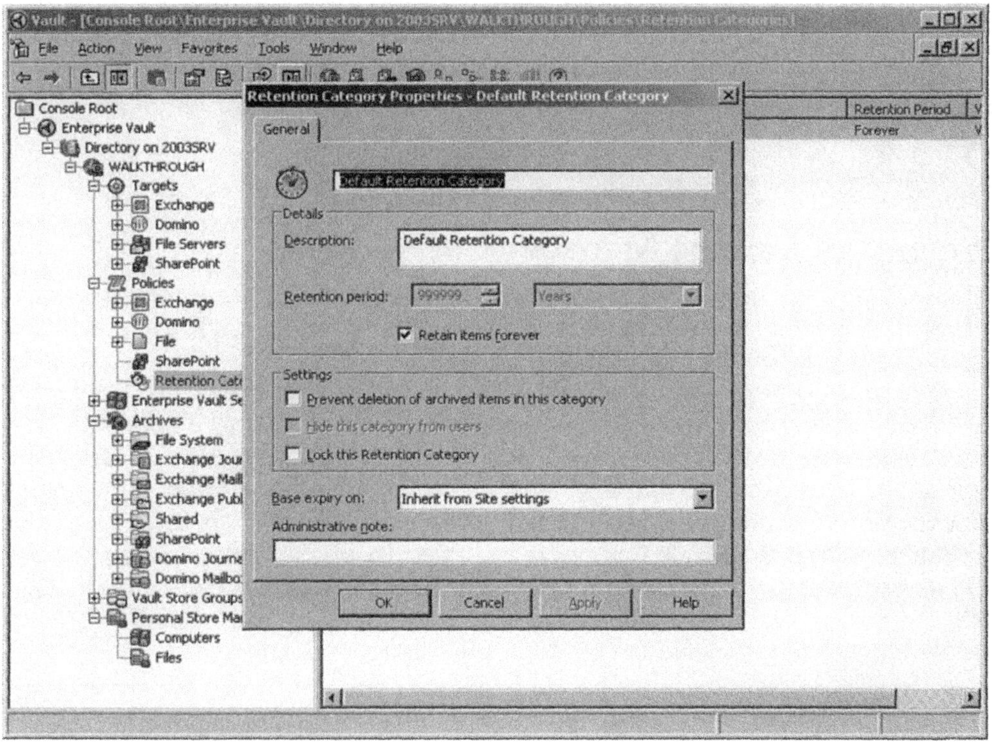

Storing, Managing, and Discovering Information

The e-mail archiving process can best be described through three stages: store, manage, and discover. Each stage is described in this section.

Storing

Archiving solutions automatically migrate files from online to near-line storage media according to a business policy. The resulting archives provide a long-term indexed repository for the storage of electronic information. Typically, these technologies employ a variety of storage management features, including the following:

■   Compression, which reduces the size of files

■   Single-instance storage, which replaces the references to identical files in a computer file system with references to a single store copy of the file

■   Deduplication, which compares electronic records based on their characteristics and removes or marks duplicate records within the data set

Tools & Traps...

Elements of Storage Management Systems

Compression, single instance storage, and data deduplication are frequently used by storage management systems to reduce the volume of stored data. Each technology uses a unique method for reducing data volume.

Compression algorithms such as zip and Run Length Encoded (RLE) reduce the size of files, saving both storage space and reducing bandwidth required for access and transmission. Data compression is widely used in backup utilities, spreadsheet applications, and database management systems. Compression generally eliminates redundant information and/or predicts where changes will occur. "Lossless" compression techniques such as zip and RLE preserve the integrity of the input. Coding standards such as Joint Photographic Experts Group (JPEG) and Motion Picture Experts Group (MPEG) employ "lossy" methods that do not preserve all of the original information and are most commonly used for photographs, audio, and video.

Continued

When several files in a computer file system contain exactly the same data, single-instance storage can replace the references to these identical files with references to a single stored copy of the file. This can potentially save large amounts of disk space in systems with many copies of the same file. Microsoft Exchange can use single-instance storage to eliminate redundant copies of a message. The reduction occurs at the Exchange Store level, so when mailboxes that receive a given message exist across Exchange Stores, each store will have one copy of the message.

Deduplication, or "de-duping," is the process of comparing electronic records based on their characteristics and removing or marking duplicate records within the data set. The definition of "duplicate records" should be agreed upon—for instance, whether an exact copy from a different location (such as a different mailbox, server tape, and so on) is considered a duplicate. Deduplication can be selective, depending on the agreed-upon criteria. (Source: The Sedona Conference)

Both outsourced and on-premise solutions exist, offering different levels of functionality, flexibility, and integration with the corporate information technology (IT) infrastructure. Other collaboration tools such as public and enterprise instant messaging, Microsoft SharePoint Server, and file-sharing environments can also be archived by some systems.

The process of archiving is usually driven by the routine application of information management policies for capturing and retaining data. Archiving systems employ four main methods of data capture:

- **Age/Quota Mailbox Archiving** Data is archived from primary applications based on the age of the information or the percentage of storage quota consumed. A quota-based policy operates in a similar fashion. However, the archiving action is triggered when a storage limit is reached in a user's mailbox or file server. For example, an age-based policy might archive all e-mail or files older than 90 days. Once archived, that data would be retained for a specified number of days, months, or years based on the user's role in the organization. After the corporate retention period passed, the data would be expired as part of the routine operation of the archiving system unless a legal hold was implemented. In contrast, with content-based archiving, data is archived from the primary application based on the content or metadata of the information. A content-based archiving policy might be created to address business requirements that are more granular. For example, all outgoing e-mail that contains the work contract should be retained for three years.

- **User-Driven** Some organizations choose to rely on a more manual approach that asks end users to categorize and archive information through the use of retention folders in the e-mail and file environments. In this scenario, an IT organization would push out retention folders with associated retention periods or categories to each user's inbox or file share. Users could then drag and drop messages or files into those folders as required.

- **Journal Capture** Journaling may be required to comply with business policies, laws, or regulations that apply to a business. Journaling retains a copy of every message that has been sent or received by the corporate mail system. Archiving technologies can be used to store, manage, and discover journal e-mail more efficiently. This type of capture is often used by highly regulated organizations, such as those governed by the Securities and Exchange Commission (SEC). For less highly regulated organizations, a hybrid approach to archiving is commonly applied. Executive or other high-risk employee e-mail would be captured through the journal while the remainder of the organization would be subject to an age-, quote-, or content-driven policy.

Managing

In addition to corporate retention policies, legal and regulatory requirements exist that require the management and preservation of electronic documents and records. These policies can be driven by specific industry requirements, such as those put forth by the SEC and the Federal Energy Regulatory Commission (FERC), or by broader directives like The Federal Rules of Civil Procedure (FRCP). The consistent and routine collection of information into the archive enables more effective information management.

Discovering

As a centralized repository of indexed content, archiving solutions can be leveraged to support early case assessments through search, analysis, and review capabilities. When litigation is anticipated, these solutions offer a legal hold function to suspend retention policies for a specific dataset. Information that must be transferred outside of the archive to litigation support providers, review applications, and third parties can be exported in native format, as load files, and in some cases through a direct technical integration.

Exploring Enterprise Content Management Technology

Enterprise Content Management (ECM) technologies are used to capture, manage, store, preserve, and deliver content and documents related to organizational processes. These ECM solutions are most frequently deployed in-house and are often part of critical business processes and document workflows.

As the need to manage ever growing volumes of data continues to challenge IT and legal organizations, ECM vendors have begun to expand their capabilities in an attempt to address all forms of electronic content—both structured and unstructured—in the enterprise.

The ECM market had its beginnings in the late 1980s and early 1990s as organizations worked to solve departmental business process challenges with stand-alone technology implementations. As these technologies began to successfully take hold in small pockets, organizations and vendors sought to integrate the various components into an enterprise-level solution for information management.

Identifying the Components of ECM

The Association for Information and Image Management (AIIM) defines the five key components of ECM as capture, manage, store, preserve, and deliver. Each component addresses a critical issue associated with managing enterprise content:

- **Capture** This function addresses the movement of content from its source into the ECM system. Capture can involve manual methods as well as automatic and semi-automatic methods.

- **Manage** This function addresses the management, processing, and use of information. Activities may include managing roles and organization, reporting, monitoring, backup and recovery, and changing or deleting records.

- **Store** This function addresses issues related to the storage of content, including the use of storage repositories and technologies, as well as retention and disposal policies, security, and audit trails.

- **Preserve** This function addresses the requirement for policies and procedures to ensure that the integrity of preserved information is retained and that such information is always accessible to users. Preserve components handle both the long-term storage and backup of static information as well as the temporary storage of information that falls outside the requirements for archiving or preservation.

- **Deliver** This function consists of three groups of functions and media: security technologies, transformation technologies, such as computer output to laser disk (COLD); and distribution, such as paper, e-mail, fax, and phone.

Reviewing Information Retention Processes and Technologies

While record retention needs and technologies vary from one company to the next, all organizations that use ESI must understand and manage according to the 2006 amendments to the FRCP. These Federal Rules require all parties involved in a litigation to have in place the processes and tools to preserve information related to actual or reasonably anticipated litigation.

Needless to say, the amended Rules impact a variety of electronic discovery issues. Consequently, businesses, IT organizations, and their counsel must become familiar with the company's ESI systems, its retention policies, and the methods for capturing information.

The rapid migration of business data from paper to electronic format has outpaced the rate of collaboration between legal and IT departments. This oversight has created a gap in the corporate information management and legal infrastructure that has played out repeatedly in courts across the United States.

Examining Information Management Failures

Court cases continue to illustrate that the management of information—especially e-mail messages—has often been overlooked. Many organizations have not yet properly integrated e-mail into a broader information management infrastructure. As a result, the question of ownership related to the management of ESI has never been clearly defined in many organizations.

Zubulake v. UBS Warburg LLC

The *Zubulake v. UBS Warburg* case became a landmark example of the potential cost of failing to preserve relevant ESI. One of the parties was unable to produce e-mail and other information during discovery and was hit with a $29 million verdict against it.

The Zubulake case was credited with identifying the growing need for changes to the Federal Rules. The message was clear. Electronic discovery had arrived, and courts were not willing to excuse failures in discovery because the evidence was in digital form.

Coleman v. Morgan Stanley

In 2004, an IT executive for Morgan Stanley provided a signed court document certifying that he had handed over all e-mails related to a suit filed by Ronald Perelman. However, 1,600 tapes were later found in a closet that had not been searched prior to the submission of that document.

The court found that Morgan Stanley failed to locate and search all of its backup tapes for relevant e-mail, even after repeated orders requiring them to do so. As a result, the judge instructed the jury to make an adverse inference regarding the missing e-mail. In effect, the court found that Morgan Stanley committed fraud against Ronald Perelman, and it became Morgan Stanley's burden to prove they had not. The jury awarded Coleman $604 million in compensatory damages and $850 million in punitive damages. The final award, which was close to $1.8 billion, was later overturned on appeal.

Whether the missing e-mail at Morgan Stanley was an honest mistake or a major effort to hide digital evidence, the lesson is clear. Mistakes such as the inability to locate data, missing backup tapes, and poor information management policies illustrate that courts believe that litigants must be aware of their obligations to preserve ESI that is relevant to pending or reasonably foreseeable litigation. In any organization where large volumes of data such as e-mail, instant messaging, Microsoft Office files, and other forms of unstructured data exist, IT managers and legal counsel need to know what data they have, where it is located, and what steps are necessary to preserve it.

Considering a Retention Policy

Organizations must establish and implement effective information retention policies. The policy pinpoints the types and categories of information generated by the organization and clarifies where, how, and by whom that information is maintained. It also includes a retention schedule that stipulates the length of time each type of information should be stored, and when and how each type of information is to be destroyed.

Organizations must establish clear and defensible retention policies to demonstrate they are attempting to meet their legal and regulatory obligations as well as their own business needs. At the same time, however, organizations must also avoid retaining information for too long. Doing so increases the risk of having to produce information that could have justifiably been expired as part of a good faith information management policy. This highlights the importance of setting a retention policy that addresses both minimum and maximum retention times and ensures that only timely and potentially relevant information is preserved.

WARNING

Retaining information for too long comes with a price. In an internal study of its response to discovery requests over a three-year period, DuPont reviewed 75 million pages of text and found that more than 50 percent of the documents it reviewed were kept beyond their required retention period. The company calculated that the cost of reviewing documents past their retention periods amounted to $12 million.

Developing a Retention Policy

Establishing a successful retention policy is a multistep process (see Figure 3.2). The resulting schedule for information retention may be a separate policy or part of a larger records and information management policy. Either way, a number of best practices have been identified to help organizations create a successful retention schedule.

Figure 3.2 Six Steps of Developing a Retention Policy

Assemble a cross functional team that includes legal, HR, records management and IT.	Gather input from stakeholders pertaining to any legal, business or regulatory requirements for the retention of electronically stored information.	Begin interim archiving with a broad and inclusive policy while particulars of the retention policy are defined.	Begin Interim archiving Develop a retention policy and schedule as well as a data map.	Institute formal retention policies and end-user training	Formalize legal hold process and training

Because the goal of developing a records and information management policy is to create a legally defensible policy that also addresses the organization's everyday business needs, the first step is to gather input from an inclusive range of stakeholders across the business. Among these should be IT representatives who are familiar with both the capabilities of the systems for retaining information and the information to be retained. It is equally important to involve legal personnel who have knowledge of the regulatory and other requirements that govern the organization's records. Additional stakeholders may also be involved at the initial stage of the process to help ensure the resulting retention periods reflect the needs and abilities of all users and of the business as a whole.

Next, organizations must identify and collect information to be retained. All information to be retained must have a retention period assigned to it and be included in a retention schedule.

Determining the actual retention periods is the next step in the development of a retention policy. Organizations must categorize their information according to the regulations to which they are subject, and then pinpoint the required minimum retention period for each category.

Once retention periods have been set, organizations may choose to begin archiving e-mail immediately. A variety of automated archiving tools enable organizations to set an "indefinite" retention period while the retention policy and schedule are being finalized and put in place. The most significant benefit of such interim archiving is that it allows the organization to quickly begin to meet legal preservation obligations. Interim archiving also gives IT teams an opportunity to better understand the technology, configure it for their environment, and share this feedback with the retention policy team. Then, when the organization is ready to implement its permanent policy, information that was already archived can be reviewed in accordance with the permanent policy and dealt with as appropriate.

After legally required categories have been addressed, the organization may then designate additional retention periods based on business needs and its perception of the potential for litigation. To that end, organizations must consider how often access to the information is likely to be needed on a regular basis and the extent to which information is either superseded by, or included in, later versions. Organizations must also consider how often information is distributed outside the organization, the potential for future litigation, the purpose of information, and its intended and actual use. Typically, setting business needs–based retention periods is sufficient to establish a defensible basis if the organization's preservation practices are challenged in the courts.

The final step in the retention policy development process is to create a written schedule that can be distributed to users and can be used as part of the legal defensibility record. Both minimum and maximum retention periods should be addressed. Organizations may choose to include a general clause stating that upon the expiration of the minimum retention period, the information will no longer be retained. The maximum retention period should also cover the disposal of any currently retained information. Once complete, the retention policy should be provided to everyone throughout the organization.

TIP

The amended FRCP rule 379f, called the "safe harbor" rule, states that "absent exceptional circumstances, a court may not impose sanctions on a party for failing to provide electronically stored information lost as a result of the routine, good-faith operation of an electronic information system." Discretion is left with the court to determine whether the information was actually lost as a result of the routine operation of an information management system or for some other reason.

The first step toward establishing a good-faith process should be a sound and reasonable information management policy effectively implemented and functioning before litigation begins. Organizations able to demonstrate that they had provisions in place for the retention, expiry, and preservation of ESI are less likely to be sanctioned for discovery misconduct.

For many organizations, there is no business or legal reason to save all electronically stored information forever. However, the amendments to the FRCP have placed clear responsibilities on the management and preservation of ESI when that data is relevant to impending litigation. Litigation holds require the suspension of any data expiry policies. By automating the management of information according to policy, technologies such as enterprise content management, records management, and archiving systems can help organizations respond to litigation holds.

Considering Technologies to Facilitate E-discovery

Today's fast changing litigation environment demands information policies and processes that support retention, expiry, preservation, and discovery. Retention processes must address the full range of ESI, including structured and unstructured content.

Discovery processes must be fast and accurate. With multiple teams of paralegals, inside counsel, and outside counsel using a wide range of review, case management, and production tools, special consideration must be paid to the processes and technologies used.

Information management technology can help organizations meet these legal requirements as they address the explosive growth in the volume and variety of information to be managed. Even as e-mail volumes continue to expand, standard mail platforms are extending to incorporate unified messaging spanning voicemail, pictures, and video. Instant messaging technologies are already in use by most employees of medium to large businesses, and its use is quickly growing. At the same time, messaging and collaboration tools are becoming more important and more pervasive across the enterprise. Clearly, addressing litigation issues demands an approach that balances legal and information technology requirements.

Legal departments should develop unambiguous information management policies that will stand up in court, with consistent automated policy enforcement where possible. They also need quick, comprehensive, and effective legal holds to prevent data destruction and spoliation sanctions and enable the rapid and efficient discovery of data to support early case assessments, analysis, and ongoing legal review. In addition, legal requires an open approach to e-discovery that helps multiple internal and external teams make the best use of electronically stored information in archives and content management systems.

IT organizations, in turn, require practical, efficient information management processes that optimize storage and minimize burdens on end users. To avoid disruption and protect productivity, IT organizations also require a proactive approach to e-discovery. A purely reactive approach presents challenges for IT when implementing legal holds and supporting early case assessments.

Examining a Technology Framework for Managing Information

In May 2005, the Electronic Discovery Reference Model (EDRM) Project was launched to address the lack of standards and guidelines in the electronic discovery market. Today, the EDRM is recognized as a viable framework for developing, selecting, evaluating, and using electronic discovery products and services. A growing number of IT and legal departments, law firms, and corporations as well as service and software providers build their approaches to e-discovery around this model.

The EDRM framework gives organizations a structure for understanding how to successfully manage information for e-discovery purposes. The model demonstrates the flow of data as it moves throughout the discovery process, marked by a series of nine "nodes" that pinpoint the stages required to process toward successful e-discovery. As this data moves from one phase to the next, the volume of data is reduced and only the most relevant content enters the final review and production stages (see Figure 3.3).

Figure 3.3 The Electronic Discovery Reference Model

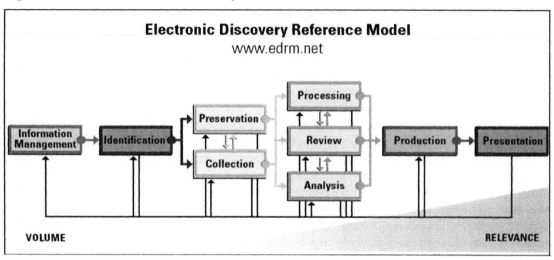

Each stage within the EDRM addresses best practices associated with a unique and critical component of electronic discovery, including the following:

- Information, or records, management
- Identification
- Preservation
- Collection
- Processing
- Review
- Analysis
- Production
- Presentation

An examination of each stage provides valuable insight into the challenges and requirements of managing information for electronic discovery.

Information Management

A comprehensive information management program is the cornerstone of a successful e-discovery process. However, while the vast majority of communications and business activities today take place in an electronic environment, many enterprises do not have document retention programs and policies in place to appropriately address how ESI is created, managed, and disposed. Fewer organizations have the tools to effectively enforce their information policies and, as a result, struggle with the discovery process.

Because a good information management program addresses all types of business records, whether electronic or not, and since electronically stored records are the dominant form today, the use of information technology systems is critical to the effective management of information. These systems support the objectives of an information management program and ease many of the challenges of dealing with electronically stored records. From capturing and automatically classifying the metadata—that is, "data about data"—associated with each record in order to meet legal requirements, to automatically handling records in compliance with federal and state regulations and streamlining the review process, these systems provide a reliable efficient way to manage information.

Tools & Traps...

Getting a Handle on Metadata

Metadata is data typically stored electronically that describes characteristics of ESI, found in different places in different forms. It can be supplied by applications, users, or the file system. Metadata can describe how, when, and by whom ESI was collected, created, accessed, and modified, and how it is formatted. Metadata can be altered intentionally or inadvertently. Certain metadata can be extracted when native files are processed for litigation. Some metadata, such as file dates and sizes, can easily be seen by users, while other metadata can be hidden or embedded and unavailable to computer users who are not technically adept. Metadata is generally not reproduced in full form when a document is printed to paper or electronic image.

Document metadata are properties about the file stored in the file, as opposed to document content. Often this data is not immediately viewable in the software application used to create/edit the document but often can be accessed via a "Properties" view. Examples include document author and company, and create and revision dates.

E-mail metadata is data stored in the e-mail about the e-mail. Often, this data is not even viewable in the e-mail client application used to create the e-mail—for example, blind copy addresses and received dates. The amount of e-mail metadata available for a particular e-mail varies greatly depending on the e-mail system.

File system metadata is metadata generated by the system to track the demographics (name, size, location, usage, and so on) of the ESI and is stored externally from the ESI rather than being embedded within it. (Source: The Sedona Conference)

Identification

At any time, a judicial order or discovery request may require an organization to preserve or disclose data. In fact, data should also be preserved and disclosed when a future or pending legal proceeding is anticipated. The challenge is, before this information can be disclosed, it must be found.

Consequently, organizations must be able to identify the individuals and business information systems likely to have information relevant to the transaction or dispute, and then determine the scope of responsive data. A litigation response plan must be established, and subsequent actions must follow to identify key witnesses and custodians of data, determine key timeframes, pinpoint keywords that will aid in searches, and single out other potentially relevant document types.

To that end, organizations should have an accurate map of their company's information systems and a diagram of its network in order to better understand document management systems, data types, e-mail systems, and other data sources. They must also consider the need for forensic data capture while taking into account the company's backup media, retired hardware, and disaster recovery systems and processes, as well as its legacy systems.

Preservation

A variety of rules, regulations, and laws now address the duty to preserve electronically stored information. Standards and guidance for preservation have been set forth by regulatory agencies such as the SEC, as well as the FRCP, case law, and the American Bar Association (ABA) Civil Discovery Standards.

Pre-preservation steps are an essential part of successful information management for e-discovery. Organizations must understand records retention policies as well as the need to designate information technology experts with whom a requesting party would work, and must know and understand their information technology architecture.

Archiving and content management solutions can help simplify the legal hold process by proactively collecting data according to policy. When a preservation order is received, archived data is more easily preserved because it has already been collected, indexed, and stored in a centralized repository.

Collection

The EDRM defines data collection as the acquisition of electronic information marked as potentially relevant in the identification phase. This information should be collected in a comprehensive manner and in a way that retains the integrity of the content as well as its form. To find data for collection, searches should span online and production data as well as offline data, archive data, and backup data—including any data that resides in backups on employees' home computers and data on backup media that is waiting to be disposed of or reused. The EDRM suggests that a good strategy to determine the location of electronic data is to leverage a network diagram to create a map of the types of data, their locations, and their custodians.

Many issues should be considered in this stage of electronic discovery. During this process, metadata must be collected and retained, and chain of custody records for all documents, data, and objects collected must be maintained in order to assure their authenticity. It is imperative that unauthorized access to the data be prevented and that any attempts to access the data be tracked.

Processing

With the evolution from paper to digital records, electronic discovery processing must now support large varieties and volumes of evidence.

Needless to say, information technology and automation are vital in ensuring that relevant data is available for review, production, and use. Technologies are now available to capture and preserve electronic documents as well as the metadata associated with collected files. These technology-based tools can automatically associate certain collections of documents with specific individuals, as well as set the parent-child relationship among source data files. Redundant data can often be automatically identified and eliminated using these tools, and keywords, date ranges, and more can be used to automatically suppress irrelevant material.

Review

Document review is another key stage in the e-discovery process. The early part of this stage is often used to sort through documents, separating responsive documents to produce from privileged documents to withhold. Later in this stage, legal teams will begin to better understand the facts of a case and be able to develop strategies based on the information collected.

Managing the large volumes of electronic documents involved in the review process requires attention to a variety of information technology issues, from planning for the appropriate hardware and software to selecting tools for review, management, and production. Advances in data storage, search technologies, and online review tools are making these tasks easier to address.

Analysis

In the analysis stage of electronic discovery, the objective is to determine relevant summary information. This may include major topics of the case, important documents, specific vocabulary and jargon, and key people.

A variety of technologies and tools of analysis are available, and they can be employed at different points in the e-discovery process. To find a good analysis tool, organizations should look for a solution that supports multiple fields, a complete set of query operators, relevance ranking, inclusive queries, and sort, stemming, and lemmatization. Other analysis capabilities such as support for derived metadata, guided navigation, and visualization can also aid in effective data analysis.

Production

With large volumes of electronic data being collected and reviewed, it is important to understand the options and variables of how that data is ultimately produced, whether in civil litigation or regulatory investigations. Types of electronic documents, as well as their formats and the media upon which they are stored and delivered, are key considerations in this stage of electronic discovery. Regardless of format, ESI must be produced in its typical form or in a form that is reasonably usable. In addition, in this stage of e-discovery, it is also necessary to ensure that production is quality-checked before data is released to the requesting party.

Presentation

While the presentation stage appears last in the EDRM, it should be thought of as the first. In other words, electronic discovery activities should begin with the end in mind to ensure that ESI can be presented most effectively at depositions, hearings, or trials.

Clearly, effective electronic discovery is tied not only to an organization's strategy for managing information but also to the technology it utilizes for information management. With the right people, processes, and technologies in place, organizations can successfully address the requirements for information management and e-discovery.

Managing Information for E-discovery

No single technology meets all of the information and e-discovery requirements in a single solution. Technologists, attorneys, and jurists have started working together to define standards. Leveraging their active participation in the EDRM Project and other standards activities, a growing number of software vendors are also aligning their solutions with complementary technologies for information management. The ability to transfer and manage data between a content and archiving solution, search tool, and collection product provides a more complete platform that eases many of the challenges of e-discovery.

Today's information management solutions provide an intelligent infrastructure for storing, managing, and enabling the discovery of corporate data from e-mail systems, file server environments, instant messaging platforms, and collaboration and records management systems. These solutions support retention policies that can ultimately help an organization demonstrate sound information management practice to the courts.

Often, these solutions offer their policy-driven retention and full indexing capabilities for hundreds of file types, from Microsoft Exchange and Simple Mail Transfer Protocol (SMTP) e-mail to Microsoft Office files, Microsoft SharePoint records, and IBM Lotus Notes Domino files, as well as encrypted e-mail, zipped files, file shares, and even obsolete and niche file formats.

To avoid file compatibility problems, many of these systems work by archiving, indexing, and retaining original content with Hypertext Markup Language (HTML) copies. A markup language uses a set of annotations that describe how text is to be structured, laid out, or formatted. HTML rendering creates a standardized version of the archived. Consequently, even if the original application associated with a file is no longer available, the file can be identified, located, and viewed. This goes a long way toward providing an indexed, centralized repository of information that supports fast cost-effective case assessment in the early stages of e-discovery.

Eliminating PST Files

One of the most valuable capabilities of a content archiving system is its ability to deal with PST files. These files can have a significant effect on the cost of the discovery process since they can be expensive to collect and, because they contain so much content, can also be expensive to review. PST files do not offer any single instance storage or deduplication capabilities, which may also result in significant processing and review costs. Also, should they appear late in the discovery process and be found to contain potentially relevant e-mail records, they create a potential smoking gun.

NOTE

Microsoft Outlook PST files are files that end users often create as private e-mail archives on their own desktop and laptop computers. These files not only waste space and are easily corrupted, but they also exist outside of the control of the organization's retention policies, resulting in years' worth of e-mail that is likely being retained longer than required.

From both an IT and legal perspective, the elimination of PST files is a best practice. Information management systems eliminate the PST problem in two ways. First, archives eliminate the need for end users to use a PST by removing mailbox quotas. Mailbox quotas are typically storage limits placed on end users by IT to control storage costs. These quotas tend to drive users toward "underground archiving" where they create their own unmanaged undocumented archives.

In addition, archiving solutions can eliminate the existing PST files by crawling the network and collecting the PST files into the archive. As these files are collected and stored in the archive, they are indexed, single instanced, compressed, and assigned a retention policy. The original PST file is then deleted. This centralization of unstructured content in the archive reduces the cost and risk of the e-discovery process by giving legal and IT a single centralized repository to store, manage, and discover all e-mail alongside other archived content, such as Microsoft SharePoint data, files, and instant messages.

In this centralized repository, legal has the ability to search, preserve, and review information that would have previously required a manual search and collection process from multiple disparate locations, such as desktops, file servers, and e-mail servers.

Legal users are able to leverage the information in archives often without IT involvement. The proactive approach of archiving enables faster access to ESI in support of early case assessments and internal investigations. Many archiving systems also facilitate the response to corporate lawsuits by providing audited workflows for the preservation, review, and marking process. This role-based process enables effective coordination of multiple teams as they prepare for "meet and confer" contact with opposing counsel.

Prior to this meeting, legal users have the ability to conduct searches against the archive as they investigate relevant custodians, keywords, file types, and date ranges. Having this view into the volume of responsive data can be advantageous when negotiating search criteria. Responsive data can be collected into cases that can also be delivered to outside counsel through virtual private network (VPN) access as well as by traditional media such as CD, DVD, and HDD.

Extending the E-discovery Platform

More and more intelligent archiving solutions now also offer integration points with other e-discovery tools to expand their capabilities. This is accomplished through an open application program interface (API). By leveraging an archiving system's open API, other applications can integrate with the archive repository both as content sources and content targets.

NOTE

An API is a language and message format used by some software applications to communicate with the operating system or some other control program such as a database management system (DBMS) or communications protocol. APIs can specify the details of how two independent computer programs can interact, such as an ECM or archiving platform and a downstream e-discovery application that may share data or chain of custody tracking.

For example, many archive solutions do not yet have the capabilities to collect active content from the desktop. As a result, archives and collection tools providers have begun to partner to provide a more complete repository of records that can centralize the retention expiry, preservation, and review of ESI. When archived data is required by third parties or external litigation support providers, manual and automated data transfers can be enabled to transfer the data. The manual approach involves copying the data onto a form of physical media for transfer; however, this put at risk the directive to maintain chain of custody reporting during the discovery process.

Indeed, chain of custody is critical throughout every stage of e-discovery. From a physical perspective, the first step in avoiding data handling errors and mistakes is to simply restrict the number of hands that touch evidence. From a technology perspective, maintaining chain of custody starts by utilizing software that includes automated robust reporting and auditing capabilities. Automating the entire process, from data collection to data review, and removing the human factor represents an important best practice for information management and electronic discovery.

To that end, an open API can enable automated and audited transfer between the archiving system and the eventual review or analysis platform. The first such integration of an archive with an analysis tool was between Symantec's Enterprise Vault archiving product and the Patterns product by Attenex. This integration eliminated the manual export process while decreasing the time, cost, and risk associated with data movement.

Content Management Systems

Enterprise content management systems typically enable organizations to manage structured information from sources such as customer relationship management applications, document management systems, enterprise portals, and enterprise resource applications according to predefined business rules, processes, and workflows.

Integrating a complementary information management system such as e-mail archiving with content management enables users of the content management system to perform in-place retention management of unstructured information, such as e-mail stored in the archive. Through direct integration, the retention policies of the content management system are transparently applied to e-mail messages, which are declared as records and then stored and managed solely by the archive.

Search and Collection Tools

While archiving systems manage the collection process for electronically stored information according to a company's records management policy, e-discovery requests may extend to include data that exists in the live environment that has not yet been subject to retention policies. An example of this type of data is a spreadsheet on which a user is working on their desktop or laptop.

For this reason, a growing number of information management systems support integration with search and collection tools to allow desktop data to be collected and imported into the archive. This gives organizations a single, centralized location for data retention, expiration, preservation, and discovery of archived data and "active" or "free range" data. The centralization of this data within an archive also enhances chain of custody reporting and decreases the risk of error by reducing or eliminating manual processes for desktop collection, retention, and expiry.

Analytics Tools

Archiving systems enable organizations to quickly conduct an initial search and review of the archive for data that is potentially responsive to a litigation request or an internal investigation. Often, corporations treat this search as a first cull of the data seeking to perform custodian, date range, or keyword-based search. Depending on the size of the case and result set, internal staff may choose to conduct the remainder of the discovery process in-house or export the data for further analysis or review.

Analytics tools automate data processing and provide powerful visualization capabilities for quickly analyzing massive amounts of ESI. If data is to be moved to an analytics system upon completion of the archiving search, organizations often must export data to portable media such as CDs, DVDs, and HDDs, and then transfer it to the analytics tool. Organizations looking to streamline this process have the option of using an integration archiving and analytics solution for advanced processing and review.

Review Tools

For organizations or legal counsel using third-party tools for review and case management, integration between the information management system and the review tool enables data to be automatically exported and updated for review. As mentioned, intelligent archiving systems provide for review by inside counsel according to a role-based workflow, and also often enable review by outside counsel through a VPN. With the archiving system maintaining a chain of custody throughout the data transfer process, this capability reduces the labor, cost, and risk of moving information. In some cases, reviewed and marked data can be returned to the repository for retention and use in future investigations.

Classifying Data

Virtually all information management tools include a data classification component. In the first stages of the information management process, classification is applied at the retention policy level and data is assigned a retention category. After all, only when data is appropriately classified can it then be intelligently filtered, retained, and discovered. This is particularly important when dealing with e-mail. Rather than treating all e-mail the same, many of these tools provide for intelligent classification and categorize messages according to their relevance to specific business purposes.

Of course, just as not all e-mail, records, or files have the same value, not all companies have the same classification needs for their information. For example, highly process-driven organizations such as insurance firms or mortgage companies may require more granular classification than businesses with more fluid interaction.

Consequently, many of today's systems for information management also provide for user classification and automated classification. Regardless of approach, classification enables staff responsible for legal compliance to quickly identify and access the highest priority communication they need to retrieve, review, audit, and produce documents. Authorized personnel can also exclude messages, such as privileged communications, when responding to a subpoena or preparing for litigation.

Tools & Traps...

Evaluating User and Automated Classification Methods

Some organizations rely on users to classify e-mail and other types of ESI as part of their daily use of the data. However, with the volume of content users interact with growing so quickly every day, productivity can suffer using this approach. Users who prefer to click, read, respond to, and move rapidly through e-mail often find it prohibitively time-consuming to be tasked with either using an application plug-in to specify meta-data with every message or ponder which folder each message should be saved to.

Information management tools that provide for user classification typically monitor user activity, identify e-mail and files that need to be classified, then prompt the user to choose from a subset of predefined classifications as needed. Because these tools are able to assign the retention categories automatically based on the classification selected by the user, policies are continuously enforced.

In contrast, the automatic classification of ESI—for example, as business, personal, or junk—eliminates the challenges of manually evaluating every item to determine whether to save or discard it. Organizations can set granular retention policies across different categories of information and determine the preferred storage media to use, which helps lower operations costs by controlling the size of archived and managed messages. Accurate automated classification of messages also provides context, thereby easing retrieval and processing.

Automated classification engines can assign tags to each e-mail or file. Each stage applies to a corresponding retention category. This determines how long the data is kept in the system before being discarded. Typically, the tagging rules are based on various customizable and predefined conditions, and flexibility is critical since rules

Continued

can be established on multiple levels. Predefined rules may include categories such as legal or financial attachments, attorney-client privilege, sexual harassment, offensive language, compensation discussions, chain mail, and more. Tagging rules also allow for certain actions to be taken on messages, including whether a message should be excluded or flagged for review.

The inclusion of classification capabilities gives organizations the ability to manage the content in their information management system more effectively and locate the information they need more rapidly.

Examining Backup, Recovery, and Security Technologies

Traditional backup and recovery solutions and security technologies are essential to effective information management. These technologies enable organizations to ensure that their information remains secure and available. However, their role in e-discovery is limited.

Evaluating the Role of Backup in E-discovery

In the context of information management, backup is critical and is often done to tape or to disk. The trouble is, however, that backups are cumbersome, expensive, and time-consuming in an e-discovery scenario. While backup procedures are intended to protect against data loss, they are not an archive from which specific pieces of information can quickly and easily be found and accessed. What's more, unless the backup provides continuous data protection capabilities to ensure real-time protection of information, backups may be incomplete or inaccurate because they do not reflect changes made between scheduled backups.

That said, restoring data from backup tape or disk may be the only option in legal cases that involve data that is no longer in use. Discovering and recovering data from tape usually requires a restore of a complete system or a subset of files and a significant amount of preparation time. It can be done, but it may fall far short of meeting regulators' demands for timeliness or accuracy.

Newer disk-to-disk-to-tape backup solutions give organizations a backup option that makes it easier to quickly restore to a specific point in time. This technology works by taking periodic snapshots of data throughout the day. Many organizations leverage such point-in-time copy capabilities to impose legal holds in document destruction.

However, from an e-discovery perspective, this approach may still be inadequate because it fails to include documents produced or archived between snapshots. It also adds risk by introducing separate security and management requirements for two versions of the same document and by injecting an unnecessary reconciliation process between those versions.

For these reasons, organizations looking for e-discovery tools are advised to opt for information management technologies, such as archiving, that are focused more specifically on speeding response to legal requests than on providing traditional data protection.

Evaluating the Role of Recovery in E-discovery

Traditional enterprise recovery solutions protect against natural disasters and full system failures by capturing and recovering applications at the server level. Within e-discovery, however, the ability to accurately recover metadata is as important as recovering business applications and documents. With traditional backup, separate content and metadata servers are susceptible to corruptions. Plus, even if the metadata database is recoverable, any data recovered will not be acceptable if the connections between metadata and a working document are corrupted.

Furthermore, creating such connections can be burdensome and difficult depending upon the number of disconnected or orphaned metadata objects. If a record or group of records is lost or corrupted—whether due to a virus, human or programmatic error, inconsistency, or isolated disruption—recovery typically involves finding the right backup tape or tapes, searching through them to find the relevant documents, and then recovering the documents without the metadata. Clearly, more granular recovery is needed.

A granular recovery solution accounts for the nature of metadata. This recovery approach locates metadata objects, validates their accuracy and authenticity, and recovers them directly back to their original state. This facilitates compliance with FRCP mandates related to the preservation and production of ESI and serves as a valuable component of an effective information management program.

Evaluating the Role of Security in E-discovery

As business evolves and connectivity drives increased mobility, online interaction, and collaboration, the risks to information increase. With people the new perimeter, the focus of security must move from infrastructure to information. Information is constantly traveling, moving across networks and from one device to another. Furthermore, a growing portion of an organization's most vital records now likely resides in e-mail systems. How can businesses make sure such information does not end up in the wrong hands? And how can they be sure their information is not only secure but discoverable as well?

Organizations must be aware of the potential impact of threats such as viruses when processing data for e-discovery. Electronic data is restored from tape or disk exactly as it was backed up or stored; therefore, a file that was infected before it was backed up will still be infected when it is restored. When dealing with electronic data that may be contaminated with malicious code, source data should be isolated before it is put into an active network or processing platform until its integrity has been determined.

Indeed, the challenges of ensuring both the security and availability of information now are a concern not only for IT departments but for legal teams as well. On one hand, information management policies must address the objectives of safeguarding the security and privacy of messages, both inbound and outbound, and preventing the leakage of proprietary and confidential information to unauthorized individuals, whether inside or outside the organization.

At the same time, overly burdensome information management policies can create unintended consequences. For example, an aggressive expiry process related to e-mail may cause users to store old messages on devices or in locations outside the reach of the organization, which makes security and e-discovery efforts more difficult.

However, just as poor information management creates risk, intelligent information management mitigates risk. To that end, organizations must take a proactive approach to information management by implementing multiple layers of security aimed at mitigating security threats while keeping sensitive information in.

For example, since information flows through a variety of channels like e-mail, instant messaging, and the Internet, organizations must ensure that it does not create added risks from viruses, worms, spam, and other unwanted content. In addition, the ease of sharing and distributing information has greatly increased the risk of losing sensitive proprietary or regulated content, even as legal requirements for information retention and e-discovery intensify the demands for information management.

A variety of technologies are available and in use today to help businesses protect their information without inhibiting its access by authorized parties. Furthermore, new tools are emerging that incorporate traditional security technologies with e-discovery and policy management technologies for more comprehensive and effective information management.

Protection technologies such as antivirus, antispam, content filtering, and data loss prevention technologies are now available together with retention and discovery or audit tools. The integration of these technologies provides a direct communication link at the critical points where data is exchanged, from the server to the gateway and archive. This enables IT to enforce policies and controls in real time and remediate jeopardous practices. In addition, consistent controls and automatic risk classifications are often provided, which help ensure that information traversing the organization's systems is not only free of malicious content but is also subject to the appropriate review and retention policies.

Summary

Archiving, enterprise content management, and other technology solutions can help organizations meet requirements for e-discovery. Archiving provides a platform for storing, managing, and enabling the discovery of unstructured corporate data from e-mail systems, file server environments, instant messaging platforms, and collaboration and content management systems. These systems use classification and retention technologies to capture, categorize, index, and store target data to enforce policies as well as tools to support legal discovery.

Enterprise content management systems also facilitate e-discovery by providing a technology platform for capturing, managing, storing, preserving, and delivering data. While many of these systems have traditionally focused on structured content, a growing number are expanding to include unstructured content as well.

A fundamental component of e-discovery technology is its support for retention policies. By automatically archiving data according to its specified retention period and schedule, these tools offer an efficient mechanism for ensuring that information is retained in accordance with legal requirements and standards. The Electronic Discovery Reference Model (EDRM) gives organizations a framework for selecting the most appropriate e-discovery technology for their needs.

A growing number of archiving systems are now expanding their capabilities by offering integration points with other e-discovery tools such as content management systems, search and collection tools, analytics, and review tools. These integrated solutions provide organizations a more robust and complete system for e-discovery.

While traditional technologies such as backup, recovery, and security are invaluable components of information management, their value in aiding the e-discovery process varies. Backup solutions are effective for data protection but do not provide an archive for e-discovery. Advanced solutions that provide granular recovery may ease the restoration of metadata in content management systems, and security solutions are an effective tool for protecting information from malicious threats before it is archived. When used together with e-discovery technologies, these traditional solutions help form the foundation of an effective technology infrastructure in an effort to meet complex requirements for managing information.

Solutions Fast Track

Understanding Archiving Technology

- ☑ Archiving solutions act as a long-term indexed repository for the storage of electronic information.

- ☑ Archiving solutions provide for the consistent and routine collection of information.

- ☑ Archiving solutions support early case assessments.

Exploring Enterprise Content Management Technology

☑ Enterprise content management systems are used to capture, manage, store, preserve, and deliver content.

☑ Enterprise content management systems frequently manage structured content.

☑ Newer enterprise content management systems may address both structured and unstructured content.

Reviewing Information Retention Processes and Technologies

☑ Information management is impacted by the Federal Rules for Civil Procedure (FRCP).

☑ FRCP rules are driving the need for information retention policies.

☑ Establishing a successful retention policy is a multistep process.

Considering Technologies to Facilitate E-discovery

☑ Information management technologies facilitate e-discovery.

☑ The Electronic Discovery Reference Model (EDRM) provides a viable e-discovery technology framework.

☑ An effective e-discovery system eases the management of data throughout the discovery process.

Examining Backup, Recovery, and Security Technologies

☑ Traditional technologies can play a role in e-discovery.

☑ Backup solutions provide for data protection, not e-discovery.

☑ Some recovery tools may aid e-discovery.

☑ Security technologies can protect information included in e-discovery.

Frequently Asked Questions

Q: What does an archiving solution provide?

A: Archiving solutions provide a long-term indexed repository for the storage of electronic information, particularly unstructured data such as e-mail and instant messages.

Q: How can archiving help in the collection of information?

A: Archiving solutions provide for the consistent and routine collection of information to address legal and regulatory requirements for document retention.

Q: Can archiving aid in early case assessment?

A: Archiving solutions can be leveraged to support early case assessments through search, analysis, and review capabilities.

Q: What is an enterprise content management system?

A: Enterprise content management systems are used to capture, manage, store, preserve, and deliver content and documents related to organizational processes.

Q: Do enterprise content management systems work only on structured data?

A: Enterprise content management systems are frequently used to manage structured content and documents.

Q: Do more advanced enterprise content management systems provide more extensive support?

A: Enterprise content management systems are being expanded to address all forms of electronic content, both structured and unstructured.

Q: What impact do FRCP rules have on information management?

A: All organizations that use electronically stored information must understand and manage it according to the 2006 amendments to the Federal Rules for Civil Procedure.

Q: What role does policy play in addressing FRCP requirements?

A: An information retention policy is critical to helping organizations address FRCP requirements.

Q: What steps are involved in developing a retention policy?

A: Establishing a successful retention policy is a multistep process that includes gathering input from stakeholders, identifying and collecting information, determining retention periods, deploying archiving (where possible), and developing a written schedule for distribution.

Q: Can information technologies aid in e-discovery?

A: Information management technologies help support policies and processes for retention, expiry, preservation, and discovery.

Q: What is the EDRM and its significance?

A: The Electronic Discovery Reference Model (EDRM) provides a viable framework for developing, selecting, evaluating, and using electronic discovery products and services.

Q: How does technology based on the EDRM aid e-discovery?

A: An effective e-discovery system based on the EDRM eases the management of data throughout the discovery process, from information management to information identification, preservation, collection, processing, review, analysis, production, and presentation.

Q: Are other traditional technology tools helpful in e-discovery?

A: Traditional backup, recovery, and security technologies are essential to effective information management, but their role in e-discovery is limited.

Q: How is backup related to e-discovery?

A: Backup tapes or disks do not provide an archive from which specific pieces of information can quickly and easily be found and accessed for e-discovery.

Q: Do recovery solutions help e-discovery?

A: Advanced granular recovery tools may serve as a component of an effective e-discovery program.

Q: Are security technologies helpful in e-discovery?

A: Proactive security technologies may work together with retention and discovery tools to enforce policies and controls and remediate risk without inhibiting timely access by authorized parties.

Chapter 4

Creating an Enterprise Discovery Response Team

Solutions in this chapter:

- **Roles and Responsibilities within a Discovery Response Team**
- **Processes for Implementing an Effective Discovery Response Team**
- **Discovery Response Team Process**
- **Implementation and Rollout**

☑ **Summary**

☑ **Solutions Fast Track**

☑ **Frequently Asked Questions**

Introduction

In today's litigation environment, e-discovery can be a daunting and often costly hurdle for many companies to overcome. The costs and potential penalties for violating the Federal Rules of Civil Procedure have finally raised awareness of this issue to the seniormost levels of many organizations. The goal of an effective discovery response team is to provide responsive information in a consistent, cost-effective, and timely manner regardless of the reason for the request. Too often, companies vary their level of effort depending on the requesting entity or the reason for the request. For example, a small employment dispute may receive little attention, whereas a request from the government is staffed with an army of people. As we learned from *Zubulake*, such inconsistency can be very costly in today's world.[1] Decisions such as *Qualcomm* have highlighted the importance of accurately identifying, collecting, and producing relevant electronically stored information (ESI).[2] Many companies find that the key to achieving this goal is to establish an internal discovery response team that follows a repeatable process each and every time a request for information is received. Companies in today's environment can no longer accept the risk of mismanaging this crucial obligation.

This chapter will provide you with a general framework for developing a discovery response team (DRT) so that your enterprise can successfully meet the challenges posed by the increasing legal and organizational demands of e-discovery. We will examine the roles and responsibilities of a DRT, who you should include in such a team, what processes you should put in place, how to clearly map out the discovery process to insure you've included everything and how to organize and prepare your core team for the organizational change management process.

Roles and Responsibilities within a Discovery Response Team

The primary function of an internal DRT is to establish and execute a discovery response plan. To ensure success, you need not only well-defined roles and responsibilities, but also well-documented processes and procedures. Although the specific roles will differ for each company, certain universal roles form a successful DRT. Of primary importance in the team organization is strong leadership and direction from the legal department and upper management. For most companies, a formal discovery response plan will be new and will require a change in management and work flow. Thus, it is critical that the impetus and direction to effectuate this change come from the executive levels within your organization.

In this age of ever-increasing demands placed on companies as a result of e-discovery, and the important of technology knowledge to fulfill these demands, the second important component of your team is strong information technology (IT) participation (whether in-house or outsourced). IT may simply assist you in locating relevant data and understanding your various systems and their retention and backup processes, or they may take a more active role and actually assist with the collection and retention of data. Whatever role you choose for them, it is important for them to be included on your team to ensure that you are meeting all of the ever-increasing technology requirements and are not falling into needless traps.

A third group that should be represented on the team is the enterprise records management team, if your organization has a separate function for records. Finally, although not directly members of the team, your discovery response process must include input from the ultimate record owners, your clients, and may also include roles filled by human resources, auditing, and third-party vendors.

Tools & Traps…

Process Mapping

To ensure that you cover all of your bases and have a consistent repeatable process, the use of process mapping when establishing your team and their roles is pivotal. Too often companies try to implement initiatives such as this in response to external pressures and do not address up front the fundamental process analysis that is required to make the team successful.

Legal Roles and Responsibilities

In the past decade, the landscape of discovery has changed dramatically. What was once a paper-driven endeavor is now focused almost exclusively on ESI and the multiple locations in which that data is stored. Due to the explosion of ESI within most corporations, the volume of data to be reviewed and produced in response to any given discovery request has increased exponentially, thus increasing the burden and cost of discovery.

Given this trend, companies are looking to their legal team as the leaders in a new age of discovery. Currently, your in-house lawyers may or may not be following consistent processes in how they respond to discovery on their individual cases. Often, you have some lawyers who are up to date on the current best practices and others who are still living in the dark ages of paper discovery and forget to look for data in the many electronic locations most users have in today's world. Lawyers who are comfortable reviewing only paper, or who think a "gig" is a job for a band, are not the best choices to head your team. Although each team will be different depending on the size of your legal department and your company, the fundamental requirements are the same. Figure 4.1 outlines some of the basic roles that we will discuss in more detail.

Figure 4.1 Discovery Response Team Roles

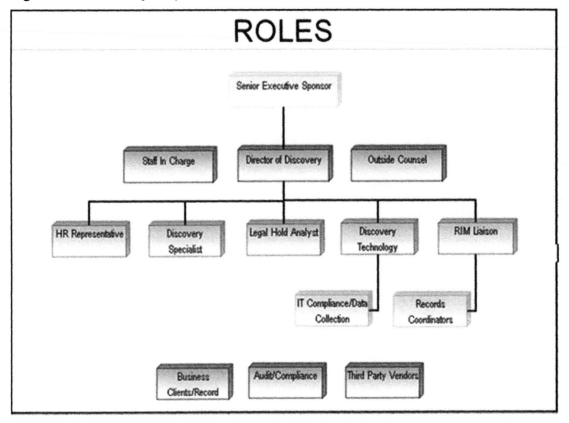

Director of Discovery/Senior Discovery Counsel

First, you need a senior-level lawyer to supervise and manage the team. This person should report to a senior executive to ensure buy-in and top down support. He is also the one who will develop and set the policies and procedures and obtain management buy-in and sign-off. Although this person does not need to have a detailed knowledge of technology, he must at least have a basic understanding of your IT systems and processes and of your records management policies, and a comprehensive understanding of the Federal Rules, as amended. The more knowledgeable this person is in these areas, the better off your team will be.

Here are some of the responsibilities you may want to include in the senior legal role:

■ Create and refine policies, procedures, and processes for the DRT, including Rule 26 compliance processes and attestations for clients.

■ Manage and update the DRT charter.

■ Oversee and coordinate the entire DRT.

- Manage the overall discovery plan and implementation.

- Manage training and education.

- Manage and ensure that the company is current with trends and rule changes.

- Lead the discovery plan for each new matter, and monitor and coordinate with in-house counsel, outside counsel, and the DRT.

- Act as a resource for in-house lawyers and outside counsel to ensure consistent stands taken in productions across all matters.

This individual may also participate in Rule 26 conferences for the company to ensure that accurate information about systems and data is relayed to the court. Having one person address these issues or "train" counsel on them prior to the meet and confer and Rule 26 conference adds yet another layer of consistency and heads off issues that may arise due to counsel's lack of in-depth knowledge of systems and processes. Finally, many companies are also utilizing this person as the 30(b)(6) designee for the company on discovery issues.

Discovery or Compliance Specialist

The second legal component of your team will be the discovery or compliance specialists. Typically, this role would be filled by senior litigation paralegals. The function of this role is broad and is the key, in many ways, to the success of your team. The discovery specialist is your front-line responder/coordinator for each discovery request. This role should report directly to the director of discovery. Here are some of the responsibilities your company may want to include in this role:

- Work with the in-house staff in charge (SIC) and the assigned paralegal to set up legal hold and identify affected individuals.

- Assist clients and the SIC in data mapping, data identification, and holding of data pursuant to Rule 26 compliance processes and your collection and preservation processes.

- Ensure that holds are up to date, and manage the hold process by ensuring timely entry of holds and revisions and follow-up with the SIC and outside counsel.

- Coordinate with outside counsel and the SIC on the discovery plan and manage implementation for specific cases.

- Work directly with external vendors on database management, hosting issues, document review, and production. Depending on outside counsel resources, may manage data review teams or work in conjunction with outside counsel. Assist with the preparation of the coding manual for production review to ensure consistency and best practices.

- Manage document productions from a high level to ensure consistent decisions companywide on form of production.

- Respond to legal hold questions from business clients.

- Assist the director of discovery with creation and refinement of policies, procedures, and processes. Assist with training and education as needed.

- Track overall vendor costs.

- Manage e-discovery vendors.

- Act as an expert on external vendor tools and usage.

The roles currently filled by your in-house legal staff will also fit into your new process. Many companies today are finding that by centralizing their discovery efforts in a core team they not only lower costs, but also reduce the risks of discovery by implementing a consistent, defensible process in each and every matter. Many in-house lawyers and paralegals are relieved to have the assistance of a focused discovery team, because the added burdens of discovery in this new era often are more than they can handle with current staffing.

TIP

When identifying legal team members focus on those with the most discovery and technology experience to shorten the learning curve. The more they understand the technology aspects of your data and its retention, the more effective they will be in working with the clients and with the IT group to ensure that all relevant data is located.

Other Legal Roles

Depending on the tools your company utilizes you may have additional roles that reside in the legal department. For example, if you utilize a legal hold system, you may have an analyst-type role that manages your legal hold tool and conducts audits on your hold process to ensure that it is functioning pursuant to your guidelines. If you outsource document review utilizing a Web-based review tool, an appropriate role is one that manages the external vendor relationships and establishes standardized review processes. Remember, this team will be a reflection of your company and one size does not fit all. For consistency and communication purposes, this role should report to the director of discovery.

Obviously, your in-house lawyers are an integral part of your discovery response plan. They are the ones with the detailed knowledge of the individual matter and will be the ones to set the scope of the discovery for their cases. Depending on how your company utilizes outside counsel for litigation, they may supplement or replace the in-house attorneys. Either way, both of these groups must be trained and brought into your plan, and execution and change management, discussed shortly, will be critical with these folks.

TIP

Start communicating early with your legal department staff and, where possible, include them in portions of the process mapping, vendor selection, or policy input. The more involved they are in assisting with the creation of the team, the easier change management and implementation will be when you roll out the new process.

The Role of IT on Your Team

The second group needed to form your successful team is IT. Although many companies choose to outsource much of the IT work related to discovery, you should consider filling some key roles with in-house IT employees. The first role to fill is that of translator. A translator would be someone in your IT organization who can talk "tech-speak" and can explain it in a language that a court, lawyer, or jury will understand. Similarly, this person must talk "lawyer-speak" and translate it into a request the technical folks can understand and respond to. This person is essentially a conduit between IT and Legal to ensure that the necessary information is being conveyed and the proper response is provided.

Have you ever asked two different IT people in your organization what you thought was the same question and received two completely different responses? Now you know why the role of a translator or liaison is a key to your success. It is important that the main IT member of your team not only be able to translate for you, but also possess knowledge of your infrastructure and enterprise content and at least a working knowledge of your key compliance and backup systems. An understanding of data preservation and collection as well as best practices for documenting chain of custody on data is also beneficial so that this individual can guide your team in proper recovery and holding of data. Some of this can be learned through seminars and published materials, but the knowledge of your internal systems is a prerequisite.

In addition to this liaison, who is delineated on Figure 4.1 as the discovery technology coordinator, you may also want to have internal IT people on your team who are involved in your key compliance systems. Some companies include, for example, an IT representative from infrastructure or enterprise security. Whether you are outsourcing or utilizing in-house resources, you will need to consider the following roles: data capture and retention; forensic imaging; investigation management; and data mapping. All will play a part in a successful response team.

One of the IT roles and responsibilities you may adopt is that of discovery technology coordinator/ IT liaison, whose responsibilities are as follows:

- Manages the IT team responsible for data collection

- Acts as the liaison to IT experts required to fulfill legal hold needs or 30(b)(6) roles

- Provides oversight of project management for electronic discovery initiatives

- Has a general knowledge of IT systems including e-mail vaulting, instant messaging systems, active directory, Oracle or similar databases, unstructured data, HR systems, and backup systems

- Acts as a liaison with outside counsel's IT department

- Understands legal requirements for data collection and production, and provides quality control of data collection, transmittal, and processing

Another IT role and responsibility you may adopt is that of IT compliance coordinator/data collection, who would be responsible for managing data collection for e-discovery activities for IT. For instance:

- Collects data required for legal holds

- Understands legal requirements for data collection chain of custody and ensures that IT conforms to requirements when collecting data

- Provides identified data to the external vendor in an appropriate format and tracks the data provided

- Updates the legal hold database (if applicable) as necessary

- Works with legal to set standards and processes for data gathering and management of hold data

- Manages internal and external resources for data gathering

- Oversees the release of data at the expiration of a hold

- Provides status reports to the team on systems and issues as needed

Your IT compliance coordinator should report directly to the discovery technology coordinator with dotted-line reporting to the director of discovery. This person will work with the SIC, discovery specialist, and paralegal on the case in their day-to-day role, but reporting should be clearly defined at the outset. In addition to these roles, many companies have recently recognized that knowledge and notification of employee transfers and terminations within your organization is critical to an effective hold process. Thus, in addition to the standard IT roles, many companies have, or are developing, a transfer/termination process for notification to the team (or Legal) when an employee is leaving the company or changing roles. Once notified, the appropriate steps can be taken to capture data, if necessary. Frequently this is managed by someone in the IT organization as a successful program has to interface between multiple IT systems such as your human resources tracking system as well as your legal hold system. Some companies utilize the IT compliance coordinator role to manage this function because that role is already integrated into the team and the person understands the goals and pitfalls. Additionally, it is often your IT organization that is managing your computer assets, so having them in the loop is beneficial. We will discuss this process in more detail later in this chapter.

Legacy data is an issue many companies are faced with due to mergers, acquisitions, and divestitures. If your IT organization has someone that specializes in these systems it is helpful to have that person as a supplement to your team to help you navigate data requests dealing with a legacy system. It is also important to educate your IT team and put a process in place for the decommissioning of legacy systems to ensure compliance with existing legal hold orders.

IT's ability to assist your legal team with the identification, capture, and production of all electronic data is crucial to the success of your team. The final piece IT brings to the puzzle is education. The more IT can educate Legal on technology, the more successful your company will be in responding to discovery. Some of the main sources of data are shown in Figure 4.2. Educate your team and legal staff on these data locations and include all types of data in your processes to ensure that you do not overlook relevant information. It is often said that a little knowledge is dangerous; however, when it comes to discovery of electronic information it is critical that you educate your lawyers on your systems and technology and provide them the IT resources. The end result will be a well-balanced team that saves your company both time and money.

Figure 4.2 Potential Data Sources for Preservation

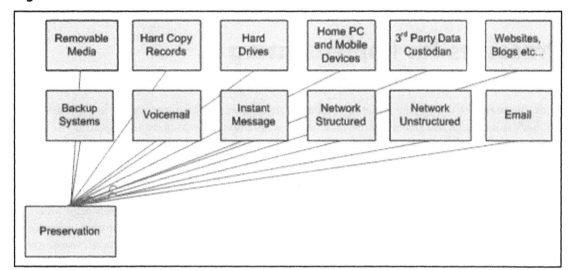

Other Team Members

Although Legal and IT may be the main focus of your initial scoping, you should not forget other very important groups that may play a role in your DRT. The output of any request for information is data. Thus, your records or information management group ("RIM") is a primary component of your team. Many companies have formalized records groups, and if this is the case in your organization, you should leverage this strength as they often have the best information about where data resides. Your records custodian may also be a frequent target of 30(b)(6) requests, and thus it is beneficial to have her on your team and to educate the team on the discovery process and your procedures. Furthermore, if your company does not have standard retention schedules and policies, that is another area for huge litigation savings. No company wants to explain why some information exists and other information for the same time period is not to be found.

Often in large organizations there are repeated requests for employment data. If this is the case in your company, having a human resources representative on your team is beneficial as a point of contact for such requests. This can streamline the gathering of data and the protection of confidential information. Additionally, in many companies the human resources group handles internal investigations and compiles information and data as a result of those investigations. It is critical that you do not overlook this source of information as you are completing your data-gathering process. Often the investigative file will have e-mails and other information that will no longer reside in your normal systems due to retention guidelines. Including them on your team ensures that this data is properly captured and is not deleted or overlooked when it is responsive to a hold. Input and support from your clients or business units is also important. The more you can include them on the front end and show them how these processes will benefit them and save time, money, and internal business resources, the more successful you will be.

Finally, you will want strong input and support from your audit or compliance group (labeled "Audit/Compliance" in Figure 4.1). Obtaining their buy-in and input on the front end of your processes will ensure that you have defensible, auditable processes. This backing will also ensure your ability to better enforce change management and compliance with the new processes and procedures.

Processes for Implementing an Effective Discovery Response Team

With the passage of the Federal Rules amendments, the burden on in-house lawyers and outside counsel has increased and become more focused. Thus, to ensure that your company is ready to respond, it is critical that you evaluate your processes and refine them to meet the new requirements, or develop them if you have none. As the recent Qualcomm decision highlights, these processes are also important to protect not only your in-house counsel and the company but also outside counsel as they navigate through production of company data. In a recent case out of the Northern District of California, *In re Flash Memory Antitrust Litigation*, the court entered the following preservation order:

"Documents, data, and tangible things shall be interpreted broadly to include writings, records, files, correspondence, reports, memoranda, calendars, diaries, minutes, electronic messages, voice mail, E-mail, telephone message records or logs, computer and network activity logs, hard drives, backup data, removable computer storage media such as tapes, discs and cards, printouts, document image files, Web pages, databases, spreadsheets, software, books, ledgers, journals, orders, invoices, bills, vouchers, check statements, worksheets, summaries, compilations, computations, charts, diagrams, graphic presentations, drawings, films, charts, digital or chemical process photographs, video, phonographic, tape or digital recordings or transcripts thereof, drafts, jottings and notes, studies or drafts of studies or other similar such material. Information that serves to identify, locate, or link such material, such as file inventories, file folders, indices, and metadata, is also included in this definition. Until the parties reach an agreement on a preservation plan or the Court orders otherwise, each party shall take reasonable steps to preserve all documents, data, and tangible things containing information potentially relevant to the subject matter of this litigation. In addition, counsel shall exercise all reasonable efforts to identify and notify parties and non-parties of their duties, including employees of corporate or institutional parties, to the extent required by the Federal Rules of Civil Procedure."[3]

Such a broad order is likely to be more common than not in this new environment and highlights why you must have the appropriate processes in place to respond to discovery. Your company may be starting from scratch but may realize that, although it may seem daunting, a focused approach that starts with mapping out your processes will give you the best chance for success. So, now that you have an idea of the roles that may be needed for your team, how do you get started? We will start from the high level and drill down through some of the processes you may need to develop.

Defining and documenting efficient, repeatable processes for your team to follow will be the lynchpin of a successful response plan. The first step before fully forming your team or starting on your process is to draft a team charter. This document will establish the goals and objectives for the team and will serve as a check point and an evaluation tool as you go forward. This is also a good starting point to formalize senior executive buy-in for your team and processes. Once you have your draft charter, you can begin to identify the team members that make the most sense for your organization. Realize that all of this needs to be flexible as you may identify additional people who are critical to your team as you go forward in the process.

Next is the process mapping step. The first process you should focus on is your high-level team process or your discovery response plan, discussed shortly. A basic flowchart showing high-level responsibilities or actions is included in Figure 4.3. This is a good starting point for your more detailed process map. Spend the time to establish robust processes at the start as it will be the key to success for your team. The time spent on the front end will save not only dollars, but also endless hours of frustration later. The objective of process mapping is to walk through every function, action, decision point, requirement, and task and assign owners or responsibility for each one. Be sure to take discovery one step at a time and think through everything that must be done. The more steps and decision points you can capture on the front end, the more quickly you will be able to accurately identify the roles and responsibilities that are associated with those steps. This will be the detailed road map for your processes and procedures. This map should also reference the processes and procedures with which your DRT will interact, even if your group does not own them.

Figure 4.3 High-Level Team Process

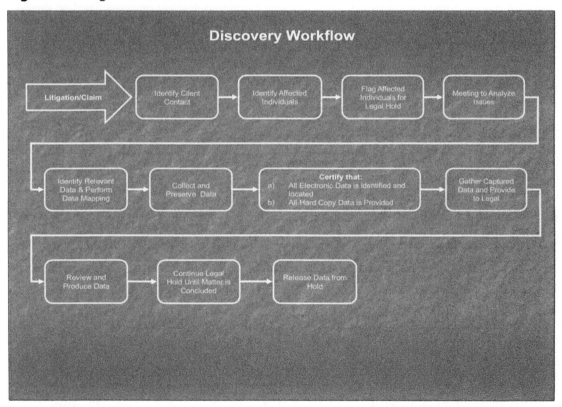

TIP

There may be processes in your enterprise that you do not own but that you touch as part of your due diligence. For example, if your company's HR department has an investigative group that gathers data in the course of their investigations, you will need a process to ensure that you are coordinating with them in the collection of relevant data in response to a request. Thus, be sure to include these data sources and external processes in your map as touch points.

In Figure 4.4, a brief example of a partial process map provides some insight regarding some of the areas you may include in mapping out your processes. Although this is clearly not an exhaustive map, it does provide a guide for developing your own. Typically, down the left-hand side of the map you will list all the roles you have identified. Then each vertical column will be an action, decision point, or step in the process. Your initial high-level process map will include other "subprocesses" that will likely be mapped out in more detail on their own process maps. One example of a key subprocess is your data collection process. Some companies may break this subprocess into multiple processes based on the type of data others may consolidate with it, especially if they outsource that role. It is important to remember to include chain of custody and defensible collection methods in this process to ensure that your data is admissible at trial.

The goal of the high-level map is to have the full picture of your DRT's goal in one document. Later in this chapter we'll discuss a few of the important subprocesses you will likely need.

Figure 4.4 A Sample Process Map

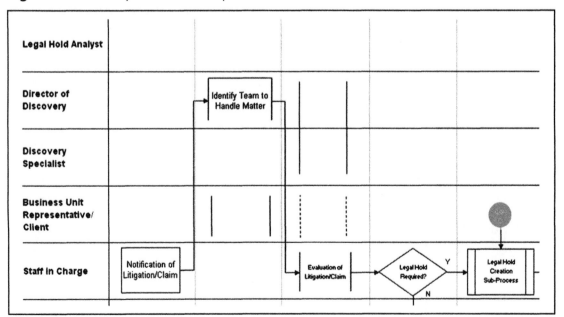

As you map out your process, be sure to keep in mind how you will audit and track each task. Defensibility is key in today's e-discovery world, and the more you build in effective documentation and audit touch points into your process, the better positioned you are to justify actions at a later date. The other benefit is that you will be able to analyze any weaknesses in your process and refine as necessary to ensure success.

Discovery Response Team Process

Many companies refer to the high-level response team process as a litigation response plan. When forming your team and establishing your goals, consider the culture of your company and your legal and IT departments. There are two primary models most companies use when forming a team and developing their litigation response plan. For ease of reference we will call them the "Do Model" and the "Assist Model." If your company has a strong culture in the legal department of individual control by staff attorneys, you may find that implementing the Assist Model is a better fit for you. Similarly, companies with more centralized control or those that have greater perceived litigation risk may opt for the Do Model.

The difference between the two is evidenced by their names. The *Do Model* of a response team is one in which the team actually handles the document discovery portion of any given case or request. The team identifies the relevant data sources, works with the custodians, and documents and gathers all of the data.

In the *Assist Model*, the team acts as a resource to the staff in charge or to outside counsel and provides guidance but does not take the lead role. It is important to look at your culture and risk level when determining which type of team is appropriate for your enterprise. Once you have determined the basic model for your team, you will begin to map out the process. The response team process is the high-level process under which all other processes and procedures will fall. It will include the legal hold process, and data capture and release processes, among others (see Figure 4.5). This overarching process is the one that gives you the big picture. If you choose to have a team that only assists with discovery, you will still include all of the necessary steps in your process; however, you will assign responsibility to the staff in charge versus the discovery team.

Figure 4.5 Discovery Response Processes

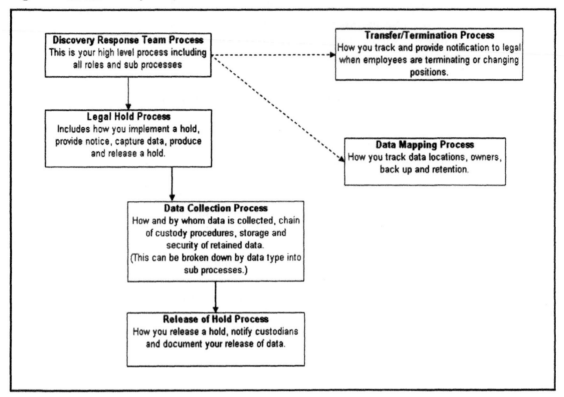

As you develop the map, think through each step of discovery. Initially, who gets notice of the case or claim? How is that notice routed to the appropriate people? What are your next steps? As you take it one step at a time, you will have not only action items, but also decision points. For example, one of your first major decision points will likely be whether a legal hold needs to be established. As you continue to walk through the process, you will include other subprocesses on your map. This is to ensure that your high-level map captures the entirety of the overall response plan. Be sure to consider third-party vendors, outside counsel roles, and other processes that you may need to touch on in responding to a request.

Having this detailed high-level process enables you to identify gaps, codependent processes, duplicative efforts, or areas of improvement in existing processes. It also forces you to look at the big picture and then gives you the ability to drill down into individual processes for the necessary detail. Finally, going through the exercise of mapping your processes will help further define the roles and responsibilities of the team members we discussed previously.

Tools & Traps...

Tunnel Vision

As you develop your processes, it is easy to focus on one area and overlook other critical steps. Be sure to start with your high-level map and discuss all the various steps, requirements, and processes or procedures that interrelate with each other. If you miss something, don't worry. This will be a work in progress, but the more you can capture at the front end, the more time and money it will save your organization.

Legal Hold Process

With the advent of the Federal Rules amendments, legal hold processes (or lack thereof) are a major risk point for many companies. Having a defensible legal hold process in place is no longer a luxury; it is a requirement. If you do not currently have a legal hold process in place, your DRT should be the group that develops, implements, and manages this process. This process takes many forms for companies, depending on their size and the volume of their litigation. Implementing and managing even one legal hold can be a technical challenge. Add to that the responsibility of tracking numerous, voluminous and often complex holds and your risk significantly increases. Tracking tools range from very basic to more complex. An Excel spreadsheet compiled and maintained internally is an example of a basic tracking tool. Naturally, all e-mail notifications with this type of tracking will have to be saved separately.

Other companies have developed in-house solutions, and still others have turned to third-party vendors for more sophisticated legal hold systems. The perfect tool should enable you to track each legal hold from issuance and acknowledgment through collection and processing and ultimately through the release process. The solution should also allow you to automate communications to custodians. Most importantly, you should have well-defined, documented processes that set out the steps taken to manage the legal hold process and define how the tool will be used in your organization. These processes will demonstrate your organization's good faith effort to meet its legal hold obligations. Whichever solution you choose, it should be based on your organization's needs and its risk profile.

Tools & Traps...

Amended Rule 26(f)

The Federal Rules now require discussion of preservation issues and other discovery issues at the meet and confer. Thus, it is important that you are at least prepared to discuss your policies and processes, including your legal hold process and data retention processes.

No matter what scale you determine is appropriate for your process, you should ensure that the process contains certain key components. First, you should implement an official policy related to legal holds. This policy should include language that the hold supersedes enterprise retention schedules and applies to not only records, but all documents and information currently existing related to the hold. Next, all holds need to be documented, including the date implemented and the reason for implementation. Documentation of your holds and the steps you take to implement them is important for defensibility down the road.

It is important at the time you initiate a hold to take the time to accurately describe the scope of the hold and the information to be retained so that the employees can accurately comply with the hold order. Then you need to ensure that all appropriate custodians are identified and notified of the hold and their obligations. It is also important that you set predetermined reminders (quarterly or bi-annually) of the hold to affected individuals to ensure that they continue to understand their obligations. As Arthur Andersen learned, random reminders can be misconstrued and only defeat your attempts at compliance.[4] All communications related to the hold should be documented and retained to defend your actions at a later date, should it become necessary. Many companies now post holds on an intranet site and have a policy that prior to disposing of records employees are required to check not only the retention schedules but also the list of legal holds.

TIP

Many companies develop templates for hold notices that are applicable to the various types of litigation they see most often. The benefit to a template is that each hold notice will contain the same basic information related to the types of documents that custodians need to consider when reviewing their information for a hold. Consistency is a key to a defensible process.

Some companies with a robust records management system are able to place holds on individual documents or entire systems. Others that are less advanced in records management are forced to rely on the individual custodians of the data to retain it. One area where companies seem to constantly fail in their legal hold obligations is e-mail. Thus, you should consider whether a process of automatic collection of e-mail should be instituted in your organization. Some companies find it is better to be safe than sorry and have instituted processes whereby all e-mail, PSTs, hard drives, and personal network shares are captured as soon as a hold is put in place. Naturally, the down side of this is that you will be keeping a lot of data that is not relevant to the subject litigation.

Another important piece of your legal hold process is the release of the hold and the associated data. For companies with serial litigation this can be a complex and delicate balancing act. For others, it may be relatively simple. The key is to have a process in place whereby you can release data when it is no longer on hold for a matter while having the ability to retain it if necessary for a separate legal hold. Again, documentation of your steps and the rationale for your decisions should be retained in the event you later need to defend your actions.

Many of the external vendors that provide legal hold software have a "Plug and Play" solution that incorporates these basic elements. Engaging in a Request for Proposal (RFP) process with such third-party vendors can be a beneficial education experience for your team and may help you to better define your needs and the holes in your process. My experience is that the tools these vendors offer are good for companies that have no automated legal hold process in place. It is only in the past year or so that many of these third-party vendors are working with companies that have an existing tool and they are replacing that tool. The data migration and work flow configurations with replacing an existing system can be more complex and time consuming than an original installation where no system exists. This being said, third-party vendors are expanding their capabilities and expertise in this area and it should only improve in the coming year.

TIP

An RFP or an RFI for a legal hold system can assist you in refining your requirements and give you ideas on process and work flow improvements that you may not have considered. The third-party vendors that provide legal hold solutions are constantly improving their product offerings and incorporating client needs into the new versions of their products.

Data Collection and Release of Hold Processes

To fulfill your preservation obligations, you need an effective process for the collection and retention of data. Additionally, it is important to look at the e-discovery life cycle and realize that you also need a defensible and documented process for the day you can release this information from hold. Many companies have focused on the former in the past year but have neglected to include the latter. This approach can have consequences if the released data should have been kept for another hold or for another reason such as a mandated retention period.

The first task of your team is to determine whether the data collection will be done in-house or will be outsourced to a third party. Obviously, there are pros and cons to each approach. In-house collection may drain already strained resources. It also brings with it the added burden of defending in-house employees' actions in the event something goes wrong. In contrast, outsourcing data collection forces you to develop clear and defined processes and ensure that the provider you use utilizes best practices. Outsourced data collection can be expensive, and many companies often utilize outsourced providers in large, complex cases and choose to rely on in-house resources and standardized processes in smaller, more manageable cases. Whichever avenue you choose, you must still develop the process and ensure that it fits with the rest of your litigation readiness plan.

As discussed earlier, documentation is critical in this process as well. Chain of custody for hard drives and media must be documented. You will need to decide what metadata will be captured and in what format the documents will be maintained. In the event you use specific systems—for instance, an e-mail storage vault—your documentation needs to be detailed down to the level of how e-mails are extracted from the system. This ensures consistent and repeatable processes.

Obviously, your IT team members will be invaluable in developing this process. Prior to mapping your collection processes, consider drafting a high-level data map of your systems and backup systems. This will ensure that as you develop your detailed collection processes you do not miss critical sources of data.

Transfer/Termination Process

One often-overlooked area in the e-discovery process is the issue of departing employees or employees who are transferring within the company to other departments or roles. This can wreak havoc on your retention if you are not in the loop, especially if you have not collected the data at the front end of the discovery process. Thus, this subprocess is one many companies are making a priority. The goal of this process is notification to the DRT or Legal of any change in status for an employee. Preferably you want to receive this notification in advance so that you have time to gather data or hard copy documents if necessary. Many employees who are leaving or changing jobs will "clean out" their offices, giving no thought to hold orders or records schedules. This can be devastating to you at a later date if that one e-mail or key document is lost. A transfer/termination process is a stop gap to prevent such behavior.

Depending on your human resource systems, your IT folks may be able to develop a basic in-house tool to accomplish this goal. The other benefit many companies have found by implementing such a process is that it also triggers appropriate access control termination which may be a gap in your existing processes. That is, some companies realize that former employees still have access or active log-in IDs to company systems and networks after they have left. For most companies, information is their greatest asset, and closing this loop greatly reduces risk.

Notification a week prior to a termination or transfer is ideal. This gives the team sufficient time to review existing holds for an employee and determine whether any additional data needs to be gathered or captured prior to the change in status. Securing PCs for departing employees and having a process for security of assets is critical. This is especially true in an employment dispute where you may need to later use the data on that former employee's PC in litigation. Having the appropriate process in place on the front end ensures that you will have documented the chain of custody and avoided any issues of spoliation.

Data Mapping Process

Data mapping is, in the most simplistic terms, knowing where your information is stored. The added emphasis on preservation obligations requires companies to have a better handle on their data systems than ever before. Thus, the burden will be on your team to establish a method of mapping out or listing your systems and the backup policies and processes for each of those systems. Additionally, this affirmative step is needed to identify retention and deletion schedules on various systems to ensure that you are able to comply with the good-faith obligation recognized in Rule 37(f) which may require you to take steps to ensure that the operation of a system does not destroy discoverable information.

TIP

Data mapping can seem like a daunting task, but don't fear. Even a basic, generic map of systems and sources of data in your company is a starting point for your team. It provides a checklist to ensure that you have reviewed all possible sources of data in response to a request.

As you begin your data mapping, start with the basic enterprise-side systems, e-mail, shared drives containing Word and Excel documents, financial systems, and so on. Once you have identified the major systems, you can often utilize your IT representatives to help you drill down into individual business systems used in departments. It is also important for you to identify systems that may be running proprietary software developed in-house. These systems may pose a particular challenge for retention and discovery.

Once you have your basic systems identified, work with your IT liaison to identify your company's backup processes and disaster recovery processes. It is important that your team understand the complete life cycle of electronic data in your company and where it may reside at any given point in time. Capturing the basic information and developing a more detailed map over time is often the most cost-efficient course of action. Companies are using various tools to capture their data maps. Some utilize a simple Excel spreadsheet. Others are beginning to use SharePoint to document the information and provide a platform for change management of the data map. Whatever solution you choose, keep it current. This information is invaluable when defending your preservation of relevant data.

Tools & Traps…

Archives

Beware the archive! Although your company may have standard processes for routinely backing up data and recycling those backup tapes, be sure to ask your IT group about archiving capabilities. Many backup systems have the capability to "archive" or back up data outside the routine schedules for specific durations. For example, an IT tech may archive a legacy system that is not longer in use and may "archive" it in the backup system and set it for 10-year retention. This data will no longer be on your active systems and you will not necessarily know of its existence absent processes to document such actions.

Review and Production Process

You have implemented the hold, mapped your data, collected responsive data, and preserved it. Now what? Don't forget about the back end of the e-discovery process as it can be an area ripe for savings. Once you have retained and tracked the data through your legal hold processes, you need a way to process, review, and produce it. For small volumes of data many utilize in-house tools or produce the data in native format. Larger volumes are where the issue arises as you need something efficient to review, tag, and produce large amounts of data. Using a professional e-discovery vendor can create efficiencies and save your company money by narrowing the amount of data that internal and external lawyers must review for production. Thus, many companies are choosing to select a converged vendor that they require all outside counsel to utilize.

The best way to begin your search for the perfect e-discovery tool or vendor for this part of your discovery response process is to send out an RFP to several vendors. Also, talk to your counterparts at other companies to see what they are using and what their experiences are. Sending out an RFP is an effective way to gather information and help you define and narrow your business requirements. Additionally, if you expect outside law firms to utilize this tool, it might be a good idea to include members from your core outside firms as part of the selection team. If you have extra time built in during the RFP process, you might consider piloting an actual case with one or two of the vendors. This will give you the opportunity to work with each vendor's project team and will also give you an idea of the underlying costs associated with each vendor.

Utilizing an external vendor for review and production has many benefits, but it can also be costly. If you decide to look at a converged vendor, be sure you are comparing apples to apples when it comes to costs. This is no easy task. Each vendor charges for different things, making it hard to compare the actual bottom-line cost. One way to best evaluate cost during your RFP is to give each vendor several production scenarios. For example, assume 300 GB of raw data; assume this is reduced by 30 percent after de-duplication; assume it is further reduced by another 60 percent after search terms are applied; and assume the resultant data is produced in TIFF format. When you have each vendor utilizing the same assumptions, you will get a better picture of the bottom-line pricing.

TIP

Because it can be difficult to compare on paper the costs and charges of the various e-discovery vendors, have each vendor price out specific data processing and production scenarios, which should give you a better means of comparison.

No matter what your choice is for review and production, be consistent and document your process. As in everything, documentation is the key.

Implementation and Rollout

You can finally see the light at the end of the tunnel. You have spent countless hours defining the roles and responsibilities of your DRT, you have been process-mapped to death, and finally it is time to tell the world about this fantastic team you have created. But how do you do that? The implementation and rollout phase of the DRT, and how you go about communicating your mission and training your legal peers and clients, is as important, if not more important, than the creation and development phases. Change management is one important aspect of the implementation and rollout phase, followed by a strong communication plan, training, education, and audit.

Hopefully, you have gotten legal peer by-in and senior-level support throughout the creation and development of your processes and procedures, so you know going into implementation that the appropriate stakeholders have blessed your team and its mission. However, even if that is the case, you must still have a plan to prepare for, manage, and reinforce change as you introduce the DRT to your organization.

Tools & Traps…

Preparing for Change

E-discovery equals change. The DRT members are charged with leading the transformation throughout the organization and the team must be sanctioned by senior management. This acceptance must then filter down throughout the organization. Senior management support is critical for your team to succeed!

Organize and Prepare Your Core Team for Change Management

The key to organizing your core team and successful change management planning is to document, document, document! Every detail of the DRT and its processes should be written down, reviewed, tested, and then blessed by senior management. Once your processes have been tried and tested, your team can feel confident when rolling out the training and communication plans. Don't expect perfection, as the rollout process will undoubtedly have unexpected glitches! Remember when you get frustrated that you are dealing with various team member and client personalities and that your team is trying to change years of ingrained work habits. You are also dealing with company data that is often in unknown locations and of an unknown quantity. However, if you have carefully thought through your processes, have worked through your test plan, and have corrected any known problems prior to rollout, you should enter the rollout phase with confidence.

Who needs to be trained on your DRT mission and its processes? The obvious people are those in the legal department and IT who will be implementing legal holds and performing the collection work, but now is a good time to think about others who might benefit from this training. What about your internal tax or audit departments or risk management or claims groups? Depending on the type of industry your organization is in, the people within these departments and other departments might benefit from being trained on the DRT and legal hold processes.

Next, you need to decide whether the training materials are going to be high-level or detailed. Because the DRT is a team made up of change agents from RIM, IT, and Legal, you should not forget about the nonlegal roles and responsibilities when establishing your training plan. If you utilize professional e-discovery and legal hold software vendors, you might include those vendors in your training plan and in your presentations to targeted groups. Additionally, don't forget to include as part of your training plan the need to train and educate a company representative to act as the company's 30(b)(6) deposition witness when electronic data storage may be an issue. Lastly, consider developing Quick-Tip Guides on your processes and procedures that can be posted on your company's intranet site or that can be laminated for easy access and referenced during training.

TIP

Getting the DRT launched requires some savoir-faire. This team will include representatives from departments who speak different languages, so keep this in mind when developing your training materials. Remember that your processes and procedures will be rolled out to legal and nonlegal groups, so be sure to explain the lingo so that those being trained will understand the terminology. Most importantly, make learning about these processes fun! Develop a theme in your training materials, turn it into a game, or come up with something creative to help you communicate your message. It might be a good idea to test your training materials on a small focus group prior to rollout so that they can provide feedback on what terminology and procedures were unclear in your materials.

Finally, it is time to develop your communication plan. Depending on the size and structure of your organization and the work habits of your peers, you need to decide whether sending out a company-wide communication is the best way to communicate the rollout of the DRT. Or perhaps it would be more productive to have your team attend various staff meetings to spread the word. This gives people an opportunity to ask questions outside the training environment. Regardless, the message should be clear that your organization takes the DRT and its processes seriously and that the expectation is compliance with all processes and procedures.

Managing Change

Now that your DRT is organized and motivated to get going, keep in mind that you are getting ready to inflict a certain amount of chaos and torture on your legal peers and clients. At least that is the way they will likely see things. Let's take a look at your client's world pre-DRT. It's likely that they had little involvement in discovery and may have been involved only from the point of verifying discovery responses, providing a few documents from their personal files or participating in depositions. Now, all of a sudden, your clients are responsible for knowing the locations of their business data, are required to have a greater knowledge and understanding of the data created within their business units, and are required to follow consistent processes for providing that data and may even be required to attest that all data has been given to the team. All this change can be a bit overwhelming.

Now, let's take a look at your legal peers and outside counsel's practices before you implemented this DRT. It is likely that your outside counsel is used to taking control of discovery and moving forward with little input from in-house counsel. Your in-house counsel is likely not used to dealing with e-discovery, and knows little or nothing about your systems and data and historically probably has not followed consistent processes regarding discovery and decisions made around discovery. Now, outside counsel and your internal lawyers are taking direction from your DRT on all issues related to discovery, and may not be too happy about it!

Why is managing change important? Proper change management around your new processes and procedures within your organization can make or break the success of your DRT. First, hopefully you included your legal group in your process planning stages so that this response team concept is not being sprung on them for the first time. Next, education and tools to assist them are beneficial to an easier transition. Shortly we will discuss some of the forms and templates that you should develop to aid your lawyers in complying with the new requirements.

Developing template letters and maintaining an easily accessible DRT procedure manual can help minimize cost and increase efficiencies. The less your in-house and outside lawyers have to brood about what they are supposed to do and how to do it, the better. This will also help you to quickly deploy the DRT into action when litigation, a claim, or an investigation is initiated. Some of the things you might include in your procedure manual include:

- Your organization's current document retention policy and legal hold policy
- Step-by-step instructions on how to set up a legal hold
- An overview of the discovery response plan and process
- A DRT contact list
- Template communications
- A Template Attestation Affidavit
- Data maps

You should consider creating template communications that can easily be updated with case-specific information. If you are using a home-grown system or professionally developed software, these templates should be electronic and automated. Regardless of whether your communications are electronic or sent out as a Word document via e-mail, you need to have a process to track the communications, who they were sent to, when they were sent, and when they were acknowledged. In the following subsections, we will discuss some examples of template communications and suggested content.

Initial Internal Notification of a Legal Hold

The initial internal notification of a legal hold should be sent to key custodians, also known as people with knowledge or potential evidence. You should also send the notification to the appropriate IT and records personnel who are responsible for retaining electronic and hard-copy data. The notice should indicate that the custodians are to retain related documents or records and the IT personnel are put on notice that certain electronic data should be preserved. Furthermore, the notice should instruct the records personnel to suspend destruction of all hard-copy records that may be subject to the legal hold.

The template should include general information that is not case-specific, such as:

- The organization's obligation to preservation of evidence
- A statement that the legal hold supersedes the current document retention policies for records subject to the legal hold
- Contact information for the case team handling the matter
- Contact information for the DRT working on the matter
- A consistent definition of data
- A detailed list of potential locations where data might exist and types of data
- A request for identification of other people who may have relevant data

Case-specific information should include:

- A high-level description of the allegations
- A description of what data and records are subject to the legal hold and relevant time period
- The procedure or process for how people should retain the data and whom to notify that potentially relevant data exists

The internal preservation letter should also include an acknowledgment of where the custodian must indicate that he received, reviewed, understands, and fully intends to comply with the internal notification of a legal hold.

Notification of a Revised Legal Hold

There may be instances in which a legal hold needs to be narrowed or broadened. This template communication should:

- Include case-specific information
- Notify the affected individual of the hold revision
- Remind the affected individual of his or her obligations related to the legal hold

Reminder of Legal Hold

Cases such as *Zubulake* have obligated in-house counsel to continuously remind custodians of their legal hold obligations. This template communication should go out on a consistent and preferably automated basis. The reminder could be communicated monthly, quarterly, or bi-annually, but your processes should be consistent across all holds as to how custodians are reminded of their ongoing obligations.

External Notification of Legal Hold

The external notification of legal hold should be a detailed list of what data your organization believes the other party must preserve, based on the type of services that the other party provided your company. This notification should require the third-party provider to acknowledge that they received, reviewed, understand, and fully intend to comply with the external notification of a legal hold.

Attestation Affidavit

The Attestation Affidavit template is a good tool to have for purposes of documenting to your collections process. The Attestation Affidavit should be executed by a business client who has responsibility and control over relevant business records. In essence, the attestation will confirm that the business unit or department has reviewed all sources of potentially relevant data and has preserved or placed on hold all identified data. It can then be used in response to a Motion to Compel or some other discovery-related or spoliation motion filed by the opposing party. The Attestation Affidavit should include the following information:

- The specific locations searched for relevant data and records
- The steps taken to identify relevant data
- A statement that all reasonable locations have been searched for relevant data
- A statement that all relevant data located has been turned over to counsel or preserved in some fashion

Response to Preservation Demand Letter

The Response to Preservation Demand template should communicate case law and best practices in response to an incoming preservation demand letter. The response should:

- Express your intent to comply with the reasonable duty of preservation
- Cite case law that discusses the reasonableness of preservation, specifically that the duty to preserve does not require companies to retain every shred of paper created, as discussed in cases such as *Zubulake v. UBS Warburg*, LLC, 220 F.R.D. 212 (S.D.N.Y. 2003)
- Discuss the validity of document destruction[5]
- Cite F.R.C.P. Rule 37(f), the Safe Harbor provision

So, how do you manage change for your clients and the data custodians? First, you will have trained the lawyers and paralegals that most often deal with the employees. This is the first step in your communication plan because these are the legal representatives they are used to working with on a daily basis. People within your organization may already be used to Sarbanes-Oxley compliance, so they are hopefully already used to change management. To facilitate and manage the changes associated with dealing with e-discovery and the implementation of a DRT, you should focus on making litigation a part of your client's daily work habits. Educate them on the importance of data management in litigation and make it real for them. If you fail to do this you may find your company in a position similar to that of Philip Morris, whose employees failed to follow the company's own retention schedules, and as a result, those employees were precluded from testifying and Philip Morris was sanctioned $2.75 million.[6]

All employees within your organization should be aware of the types of information they create and which must be disclosed in litigation. The aforementioned templates will assist in consistent communications to employees about holds and their responsibilities. Another avenue many companies are exploring involves company-wide training on smart communications and records. All employees within your organization should be educated on the pitfalls of sending careless communications and of not following your organization's record retention policies. This training gives them some real-world insight into litigation and the effects their everyday work can have on your company in the event of litigation. The more you can focus employees on working effectively and communicating smartly, the easier your change management process will be.

Reinforcing Change

Now that you have prepared your core team for change, trained your legal peers and clients, communicated the mission to your organization, and have a plan in place to manage change, the final piece of the implementation and rollout puzzle is reinforcing that change. You will need to have a plan to collect and analyze feedback from your clients, peers, IT, and the records personnel as well as a process and procedure to benchmark your results and audit your processes. At some point, senior management will want to see the "bang for their buck" related to this project, meaning they will want reports and information about how the DRT and legal hold processes are creating efficiencies, saving the company money, and increasing shareholder value. You might consider selecting a few key tasks within your DRT, legal hold, or data collection processes and score-card or set up a monthly audit to help you identify any gaps.

TIP

You might want to formally or informally survey your peers and clients six months after implementation and rollout to judge their understanding of the process, procedures, and various communications associated with your DRT and legal hold processes.

Summary

Pat yourself and your DRT members on the back for successfully implementing and rolling out the DRT and legal hold processes and procedures that will ensure that your organization is litigation-ready and able to meet every challenge in this new world of e-discovery.

For all of these processes you can find good information in many locations. For instance, http://www.edrm.net/ contains work flow examples. General Counsel Roundtable and the Sedona Conference are also good sources for materials, information, and, in some cases, templates. In June 2007, the Sedona Conference published the second edition of the *Sedona Principles: Best Practices Recommendations & Principals for Addressing Electronic Document Production*. This publication has a wealth of information and tips you should review prior to developing your DRT. Additionally, don't hesitate to talk to your counterparts who are facing the same issues you are. You may be surprised at how willing they are to share good processes and lessons learned.

Solutions Fast Track

Roles and Responsibilities within a Discovery Response Team

☑ The primary function of an internal DRT is to establish and execute a discovery response plan.

☑ For most companies, a formal discovery response plan will be new and will require a change in management and work flow.

☑ Your IT compliance coordinator should report directly to the discovery technology coordinator with dotted-line reporting to the director of discovery.

Processes for Implementing an Effective Discovery Response Team

☑ Defining and documenting efficient, repeatable processes for your team to follow will be the lynchpin of a successful response plan.

☑ The goal of the high-level map is to have the full picture of your DRT's goal in one document.

☑ Defensibility is a key in today's e-discovery world, and the more you build effective documentation and audit touch points into your process, the better positioned you are to justify actions at a later date.

Discovery Response Team Process

☑ When forming your DRT and establishing your goals, consider the culture of your company and your legal and IT departments.

☑ There are two primary models most companies use when forming a team and developing their litigation response plan: the "Do Model" and the "Assist Model."

☑ Having a defensible legal hold process in place is no longer a luxury; it is a requirement.

Implementation and Rollout

☑ The implementation and rollout phase of the DRT, and how you go about communicating your mission and training your legal peers and clients, is as important, if not more important, than the creation and development phases.

☑ The key to organizing your core team and successful change management planning is to document, document, document!

☑ Proper change management around your new processes and procedures within your organization can make or break the success of your DRT.

Frequently Asked Questions

Q: What is the best way to get started forming a DRT?

A: Draft a charter. This document will force you to define your goals and objectives and will give you the executive mandate you need to proceed.

Q: Who should be included on a DRT?

A: This may vary based on your organization, but at best, you'll need a senior-level lawyer to supervise and manage the team; other legal team members with discovery and technology experience; an IT professional who is proficient in communicating in both legal and technical terms and who understands your infrastructure and enterprise content, key compliance, and backup systems; someone from your records management group; a representative for human resources for cases that deal with employment data; and someone from your audit or compliance group.

Q: How detailed should our data mapping be?

A: As you begin your data mapping, start with the basic enterprise-side systems, e-mail, shared drives containing Word and Excel documents, and financial systems. Once you have identified the major systems, you can often utilize your IT representatives to help you drill down into individual business systems used in departments. It is important that your team understand the complete life cycle of electronic data in your company and where it may reside at any given point in time. Capturing the basic information and developing a more detailed map over time is often the most cost-efficient course of action.

Q: What's the best method for implementing a DRT?

A: Start at a high level with your requirements and a broad view of the litigation or discovery response process. Once you have established a high–level, general process that includes each step of your response, identify the roles that will be necessary to put that process into action. Then start working on your detailed processes, such as your legal hold, data collection, or data mapping processes. By working from the top down, you will have a better chance of capturing all of the necessary steps and requirements.

Q: Why is a change management process important?

A: Proper change management around your new processes and procedures within your organization can make or break the success of your DRT. Training and communication will be the key. The easier you can make your new processes, the more likely people will be to comply.

Notes

1. *Zubulake v. UBS Warburg, LLC*, 220 F.R.D. 212 (S.D.N.Y. 2003).

2. *Broadcom v. Qualcomm*, 2008 U.S. Lexis 911 (January 7, 2008).

3. *In re Flash Memory Antitrust Litigation*, 2008 WL 1831668 (N.D.Cal.).

4. *Arthur Andersen LLP v. United States*, 544 U.S. 696, 704 (2005).

5. *Arthur Andersen LLP v. United States*, 544 U.S. 696, 704 (2005).

6. *United States v. Philip Morris USA Inc.*, 2004 WL 1627252 (D.D.C. July 21, 2004).

Chapter 5

The Focus of IT within a Discovery Response Team

Solutions in this chapter:

- IT Steps to Prepare for Discovery Readiness

- Managing Data Collections for Legal Holds

- Creating Data Profiles and Mapping the IT Environment

- IT/Discovery Liaison Roles and Responsibilities

☑ Summary

☑ Solutions Fast Track

☑ Frequently Asked Questions

Introduction

This chapter expands on the preceding one by presenting best practices for managing the technical components within a discovery response program. Critical to the creation and management of a successful discovery program is the relationship between the legal and information technology (IT) departments; the key to this will be IT's ability to translate technical concepts for the legal team. In addition, the ability to facilitate data collection, oversee project management and vendor management, and identify sources of electronically stored information (ESI) will also be important. Because you will have limited technical resources, it is essential to develop a clear understanding of your business's legal and regulatory requirements, data management practices, and the enforcement of your policies and procedures. The ultimate goal is to streamline the discovery practices throughout your organization and ensure that electronic evidence can be produced in a defensible and admissible manner.

IT Steps to Prepare for Discovery Readiness

Even though the legal team is typically challenged with creating a reliable discovery readiness protocol, IT should be as interested in helping to shape this protocol. Increasingly, the responsibility of managing technical aspects of discovery efforts falls within the IT group. If you are part of the IT senior management team, you need to start thinking about which key employees can best assist the overall discovery readiness process.

NOTE

Even the perception of possible litigation requires that your company must preserve potentially responsive ESI. Because of this mandate, the ability to efficiently identify, preserve, and collect ESI is paramount to the success of your program. Knowing where information resides, understanding the standard policies and procedures that should be ceased for a litigation hold, and having the ability to communicate a hold to potential custodians are just a few steps that can drive an efficient response.

From the IT team's perspective, a standard protocol should lay the groundwork necessary to:

- Identify and manage standard corporate policies and procedures, forms, and case-tracking information within a central repository.
- Assess the technical environment.
- Identify gaps within the existing discovery program.
- Leverage litigation support systems.

Creating a Central Repository for Corporate and Case Information

This section of the chapter focuses on what documentation you could create—including policies and procedures, case information, and other documentation—that should be readily accessible to all discovery team members. Outside counsel, vendors, and consultants will often request such information. The ability to provide outside team members with current documentation in a timely manner will help to expedite the overall process. Although it is not always necessary for outside teams to acquire such documentation, it can be essential if one or more of these teams are to testify, conduct a deposition of a former employee, or relay any information to the courts, opposing parties, or a government entity. Figure 5.1 lists some of the more valuable components IT should initially consider for its documentation.

Figure 5.1 Sample Readiness Document Checklist

☐	Identify written policies: • Regulatory (state, federal, or industry-specific) • Litigation • Internal retention policies
☐	Determine enforcement of policies: • End-user training • Acknowledgment of policies by end-users • Other actions related to policy enforcement/adherence
☐	Assess your litigation hold communications and program: • Preservation notice distribution • Preservation notice acknowledgment/receipts • Identify who is preserving and collecting ESI, including the methods by which this is being completed
☐	Identify internal investigation processes: • Confidential investigation policies and procedures • Steps taken to respond to government inquiries or investigations
☐	Determine the nature of suits: • Volume of annual matters in which your company is involved, including plaintiffs, defendants, and third parties • Types of lawsuits or matters, such as government, IP, product liability, natural-resource damages, and so on
☐	Identify more specific policies related to IT (see "Creating Data Profiles and Mapping the IT Environment" later in this chapter for further details) • E-mail • Backup tapes • User-created files/ESI • Databases

Following the identification and collection of the general information listed in Figure 5.1, creating a central repository that is available to both the legal and IT team members will provide easy access to this information. In addition to maintaining current versions of the documents in one location, the repository should also enable tracking of document versions and the users who check in and check out documentation. By creating a collaborative environment to host these documents, your overall discovery readiness program will be one step closer to becoming a streamlined process.

TIP

Although homegrown document repositories or management systems can provide some unique features, commercially available applications might actually be more cost- and time-efficient. For example, just to name a few, consider Microsoft SharePoint, Google Enterprise, or applications by Open Text or Symantec. Additionally, many of the legal case management applications similarly contain the ability to store and manage documents collaboratively. Prior to implementing a solution for hosting your documentation, it would also be prudent to confer with your legal team for their recommendations.

Assessing the Technical Environment

Addressing documentation identified in the checklist from Figure 5.1 is just the first step in creating a sound discovery protocol. Next, your team should assess the technical environment within your organization. To the layperson, this means obtaining and/or creating documentation to provide the legal team with a better understanding of the electronic surroundings in your organization. And, if you have not already done so, this documentation will identify individuals with knowledge of the IT systems containing ESI. If you happen to work in the IT department, one of these individuals will likely be you. Don't forget to include other key personnel, as you will need their expertise and input as early as possible in the process. To fully understand all of the different systems, it will often be necessary to go beyond IT and involve the legal department, business unit managers, and possibly discovery experts.

NOTE

A *discovery expert* helps to assess the technical environment by providing guidance. Experts are able to: 1) determine what could be considered readily accessible forms of ESI; 2) create cost assessments for the recovery of inaccessible forms of ESI (i.e., when archived forms of media or backup tapes are utilized for the purposes of legal holds); 3) identify potential collection methodologies specific to your environment; and 4) possibly provide guidance regarding forms of storage that can be captured to ensure defensible and admissible evidence.

When assessing the technical environment—short of undertaking a complete data profiling and mapping exercise as outlined later in this chapter—you will need to create or collect information as it relates to the following network diagrams:

- Desktop or laptop standards

- Database systems

- E-mail system specifications

- E-mail archiving system specifications

- Document management system specifications

- Backup tape or archiving system configurations and details

- On-site and off-site media storage

Determining the Elements of the Gap Analysis: Asking Questions

Questions are important. Without them, we would never have answers. Therefore, this section of the discovery readiness process outlines questions to ask within your organization. This step is vital because it will start the gap identification process. Note that this is not an exhaustive list of questions, but it is geared toward providing you with a snapshot of the types of questions you might want to ask regarding e-mail and user-protected files/ESI.

- Does a written e-mail retention policy exist? If so, what does it outline and how long has it been in existence?

- Who is responsible for maintaining the e-mail policy and how frequently is it reviewed for updates?

- Do you have an e-mail archiving system in place? If yes, what is it and how does it work? Who maintains the system?

- If you have an e-mail archiving system installed, have you tested your ability to search for potentially responsive e-mail messages? If yes, have you also tested the accuracy in extracting these e-mail messages from the archiving system?

Tools & Traps...

E-mail Retention Systems

E-mail management is critical to every organization and is typically augmented through e-mail archiving applications. Utilizing these systems for the purposes of e-discovery can seem like an obvious choice, but often the desired results are not so easy to obtain. Although such systems may be fine for archiving, you must carefully consider their adequacy for searching and retrieving messages during a time-sensitive legal response in which the accuracy and completeness of results need to be defensible.

The following is a practice example of how the accuracy and completeness of results from an e-mail archiving system might be established:

■ You search your e-mail archiving system for any messages containing the keyword "fraud."

■ The e-mail archiving system identifies 1,000 e-mail messages with the word "fraud."

■ You select the potentially responsive e-mail messages and choose the option to extract these messages with their attachments.

■ Upon extraction, your e-mail archiving system creates one Microsoft Outlook (PST) file containing the keyword results.

■ Because you are extremely diligent and track your results for every keyword, you examine the PST file to ensure that 1,000 messages were indeed extracted.

■ As a result of your verification methods, you identify that only 850 messages were actually extracted.

This practical example could be experienced due to message corruption, viruses within the messages or attachments, or issues related to the e-mail archiving application itself. The point here is to document your results carefully, notify the legal team immediately, and then identify the means to potentially resolve the issue.

■ Do you destroy messages over a certain age? If so, what is the timing—after 30, 60, 360 days?

■ Are e-mail messages purged after a certain point? If so, what is that timing?

■ How are e-mail messages backed up, especially if an e-mail archiving system does not exist?

■ Are your inbox items handled differently than sent items?

- If a litigation hold notice is distributed to an end-user, is there a method to automatically identify potentially responsive messages and/or does the end-user have the ability to save the potentially responsive messages to a dedicated area within the e-mail system?

- What type of enterprise content management (ECM) systems/applications are in place? What, if any, applications or appliances are being utilized?

- If ECM does exist, how is user-created ESI categorized?

NOTE

Although many applications offer ECM solutions, some examples of companies that provide a suite of tools include Open Text, IBM, OnBase, Oracle, Ademero, and EMC. Additionally, several associations, including the Association for Information and Image Management (AIIM), the Document Management Industries Association (DMIA), and the Association of Records Managers and Administrators (ARMA International), provide guidance for end-users to understand the challenges associated with managing documents, content, records, and business processes.

- Do regulatory statutes or laws exist in which your type of organization is specifically required to retain documents/records? If yes, it is recommended that you outline these requirements and identify time frames in which documents or records must be retained.

- Are you able to easily identify documents or records throughout the organization? If yes, how is this accomplished?

- Have you determined when a document becomes a "record"? If so, outline the guidelines surrounding that decision-making process. Also, identify whether the process is automated within an ECM system or through some manual form of document management.

- Is it possible to confidently determine whether records are deleted in a timely fashion, such as when they become outdated through policies or are no longer required for other reasons?

Performing a Discovery Readiness Gap Analysis

A gap analysis is sometimes the most difficult task to accomplish, for a couple of reasons: (1) there is no perfect method to identify all the gaps that could exist in a program or process; and (2) the components being considered may not be consistent. You can use the following procedure to aid in assessing collected information and associated systems:

1. Are requirements for litigation and compliance aligned? Because the same data can be subject to risk from both litigation and compliance, it is critical to ensure that a company's data retention provisions fully address the entire range of these requirements. Failure to do so can result in gaps or opportunities for errors, which could translate into increased risk and cost for a company.

2. Is the company's ECM system readily searchable and are the exported results consistent with the search results? Archiving data is one thing, but efficiently searching and producing that data is quite another. Even if the application has robust search capabilities, the extraction or export mechanisms could still be limited and thus can expose the company to greater risk.

3. Are the company's data retention policies adequately defined and enforced? With the complex nature of multinational business along with the variation between legal and geographic jurisdictions, failure to have defined and enforceable retention policies can call into question the integrity and authenticity of produced data, which can subsequently render any such data as inadmissible and thus expose the company to greater risk.

4. Are end-users (potential custodians) allowed to copy or save ESI to loose media (i.e., external hard drives, flash drives, floppy disks, or CD/DVDs)? If it is determined that users are saving ESI to external locations for no reason other than because they are simply able to do so, you should plan an annual cleanup day to eliminate any unnecessary loose media.

5. Does an e-mail purging schedule exist, and if so, how is it managed? If possible, identify reasonable purging schedules that you could initiate. It is not recommended that you start this practice until such time as you are absolutely certain that doing so will not disrupt a litigation hold or cause any issues related to regulatory requirements.

6. Have backup tapes been remediated? Not to be confused with traditional and often costly restoration services, *tape remediation* is a new area that enables companies to cost-effectively search their backup environments. We describe some technologies for doing this, such as those from Index Engines, later in this book. Although tape remediation can be beneficial for companies, these efforts must be managed within a properly documented process. Most importantly, you will need to identify whether your backup tapes are considered readily accessible or inaccessible. The determining factor for accessibility is typically the cost burden associated with restoring backup data. As cost-effective tape search technologies improve, courts and governing bodies will increasingly consider backup tapes as accessible, and any arguments otherwise will likewise be increasingly difficult to defend. This is an area where your organization should consider the potential advantages of proactively planning for a solution that would enable searching of backup tapes and thus facilitate the overall e-discovery process. Not doing so may result in you having to scramble at the eleventh hour to comply with a court order or other mandate.

Leveraging Litigation Support Systems

Throughout the entire process of creating a discovery response team, assessing your current state of discovery readiness, and mapping out data locations, the end game should be to determine the following:

■   What systems do we currently have internally in support of the litigation and discovery process?

- What systems should we purchase or acquire to utilize internally to reduce risk, minimize costs, or speed response times?

- What internal human resources are available to assist in supporting these systems or for responding to discovery requests?

- What outside resources are required to diligently and defensibly respond to discovery requests?

By answering questions regarding current and future systems, your team will be better prepared to respond to discovery requests. Remember, outside consultants are available to assist in this process with guidance on best practices and recommendations for corporate systems. Although the industry is not completely equipped with an overwhelming number of e-discovery corporate systems, it might still be worth considering which systems could benefit your organization. Once you've considered your options and understand the greatest pain points, then it will be time to consider the appropriate systems and outside resources you can leverage for implementing your litigation support framework.

Managing Data Collections for Legal Holds

This section of the chapter identifies some tools you can utilize for collecting or managing ESI and how to do so in a defensible manner. It is important to consider not only the internal human processes associated with use of these tools, but also the applicability of new technologies as they become available. More and more, litigation hold and preservation processes are being automated. For example, PSS Systems provides an automated legal governance solution for global corporations which have large volumes of information subject to a diverse range of laws.

Let's take a moment to look at what PSS Systems can do. The company's Atlas LCC module helps litigation departments respond to the challenges of broad preservation obligations and, in conjunction, its Atlas ERM module helps companies to define and implement rational information retention processes that can ultimately reduce the volume of information being managed. The overall Atlas platform also provides a reference map of the corporation, its employees (past and present), and all the diverse systems and data stores across the enterprise. In addition, Policy Atlas portals can help business and IT staff members understand their ongoing legal obligations, and Policy Enforcement Services can automatically distribute legal holds, collection requests, and retention schedules for all the various systems that may contain relevant data. The automation and integration of the Atlas platform have made it a de facto standard for legal holds and retention management software such that PSS Systems is currently the recognized subject-matter expert on business systems for addressing preservation, retention, and privacy burdens. Although specific to the Atlas platform, the following model (see Figure 5.2) does present all the components generally needed for a legal hold.

Figure 5.2 Sample Legal Hold and Retention Policies Workflow

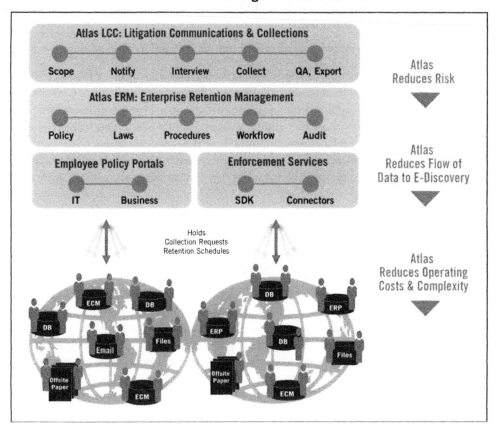

Because PSS Systems provides a full suite of software for addressing the entire legal hold process, the next several pages of this chapter will use its platform as an example to provide additional insight into the overall legal hold process. Figures 5.3 through 5.7 will also illustrate how using this software can augment the process.

To begin, the Atlas platform includes the following key components:

■ Atlas LCC Dashboard

■ Atlas LCC Hold Notices

■ Atlas Employee Portal

■ Policy Atlas for IT

■ Atlas Legal Library

Visibility to the overall process is the key to managing that process. As show in Figure 5.3, the Atlas LCC Dashboard presents tremendous intelligence regarding the litigation and discovery workload that can be readily tapped to reduce cost, improve case strategy, balance staffing, more effectively charge back to business units, and optimize data management to gain better control over cost and risk. Context-based information is easily accessed throughout Atlas LCC. Dashboards for attorneys, managing attorneys, paralegals, and discovery delegates also provide a high-level view of work in progress and any exceptions that need attention.

Figure 5.3 Demonstration of a Streamlined and Integrated Dashboard: Ability to Track and Monitor the Discovery Workload

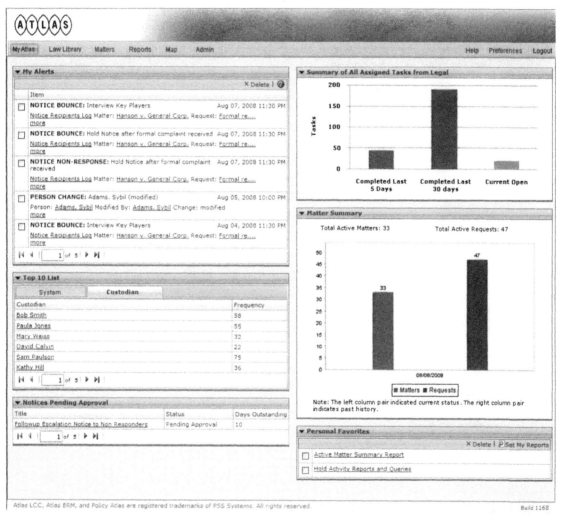

To facilitate the efforts of participants in the legal hold process, the team needs to be able to easily set reminder intervals, response requirements, time periods for compliance, and escalation paths for noncompliance, as shown in Figure 5.4 for Atlas LCC Hold Notices. Atlas provides templates for headers, footers, and notice text that can eliminate the need for typing and can provide consistency across matters. The application can also automatically personalize each notice, and fill in the matter name, due date, attorney, paralegal team, or other routine information as it sends out the notice. Noncompliance with notices can also be tracked automatically and discovery team members can be alerted via both e-mail and their dashboard regarding those employees who need follow-up attention.

Figure 5.4 Demonstration of Tracking Legal Hold Compliance and Noncompliance

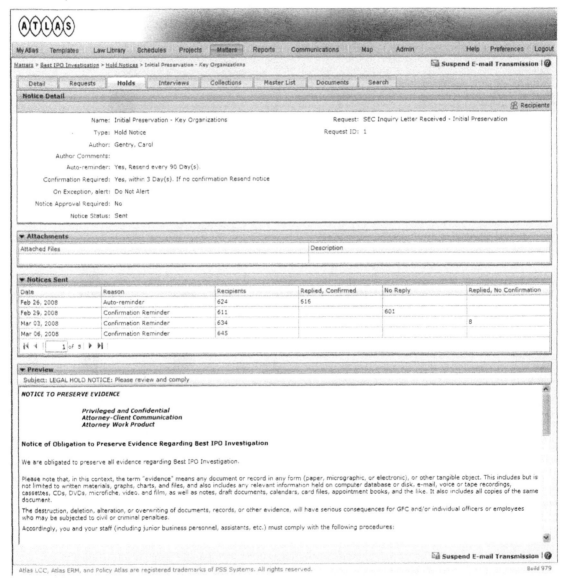

Continuing awareness of hold duties has also become critical for individual custodians who now receive more hold notices and reminders than ever before. The Atlas Employee Portal enables employees to always access, via the intranet, their own holds and applicable notices. This self-service capability is increasingly important as employees receive more legal communications but lack the time to organize them and track their ongoing duties. As shown in Figure 5.5, Atlas addresses continuous communications through its employee portal. This is a critical capability for any team to ensure that all project or case stakeholders have seamless communications.

Figure 5.5 Sample Employee Portal Allowing Seamless Communications

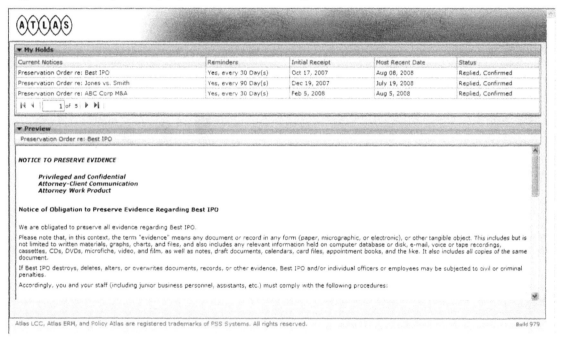

IT is a critical stakeholder in ensuring that legal obligations for information are ultimately addressed. Policy Atlas for IT presents legal holds, collection requests, and retention schedules in an IT context to simplify and ensure compliance, increase efficiency, and avoid over- or under-retaining information. This module also provides a dashboard for coordinating all IT discovery activities including work queues as well as providing an easy legal hold lookup for systems and custodians to prevent mishandling data. Policy Atlas for IT also organizes and presents legal instructions by due date, system, data area, and staff member. With Policy Atlas for IT (shown in Figure 5.6), you will also be able to catalog the company's systems by country and business unit with accessibility, data formats, discovery and preservation capacity, privacy capabilities, and related governance attributes.

Figure 5.6 Monitoring That Closes the Gap between Legal and IT

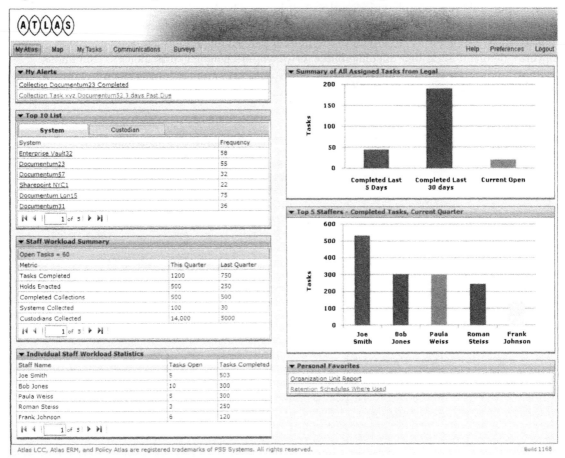

Finally, you need to be able to capture all relevant laws that dictate legal requirements for data, including privacy and data protection laws, discovery rules, and retention laws. Atlas Law Library (shown in Figure 5.7) can do this. It also serves as the central catalog for internal protocols and opinions and briefs from outside counsel on the retention, discovery, handling, and privacy of data within a company. The Law Library should help companies to reconcile the conflicts between discovery, retention, and data protection laws. Gathering this information is extremely time-consuming, so its availability within an application allows the team to focus on monitoring and enforcing legal holds, managing data collections, and sending data to outside counsel in a more timely manner.

Figure 5.7 Added Value within a Legal Hold Application: The Law Library

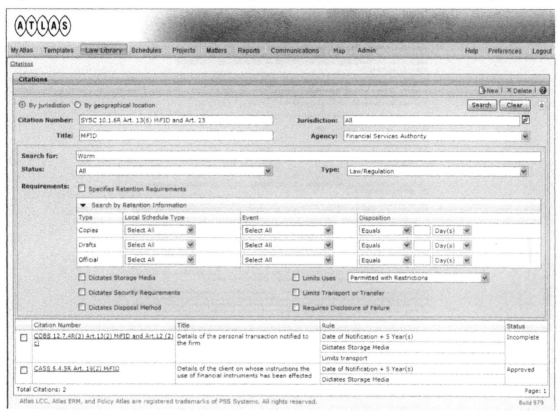

Other companies provide solutions with similar functionality for managing legal holds. One such company, known as WorkProducts, created an appliance to manage litigation hold, preservation, and corporate collections. Its appliance, called MatterSpace, has a component or feature called Preservation Hold Notification & Requested Acknowledgement which can send a notification to the identified data custodian's e-mail inbox, such as that shown in Figure 5.8.

Figure 5.8 A Sample Preservation Hold Notification from WorkProducts' MatterSpace

From: slilley@workproducts.com [mailto:slilley@workproducts.com]
Sent: Friday, June 20, 2008 10:55 AM
To: adias@rpwb.com; kschuler@onss.com; skauff@rpwb.com
Cc: apack@ds3datavaulting.com; slilley@workproducts.com
Subject: MATTERSPACE DEMO SAMPLE - PRESERVATION HOLD NOTIFICATION & ACKNOWLEDGEMENT

HOLD LETTER RE: Notice of Civil Action No. 11900, Standard v. West(D,DC 2008):
1. Request for Preservation of Electronically Stored Info.
2. Request for Cessation of Destruction/Retention Practices
3. Request for Documentation of Failure to Preserve

This correspondence is offical notice of the pending [or imminent] lawsuit concerning the following:

Standard v. West, Civil Action No. 11900
Mike Roberts, CFO
Sally Short, Secretary
Irwin Box, CSM
Chip Anderson, Security Manager
Derrick Mosely, CSR
Anne Usly, CSR
Kim Smith, former CSR

I. YOU ARE HEREBY DEMANDED TO PRESERVE ALL ELECTRONICALLY STORED INFORMATION CONCERNING THE ABOVE-LISTED PERSONS.

State and Federal Law and the applicable discovery rules require preservation of all electronically stored information, in any format it may exist. Specifically, you must look on [or in] your computer drives, floppy disks, tape drives, flash drives, file servers, zip drives, storage cards, etc. Further, you must check all software programs and file locations which include, but is not limited to, word processing applications, database applications, email, etc.

Your duty to preserve electronic data also includes people, places, and things over which you exert control. Consequently, you are obligated to preserve electronic information held in remote storage or offsite locations, held by directors, officers, records retention personnel, contractors, etc., and data held on your behalf by third-party vendors.

II. YOU MUST IMMEDIATELY CEASE ALL DOCUMENT STORAGE AND DOCUMENT DESTRUCTION POLICIES AND PRACTICES AS IT PERTAINS TO RELATED ELECTRONICALLY STORED INFORMATION

Applicable federal and state law further requires that you cease all document retention and/or document destruction policies or practices to the extent such policy or practice impact in any way whatsoever electronically stored data concerning individuals listed above. This is a case in which electronically stored information, such as email, will be critical to the discovery process and various critical evidentiary matters.

III. ANY LOSS OF RELEVANT ELECTRONICALLY STORED INFORMATION MUST BE DOCUMENTED

Should, for any reason, electronically stored information concerning, discussing, or relating to the individuals listed above is lost, destroyed or is otherwise not preserved, provide a detailed written explanation by the person involved and their direct supervisor of the nature of events - including date and time - that caused the loss, with a description, the amount of, and steps taken to recover, retrieve, or reconstruct the information not preserved, and the steps taken to avoid further loss of data.

Please click below to complete the acknowledgement of receipt of this letter, which will be received electronically by the legal department and/or legal counsel. Call Bill Smith at 703-222-0000 in the legal department should you have any questions.

MatterSpace Mail ID - 58
Click here to acknowledge this email

The MatterSpace appliance also allows the administrator to track legal hold notifications, as shown in Figure 5.9.

Figure 5.9 A Sample Preservation Communications and Hold Audit Report from WorkProducts' MatterSpace

1 of 3 | 100% | Find | Next | Select a format | Export

Communications Report

ID	Member Name	Subject	Date Time	Matter Space Name
2	Steve Lilley (Slil1)	Test Mail 2 Lorem Ipsum	1/21/2008 5:07:44 PM	Standard v. West
		To - Gus Lee (bob@elston org) : Not Acknowledged		
		CC - Deepak Sinha (manisha chabbra@gmail com) : Not Acknowledged		
3	Steve Lilley (Slil1)	Bus. Description	1/28/2008 5:30:16 AM	Standard v. West
		To - Steve Lilley (slilley@workproducts com) : Jan 28 2008 5 32AM		
4	Steve Lilley (Slil1)	Preservation Hold Notice	1/28/2008 10:59:36 PM	Standard v. West
		To - Steve Lilley (slilley@workproducts com) : Jan 28 2008 11 05PM		
5	Steve Lilley (Slil1)	Preservation Hold Notification & Acknowledgement	1/29/2008 12:18:18 AM	Standard v. West
		To - Brad Harris (bharris@fosinc com) : Not Acknowledged		
		To - Charles Skamser (cskamser@trialgraphic com) : Not Acknowledged		
		To - Charlie Belot (balot@onlinesecurity com) : Not Acknowledged		
		To - Deepak Sinha (manisha chabbra@gmail com) : Jan 29 2008 12 51AM		
		To - Michael OnlineSecurity (michael@onlinesecurity com) : Not Acknowledged		
		To - Sophia Lilley (slilley@workproducts com) : Not Acknowledged		
		To - Torey OnlineSecurity (torey@onlinesecurity com) : Not Acknowledged		

Tracking Evidence

The first critical step when it comes to tracking evidence is to establish a case file, which will hopefully be maintained in electronic form. The case file is where you can place your evidence-tracking forms, photographs, acquisition forms, Chain of Custody (CoC) forms, and other materials relevant to the case. It should be stressed that every piece of evidence must have an associated CoC form for the effective management of data collections. This is not to say that every individual record must necessarily have a separate CoC form, but rather that each unit of media, container, and so forth for the associated records must be tracked through such forms. Figure 5.10 provides an example of a CoC form.

Figure 5.10 A CoC Form

Company Name – Chain of Custody Form			
Date Case Initiated		Time Case Initiated	
Case #		Purpose of Custody	
Media Details			
Evidence ID #		Description	
Manufacturer		Model #	
Serial #		Custodian Name	
Chain of Custody Tracking			
Date/Time	From	To	Reason/Notes
Date and time when custody was exchanged	Name/Organization	Name/Organization	
	Phone #	Phone #	
	E-mail	E-mail	
	Signature	Signature	
Date and time when custody was exchanged	Name/Organization	Name/Organization	
	Phone #	Phone #	
	E-mail	E-mail	
	Signature	Signature	
Date and time when custody was exchanged	Name/Organization	Name/Organization	
	Phone #	Phone #	
	E-mail	E-mail	
	Signature	Signature	

Page ____ of ____

Chain of Custody Form # _____

For large volumes of evidence or large case loads, it is essential to create a database that tracks all of these forms. If you are unable to create such a database, simple evidence workbooks can represent a handy alternative. As demonstrated in Figure 5.11, necessary fields within an evidence-tracking sheet could include (but are not limited to): 1. the CoC form tracking ID or number; 2. the evidence number for that piece of media; 3. the date the evidence was collected; 4. the type of media collected; 5. the serial number for the piece of media or evidence; 6. the size of that media in gigabytes (or some standardized volume), which is also a good method for summarizing the total amount of evidence in your possession or that has been collected; 7. the name of the person who collected the evidence; and 8. additional notes, such as issues encountered when you collected the media.

Figure 5.11 An Evidence-Tracking Log File

CoC Form#	Evidence#	Date Collected	Type of Media	Serial Number	Size (GB)	Collected by...	Notes
OR-1874	08-OR-34-0001	08-Jun-26	SATA Hard Drive	WDS0001435	160.00	Don Jones	Hard drive looked like it was previously removed from the computer.

You should also determine standard conventions for these fields to allow for systematic and seamless tracking from case to case. The following tip lists good rules of thumb to follow when creating an evidence-tracking log.

TIP

When you are creating an evidence-tracking log, you should follow these rules of thumb:

The CoC form number could comprise the first two initials of your company name, followed by the number of the actual form that was completed. In our example, we use OR-1874. The letters "OR" represent the first two initials of the company name and the number "1874" is sequentially the next number available for a CoC form.

The evidence number could be the last two numbers of the current year, followed by your company's initials, followed by the case number (which might be longer in some cases), followed by the actual reference number for the evidence (based on numbering from 0001, 0002, 0003, etc.).

The date collected could be in the form of a short date, such as YY-MMM-DD (representing the year, month, and date).

The type of media should be standardized with terms such as SATA hard drive, ATA hard drive, SCSI hard drive, CD-ROM, flash media, and so forth. If you were to just use "hard drive" as the identifier, you would have to also reference each individual piece of media every time there was a need to determine the different types of media collected.

Serial numbers should be recorded exactly as they were recorded on the CoC form. Double-check the serial numbers as they are the most unique identifier available.

The size in gigabytes is a good calculation to use because it allows you to numerically track and summarize the total amount of evidence collected throughout the case. Note that this might not be the actual amount of user-created ESI being sent for processing (such as due to compressed archive files), but this at least allows you to approximate how much data was captured.

"Collected by" is critical in the event that you need to ask additional questions of the person who collected the media. Even if this is being collected by someone outside the organization, make a note of the person's company and full name. In the Notes section you can add details, if necessary.

Notes are a quick method to reference specific issues or concerns you might have encountered while collecting the media. Although this section is not going to contain complete details regarding the actual issues, it is useful for tracking any general concerns.

Tracking the Collection of ESI

Similar to tracking evidence, it is always necessary to document particular items in relation to the actual ESI being collected. Here we will focus on some general guidelines to efficiently and effectively track the actual ESI. Figure 5.12 shows a general form you can utilize when collecting evidence. These types of forms typically include very specific information regarding the ESI, such as (but not limited to) media serial number, manufacturer, model number, type of media, method used to collect that piece of evidence, and specific software and hardware utilities utilized to collect the evidence. The sample form shown in Figure 5.12 is specifically intended for recording details when collecting evidence from a single end-user desktop or laptop.

Figure 5.12 A Sample Hard Drive Collection/Acquisition Form

General Information			
Case Name		Case #	
Project Manager		Name of Lead Attorney	
Project Manager Phone		Lead Attorney Phone	
Project Manager E-mail		Lead Attorney E-mail	
Custodian Name		Evidence #	
Custodian Computer			
Manufacturer		BIOS Date/Time	
Model Name/#		Actual Date/Time	
Serial #		Computer Type	
Condition/Status		Other Identifiers	
Custodian Hard Drive			
Manufacturer		Capacity/Size	
Model Name/#		Type of Drive (ATA, SATA, SCSI...)	
Serial #		Jumper Settings (if applicable, master, slave)	
Other Identifiers			
Other Custodian Media			
CD/DVD	Label/Description		
External Hard Drive	Make/Model/Size/ Serial #		
Zip Disk	Label/Description		
Flash Media/Thumb Drives	Make/Model/Size/ Serial # or ID		
Personal Digital Assistant	Make/Model/Size/ Serial #		

Continued

Figure 5.12 Continued. A Sample Hard Drive Collection/Acquisition Form

BlackBerry	Make/Model/Size/ Serial #	
Mobile Phone	Make/Model/Size/ Serial #	
Acquisition Information		
Acquired By		Acquisition Method	
Evidence #		Acquisition Date/Time	
Evidence File Name (if applicable)		Audit Trail Attached	
Image Start Time		Software Version	
Image Complete Time		Purpose of Image	
Image Backup Location		Was the image successful? If yes, state verification method.	
Location where acquisition was performed			
Notes:		

As with collecting individual hard drives, it is necessary to track evidence collected from servers, backup systems, and other locations. Figure 5.13 is a sample spreadsheet you can use when collecting evidence from a server. You can customize this form to fit the needs of any type of non–hard-drive collection (see Figure 5.13).

Figure 5.13 A Sample Server ESI Collection Form

Case Name		Case #	
Project Manager		Name of Lead Attorney	
Project Manager Phone		Lead Attorney Phone	
Project Manager E-mail		Lead Attorney E-mail	
Custodian Name		Evidence #	
Server Name: _____			
Date/Time		Person Collecting ESI	
Manufacturer		Model Name/#	
Serial #		Functionality/Purpose of Server	
Operating System		Version/Service Pack	
Software Installed		Purpose of Collection	
Utilities Utilized to Collect ESI			

Relevant Custodians	**Last Name/First Name**	**Size of ESI**	**Type of Evidence**

Additional Notes:	

TIP

If you document your collection efforts in hard-copy format, it is recommended that you either transfer that information to an electronic version or at least scan the hard copy into an electronic form. It is very useful to have such documentation stored electronically to expedite providing it to counsel as needed or requested. It will also allow you to better organize your documentation according to each case.

Creating Data Profiles and Mapping the IT Environment

Data profiling (or mapping) is a type of process for examining data available in an existing source. In the area of e-discovery, you apply this approach by examining existing ESI sources (such as databases or files) to collect information about them. Through the process of data profiling, the practitioner identifies metrics concerning the ESI (size in gigabytes or terabytes, frequency or number of each file type that exists in the environment, and/or an estimated number of pages), and determines its accessibility, identifies legacy forms of ESI and their accessibility, outlines methods to capture the ESI, and establishes standard practices for maintaining all of this information.

At the core of the e-discovery program, the IT team needs to identify locations, frequencies, and volumes of ESI early in the process. By doing this early or before litigation begins, counsel is afforded the ability to make earlier case strategy decisions, negotiate accordingly, and determine costs related to an e-discovery plan. Creating a data profile of your desktop and network systems does require a significant amount of time and effort; however, the steps in Figure 5.14 can enable your team to move through the process as quickly as possible.

Figure 5.14 Data Profiling Project Phases

Phase I – Collection of Organization's Information	Phase IIA – Enterprise Systems	Phase IIB – Data Discovery
• Corporate Details • Employee Counts • Branch/Field Office Details • Organizational Chart • Collection of Policies & Procedures (RIM, DM, ILM)	• IT Interviews • Collection of Network Infrastructure Information • Collection of Desktop System Information • Identification of Proprietary Applications • Assessment of Structured vs. Unstructured Data Identification of File Types, Volumes & Frequency • Historical/Legacy Details • Risk Assessment	• Identification of File Types on Desktops and Laptops • Identification of File Types stored on Loose Media and External Devices • Identification of File Types stored on Network Devices • Identification of Email Volumes • Identification of Hard Copy Vaults/ Storage
Phase III – Custodial Information	Phase IV - Reporting	Phase V - Presentation
• Custodian Interviews • Assessment of Loose Media • Risk Assessment – End User Practices • Laptop/Desktop Standards and Specifics • Historical/Legacy Details	• Executive Summary & Realizations • Findings • Considerations/Suggestions – Risk Identification • Compilation of Appendices	• Presentation Creation • Presentation to Stakeholders • Modifications
		Phase VI - Maintenance
		• Update and audit the report on an quarterly basis

TIP

When you are creating data system profiles, experience has shown that it is critical to conduct thorough business–unit-specific and end-user interviews. As with any research project, your human resources and knowledge are a critical and necessary component to that research. Talking to the people who, on a daily basis, deliver business-related services or products will usually provide information that is often unavailable through other means.

Phase I: Collecting Organizational Information

Although collecting data about your organization might seem like a trivial task, it occasionally proves to be quite daunting. Within larger organizations, it is a plus if you start by identifying business units and then working within those business units to collect the necessary documentation. However, this is not to say that it's necessarily any easier within a smaller organization. For example, an organization with 5,000 employees or less might have fewer business units, but it also might be less structured, which would potentially make it more difficult to determine where responsibilities reside. Therefore, a key component in the process is to assign someone who can efficiently facilitate this phase of the process. The last thing you want to do is create a bottleneck when the real goal is to learn more about the organization and its business operations to facilitate the next phases. Generally, you will want to identify the following information about your organization:

- **General corporate/organization details** This could include background about divisions within the company, their purpose, and anything special about partnerships or vendors that may utilize systems within the company.

- **Employee counts** Detail this information by location, because this will provide further details later in the project when you assessing actual system information.

- **Branch or field office locations** Document the addresses, primary contacts, and any other specific details about each location.

- **Organizational chart** Even at the highest level, this information can assist with identifying the key business units and key players.

- **Collection of policies and procedures** Although not always enforced, documentation of information management policies and procedures globally and by business unit will provide useful insight.

One important rule of thumb during Phase I is to ensure that you do not under-collect documentation and details. Later in this project it may be useful to be able to refer back to policies that perhaps seemed unimportant initially. Document as much information and collect as many policies and procedures as you can to avoid having to go back and research this information later on.

Phase II: Collecting Enterprise System Information and Data Discovery

In Phase II, which includes the collection of enterprise system information (Phase IIA) and data discovery (Phase IIB), you will outline the actual systems and ESI of the organization. Because it is sometimes necessary to conduct Phases IIA and IIB simultaneously, these steps are broken down into their subsequent elements. Oftentimes, as you are learning about enterprise systems, it is also necessary to utilize data-cataloging applications or appliances over the network to confirm your Phase IIA findings. Although you are not required to simultaneously perform Phase IIA and IIB efforts, experience has found that doing so can save substantial time.

Phase IIA: Collecting Enterprise System Information

You can now start to collect technical details regarding the infrastructure you are profiling. This is also when you will lay the groundwork for how well the technical team documents its systems and maintains that documentation. This phase will also provide guidance in further identifying unknown system locations and updated technology. Table 5.1 lists the key components of this phase. The list for verification of documentation is included to serve as a guideline for you to create a checklist of documentation useful during this process. We will not discuss the IT/Legal Communications portion in detail here, as we discussed this in the preceding chapter.

Table 5.1 Phase IIA Components Summary

Verification of Documentation	Interviews	IT/Legal Communications
Backup policies and procedures	Server information	Litigation hold communications and acknowledgment practices or systems
	Maintenance practices	
Network diagrams/topologies	Policies and procedures specifically focused on employment separation, retired hardware	Frequency of legal/IT team members
User access control information		
		Practices enforced as a factor of litigation
Username lists that log on to the network		
	Storage requirements and practices	In-house forensic or data collection technologies/teams
Shared folder listings from file servers		
	Collaboration, portals, and project management applications	IT members within the litigation or discovery response team
Standard software and hardware list for users		
	Desktop/laptop information and ESI	Training provided to IT regarding litigation hold practices or preservation
Tape backup inventory		
Security policies and procedures	Remote user access	

Continued

Table 5.1 Continued. Phase IIA Components Summary

Verification of Documentation	Interviews	IT/Legal Communications
Disaster recovery plan	Mobile computing components	Identification of previous 30(b)6 witnesses
Acceptable use policies and procedures	Unified messaging	
Business continuity plan or COOP	Structured data	
Document retention/archiving schedule	Unstructured data	
Regulatory compliance documents/policies	Backup systems	
New end-user training documents	Legacy systems	
Litigation hold policies and procedures		
Remote user policies and procedures		
List of databases		
List of mainframe applications		
List of proprietary applications		
List of Web-based portals, FTP sites, or applications managed internally		
Litigation readiness policies and procedures		
Discovery readiness policies and procedures		

If you are tasked with creating a data profile, it is extremely important to conduct thorough IT interviews, which provide an enormous amount of information. Even if you are a full-time employee tasked with this responsibility, you will be amazed at how much information you can gain by conducting thorough interviews. Consider the following sample questions to ask when creating your data profile.

For instance, to find out information about servers, you'll need to ask the following questions:

- How would you describe the computer system, storage, and network environment from a high level?

- What is the total number of servers, including e-mail, file, database, Internet, portals, security, voice mail, fax, antivirus, mainframe, and e-mail Web access servers?

- What network operating systems are used in the organization?

- What server applications are used in the organization?

- Who are the key individuals responsible for maintaining the systems (e-mail, proxy, security, backup, deployment, etc.)?

- Has anything been done to alter the use of the system(s) in response to recent discovery requests?

- Are the primary servers located at the headquarters or another location? If another location, what is that location (centralized or decentralized)?

- Can you provide a topology including all server locations? (Don't forget any backup or disaster recovery sites.)

- If the company has multiple locations, do you have a wide area network (WAN)?

- If a WAN is utilized, how would you describe connectivity to remote offices?

- How many e-mail user accounts exist?

- Do any users not use e-mail and have access to the network for only specific functions (e.g., ERP, CRM, mainframe, middleware)? What do these users access?

- Are standard drive letters mapped to each user's desktop or laptop computer? If so, what drive letters are utilized and what purpose do they serve?

- Does each user receive a home directory or some area designated specifically for that user to store ESI on a file server? If yes, what letter is assigned, what is the standard amount of space, and what is the standard naming convention for these folders/directories?

Ask these questions to find out information regarding maintenance practices:

- How often are servers upgraded?

- Have any servers been replaced in the past 12 months or during any period of litigation? If yes, describe the location or status of retired servers as well as mechanisms utilized to preserve evidence.

- How often is maintenance performed on e-mail and file servers?

- Have any computer hardware upgrades been performed in the past 12 months? If yes, did you track the upgrades, and what was done to preserve potentially responsive ESI?

- Have any computer software upgrades been performed in the past 12 months? If yes, did you track the upgrades, and what was done to preserve potentially responsive ESI?

- Are any utility applications used on local machines or servers?

- Are any disk-cleaning applications used on local machines or servers?

- Are there routines on servers that control purging of logs or other maintenance information?

Ask these questions to find out information regarding policies and procedures:

- When an employee separates from the organization, what steps are taken to preserve his or her ESI?
- If there are specific steps to preserve ESI, what utilities are utilized?
- Do users receive any sort of training or briefing when they receive a new computer? If yes, please describe or provide the name of the person responsible for training.
- Is there a help desk application to track end-user issues, maintenance, or upgrades? if yes, what is it?
- Are employee directories purged when an employee separates from the company?
- Are passwords and access codes revoked when an employee separates from the company? Specifically, what steps are taken to ensure that the employee's ESI is secure?
- Are workstations reassigned to new employees? If yes, is a tracking mechanism in place? If yes, how are hard drives handled (wiped, f-disked, no action is taken, etc.)? And if something occurs, is the ESI preserved in a particular manner and tracked for easy identification?
- How would you describe the retirement and disposal process of old equipment?
- How would you describe how old disk drives are disposed of before destruction or sales (e.g., shredded, degaussed)?
- Do any outsourced contractors service, upgrade, or store your data/systems? If yes, what function do they serve and who are they?
- Are any logs kept for the deployment or destruction of systems?

Ask these questions to find out information concerning storage requirements and practices:

- Where can users store ESI (e.g., home directory, shared directories, hard drives, external media, and personal devices)? Can users save information in additional locations?
- What forms of near-line or offline storage are available to the organization?
- What collocations does the organization utilize, including location, address, primary contact, and how ESI is actually replicated?
- In the documentation requirements, the team provided a list of server specifications outlining storage details. Is additional information available related to storage systems? If so, please describe the environment(s).

Ask these questions to find out information regarding collaboration, portals, and project management applications:

- What are the names of all portal collaborative, project management, or business intelligence applications installed within the organization? Who accesses that information? Specifically, which departments or business units have access to these applications? Are files saved to these locations?

- What is the security policy regarding access to these sites? Do you need to be logged on to your network, or is there another method in which users can access these locations?

- Does the organization support FTP sites? If yes, who has access to these sites? Who outside the organization can access the sites? What types of files are stored on these sites? Are these sites secure with Secure Sockets Layer (SSL), https://, single-sign on, or Active Directory?

- Are there any sites in which a user could store information that is located on a vendor or consultant's portal? If yes, please indicate the primary contacts for managing this information.

Ask these questions to find out information concerning desktop/laptop information and ESI:

- What is the standard desktop/laptop operating system? Do employees follow specific install details which could affect storage of ESI on desktops/laptops?

- Is hard drive encryption used? If so, describe the methods used.

- What standard desktop and laptop manufacturers and models are used throughout the organization?

- What standard desktop application suite is utilized throughout the organization?

- What other production software do end-users utilize?

- What proprietary applications do end-users utilize?

- What other details regarding the end-user environment could relate to ESI and the need to collect that information?

- If known, what metadata is captured for each end-user type of created ESI?

- Can end-users store ESI to their local hard drives or external devices?

Ask these questions to find out information regarding remote user access:

- Is remote access granted to all end-users or just specific end-users within the organization? Please explain who has remote access and details surrounding their capabilities.

- Do all e-mail users receive access to e-mail through the Internet or a Web interface? Please provide details.

- What applications are utilized to manage remote access (e.g., Citrix, virtual private network [VPN])?

- What other details are necessary to understand end-users' ability to access the network or computers remotely?

Ask these questions to find out information regarding backup systems:

- Does a document exist that outlines the standard backup policies and procedures for the organization? If yes, please provide the most current electronic version.

- What is the backup environment for the entire organization (e.g., tape, disk, other)?

- What systems and computers are backed up? What are the backup schedules as well as the rotation schedules for media?

- What applications are used to archive and back up the data?

- Is there a standard backup media retention policy? If yes, describe it in detail.

- Is any data archived to another medium? If yes, describe it in detail.

- How are files removed or deleted from the system?

- Is the backup system solely utilized for disaster recovery purposes? Or does the system have a purpose for litigation or compliance? Describe in detail.

- What hardware is utilized as a backup system? What software and versions are utilized?

- If tapes are used, what types of tapes exist within the organization (legacy and present-day formats)?

- Are legacy backup tapes stored off-site? If yes, where are they stored and what level of organization exists for these tapes (labels, tracking systems, packaged as a set, etc.)?

Phase IIB: Data Discovery

As long as a network topology exists for the organization, the data discovery portion of this project can effectively identify the most frequently used unstructured data types, their associated volumes, and maybe even an estimate of their pages. If the network topology is not current, updates to this documentation will be necessary to identify new systems and determine the true size of the infrastructure. For our purposes here, let's assume that a current network topology is available. Several tools can enable the specialist to connect to a network and identify file types, their volumes, and possibly even the number of estimated pages. Figure 5.15 displays an appliance from Deepdive Technologies that enables users to provide detailed search results of certain file types with metadata. During your data discovery phase, appliances such as this will assist you in preparing detailed reports regarding the volumes and sources of ESI.

Figure 5.15 Deepdive Technologies' DD300 Search Results by File Type with Metadata

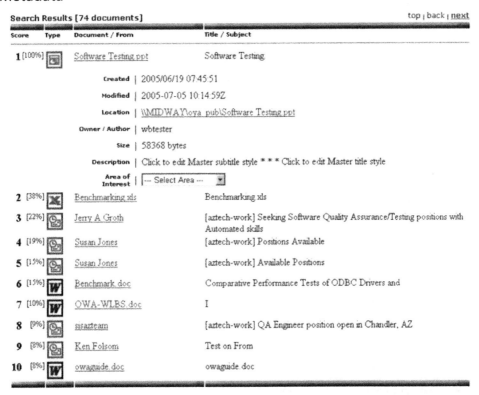

Phase III: Collecting Custodial Information

Custodians, even prior to litigation, are often very resourceful in providing details regarding the IT environment. Because of their interactions with the different types of ESI required to accomplish their business objectives, as well as their ability to store ESI in places unbeknownst to IT, their insight is generally very helpful.

WARNING

Regardless of the timing of a custodian or end-user interview, it is prudent to conduct multiple interviews with various individuals from the same department or business unit. Because of the way different users interact with their hardware and software, this approach could identify areas that would otherwise be missed through a more limited number of interviews. End-users (and the eventual custodians) might know something about legacy data that IT has never encountered, perhaps, for example, because the current IT personnel were not employed within the organization five, 10, or 15 years ago. From experience, end-users are sometimes able to provide the actual receipt of sale or destruction for legacy systems, which is just one example of the wealth of useful information that can be acquired in this way.

Phase IV: Reporting

For anyone who prepares detailed reports, the key to this phase will be the ability to manage previously collected information prior to generating a report. As you move through the project, it is essential that you electronically record as much information as possible. Data profiling and mapping reports will typically need to include the following components:

- Section 1: Summary
  - Introduction
  - Executive Summary
  - Realizations and Recommendations
  - Organizational Details
- Section 2: Technical Details
  - Retirement and Migration Summary
  - E-mail Hardware and Applications
  - General Hardware
  - Software Applications
  - Server Applications
  - Office Productivity Applications
  - Database System Summary
  - Standard Desktop Information
  - Network Infrastructure Details
  - Backup Systems
  - Documentation Checklist
- Section 3: Interviews
- Section 4: Proprietary Applications
- Section 5: Legacy Details
  - Timelines Displaying Implementation of New Systems
- Section 6: Data Discovery Details
  - Comprehensive ESI Summaries
  - Metadata Analysis
  - Risks and Recommendations Assessment

- Section 7: Appendices
  - Relevant Documentation
  - Inventories
- Section 8: Table of Figures

Phase V: Presenting Findings

Because of the volume of information collected and the findings reported from the project, presenting these findings to the team is a great means for continued conversation about the project. Not only will this alert stakeholders to potential pitfalls, but it can also facilitate an understanding for the team about the necessity to maintain this documentation. Therefore, your presentation should include topics such as an introduction to the team, a summary of ESI throughout the organization, accessible versus inaccessible ESI considerations, pitfalls or risks identified, and methods for mitigating those risks. With a very thoughtful approach, you will be able to address backup tape inventories or other identification steps, training for end-users to limit storage of ESI to external media, and even methods that could be implemented to improve your ability to search for potentially responsive ESI. For more information on this phase of the process, see Chapter 7, which discusses software and methods you can use to identify and search networks.

Phase VI: Maintaining Collected Information

You need to assign someone to manage the maintenance of all the information accumulated as a result of this project. If this type of project were conducted through a consultant or vendor, it would make sense to obtain the document collection (in native format) to avoid any additional fees. However, if the organization decides to maintain this information internally, make sure it has the necessary tools and resources to update its records on a quarterly basis.

IT/Discovery Liaison Roles and Responsibilities

Working as an IT discovery or IT/legal liaison is no easy task. It is critical that the person who holds this position be able to blend skills from previous legal, IT, forensic, or discovery experiences with his or her ability to communicate effectively. It seems as though corporations are commonly hiring individuals who have technical, legal, or a combination of these skills to fill these big shoes. As mentioned previously, the IT/discovery liaison has multiple roles and responsibilities. Clearly defining these roles and responsibilities is critical to the success of this role. In addition, the forms and tips provided in this chapter should help to prepare your IT/discovery liaison to conduct a successful program.

To fulfill legal hold or 30(b)(6) requirements, it will be necessary to take a good look in the mirror. If you have not previously provided testimony or if you feel that your skills might not match the needs at hand, acquire other resources that can assist you. In some cases, you'll want to solicit testifying experts or subject matter experts (who qualify as experts in the courts). You will, of course, want to carefully select these folks. If you decide to provide the depositions yourself, ensure that you answer every question as succinctly as possible, providing only the information that relates to the specific questions being asked. Try not to over-elaborate, as doing so can provide valuable insight and opportunities for the opposition. Look to your counsel for guidance regarding reports or other documentation that should accompany you during the deposition.

The project management role in this process will be a job in and of itself. Project management requires attention to detail and places a large demand on your time. Therefore, look to others to assist with project management responsibilities. A key factor in selecting an outside consultant or vendor is to look for reputable experience in project management and process control. Don't limit your selection based on a company's astounding technology. Ensure that the company's support mechanisms are equally well tuned. Your choice in this regard can lead to the success or failure of your discovery response, simply based on how the project is managed and controlled.

All in all, the responsibilities of a liaison should be to do what liaisons are supposed to do: communicate, transmit information, and ensure that teams work together. One of the biggest hurdles for most liaisons has been to identify who is responsible for what. If you make tackling this challenge your number one goal, success will likely be on the horizon.

Summary

Effective management of the technical components within a discovery response program depends on the relationship between the legal and information technology (IT) departments, and the key to this relationship will be IT's ability to translate technical concepts for the legal team. Even though the legal team is typically challenged with creating a reliable discovery readiness protocol, IT should be as interested in helping to shape this protocol. Increasingly, the responsibility of managing technical aspects of discovery efforts falls within the IT group. Your e-discovery documentation—e.g., policies and procedures, case information, etc.—should be readily accessible to all discovery team members. Remember to create a check list such as the one included in this chapter for addressing various documentation components. After you address these components, your next step is to assess the technical environment within your organization (i.e., obtaining and/or creating documentation to provide the legal team with a better understanding of the electronic surroundings in your organization). Remember to ask a series of questions to start the gap identification analysis within your organization. These questions should address e-mail retention polices, e-mail archiving policies, and so on. Remember to follow the steps outlined in this chapter for preparing a discovery readiness gap analysis. You should decide what tools to use for ESI collection and management and then you'll need to create a case for tracking evidence that has been collected. You also need to track ESI that has been collected.

To create a data profile and map your IT environment, you'll need to follow the steps outlined in phases I through VI of this chapter. You'll also need to assess your role as an IT discovery or IT/legal liaison. Remember that your goal during all these processes is to streamline the discovery practices throughout your organization and ensure that electronic evidence can be produced in a defensible and admissible manner.

Solutions Fast Track

IT Steps to Prepare for Discovery Readiness

- ☑ Attempt to link the discovery readiness plan directly to compliance and other requirements within your organization.

- ☑ Take a step back and assess the entire environment to ensure that you create a diligent approach which utilizes the proper technology and resources.

- ☑ Cut costs by identifying existing technologies that could reduce your need to hire outside consultants and contractors. However, do this only when it does not increase risks.

Managing Data Collections for Legal Holds

- ☑ Create forms for tracking and due diligence. This will avoid confusion regarding evidence, its storage location, and the owner of custody at any particular time.

- ☑ Manage your forms in a database environment, especially if you have too many of them or if you need multiple individuals to utilize the various forms.

☑ Document, document, document. You'll hear this mantra a number of times throughout this book, but when it comes to managing data collection and evidence, nothing is more critical.

Creating Data Profiles and Mapping the IT Environment

☑ Interview more than just the IT team. Talk with business unit leaders to ensure that you learn about business-specific and legacy applications.

☑ Identify data sources in every possible location to avoid surprises during litigation. Although new sources will always become available, keep your data profiles current to ensure that your information will remain current.

☑ Collect policies and procedures to ensure that they are the latest versions and to determine whether they contain useful information during litigation. Check to see whether the documented policies actually match the actual practices. Many times, you'll be surprised that they don't.

IT/Discovery Liaison Roles and Responsibilities

☑ Manage communications between the legal and IT teams to ensure integration of solutions as well as timely responses from team members.

☑ Be sure to involve legal and IT team members when selecting e-discovery technologies, vendors, or consultants.

☑ Make it a habit to perform quality control measures on evidence tracking and management, whether performed internally or by outside resources.

Frequently Asked Questions

Q: What are the five primary steps in creating a discovery readiness plan from the IT perspective?

A: Create a checklist that outlines the items required for the project, assess the technical environment, ask questions that lead into a gap analysis, perform the gap analysis, and leverage litigation support systems.

Q: Apart from setting up manual litigation hold practices, what other methodologies could be employed?

A: Newer technology exists to allow companies to manage their litigation hold and preservation practices by leveraging automated systems. These newer technologies allow an administrator to set up litigation hold communications requiring an end-user to acknowledge the notice. Additionally, these systems have an escalation process in place to notify managers when a custodian does not respond.

Q: What types of forms are necessary for tracking evidence and data collection?

A: It is recommended that evidence is tracked diligently as a tool to ensuring that your evidence is admissible. Therefore, it is a good rule of thumb to utilize a Chain of Custody form, maintain an evidence-tracking log or database, and complete all ESI/media collection forms.

Q: When you are conducting a discovery readiness gap analysis, what are the most critical steps?

A: Conducting a discovery readiness gap analysis could include a variety of steps based on your organization's needs. However, some standard steps include: 1) ensuring that your litigation and compliance requirements are aligned; 2) testing your enterprise content management system(s) for search and export functionality; 3) considering the state of your backup tapes and whether a tape remediation program is warranted; 4) identifying forms of loose media to decide how to handle these items; and 5) considering the use of purging programs, whenever possible.

Q: What would be considered a useful litigation readiness checklist of documents from the IT perspective?

A: It is necessary to identify all the documentation you have created over time. This provides an important foundation for determining whether policies and procedures exist in writing, and if those same policies/procedures are actually enforced. A useful checklist includes: 1) collection of written policies; 2) a litigation hold communications plan; 3) internal investigation steps and procedures; 4) identification of the nature of suits, including copies of complaints or orders; and 5) IT policies and procedures (which also overlaps with other topics discussed elsewhere in this chapter).

Q: What are the primary steps when considering a data cataloging project?

A: Even though you have flexibility for each of these projects, important steps include: 1) collecting organizational information; 2) identifying enterprise systems; 3) discovering the forms and volumes of ESI located within an organization; 4) collecting information related to individual business units and potential custodians (end-users); 5) thoughtful reporting; 6) presenting information to stakeholders; and 7) forming a maintenance plan.

Q: What are some key considerations when creating a discovery readiness program from the IT perspective?

A: Although you will work with your legal team to align both teams' goals, some items will directly relate to IT. These could include: 1) checklists that outline items required for the project; 2) an assessment of the technical environment; 3) questions that you will want to ask to enable performing a gap analysis; 4) conducting the gap analysis itself; and 5) your ability to leverage litigation support systems.

Chapter 6

Defensible Data Collection Techniques in the Enterprise

Solutions in this chapter:

- "A Day in the Life": Defining the Enterprise

- What Does Defensible Mean?

- The Defensible Protocol: Considerations in Planning

- Defensible Tools: How Will You Collect?

- Collecting Data from Database or other Structured Systems

- Defensible People: Consultants, IT, Custodians, Oh My!

☑ Summary

☑ Solutions Fast Track

☑ Frequently Asked Questions

Introduction

Dnzzzzz Dnzzzzz

    Dnzzzzz Dnzzzzz

    Jane's BlackBerry has been buzzing relentlessly for the past 15 minutes. Her husband, George, has been trying to wake her, but she keeps insisting he's dreaming. Finally, Jane stumbles from bed to her programmable coffee machine and a fresh cup of coffee. "Now, there, at least, is some useful technology," she thinks to herself as she finally opens her eyes enough to see the screen of the BlackBerry.

    It's 6:30 A.M. and Jane already has 10 e-mail messages.

    Unable to face the prospect of reading them all on the tiny screen and typing out the inevitable long response, she shuffles her feet into the den and uses her personally owned home computer to log in to work via Citrix so that she can have the comforts of a big screen and full-size keyboard from which to work. The first e-mail asks for a document on the accounting department's file share, which she can access remotely on the company's *T:* drive. One down, nine to go....

    Jane also remembers that she couldn't access Citrix last night and has a memo saved to her home computer that she intends to e-mail to herself to ensure that she has a copy on her work computer.

    Sound familiar? As technology has become more prevalent and sophisticated, we have moved away from an environment where business documents are confined to the workplace to a world where company data can be accessible virtually anywhere and is found in many formats. When the time comes to provide electronically stored information (ESI) to a requesting party for electronic discovery (e-discovery) requests, how do you navigate the increasing complexities and collect the responsive ESI in a sound and defensible manner?

"A Day in the Life": Defining the Enterprise

After Jane deals with those first 10 e-mails of the day and heads to the office, she sits at her office desk with her hastily grabbed breakfast to find the voice-mail light on her phone glowing. One message had been misdirected, so she forwards it to another department. She saves another message to deal with later—something from the legal department about not deleting some documents and e-mails, not something she has time for now!

    She logs in to her office computer and is automatically logged in to Omni Pod, her company's Instant Messaging (IM) client. George IMs her right away, asking about that link she sent him yesterday for the Web site of a local toy store so that he can get a birthday gift for their nephew, on the way home from work. Now, what was the name of that place? Luckily, the history function of this thing is turned on by default, so she can just pull it up again! If it wasn't for that, she would lose track of half the things her assistant asks her.

    Like that thing she was supposed to do this morning with her computer. What was that? Oh, yes. She has a new computer with a bigger hard dive on order, but in the meantime she needs more space on her current computer. The information technology (IT) department showed her how to move files to the *H:* drive (they kept calling it "home"), but she would rather just delete a lot—getting rid of older files and moving others. While she was at it, Jane noticed an old folder on the *H:* drive that could be discarded and she emptied the Recycle Bin. Oops—she really should not have deleted that last folder from the *H:* drive. Where did she put the number for IT?

Jane explains to Jackie, in IT, that she accidentally deleted a folder from the *H:* drive. Jackie asks whether she deleted the Recycle Bin, and of course, Jane cleaned it out. Jackie sends Jane a form to complete for the data retrieval request. As they are speaking, Jane also mentions that she has a number of project CDs to destroy. Jackie explains that there is a special bin outside the IT office marked "CD disposal" and that Jane could just dump them in there.

With that little fiasco behind her, Jane fields a request for some reports from one of the accounting databases. By the time she compiles all the requested reports, they are too large to easily send over to the requester via e-mail. She could use a little walk anyway, so she grabs one of the department thumb drives, copies the reports onto it, and walks them across the building to Roy.

In this day and age, there is nothing unusual about the amount of ESI Jane has interacted with before lunch. If Jane was a custodian in litigation and my team needed to look at where she has access to locate responsive data, how many places would we potentially have to look depending on the scope of the request? Let's make a list based on Jane's actions for the first half of her day (see Figure 6.1):

- BlackBerry
- File server: group network share (*T:* drive)
- Personal home computer
- Work and personal e-mail
- Voicemail server
- Work computer
- IM server
- File server: personal network share (*H:* drive)
- Backup tapes
- External media

Tools & Traps...

Swapping Computers

One situation that is often overlooked during preservation and collection is computer "swapping". What happens when an employee leaves, and her computer is put back into the pool of available computers? What about in Jane's situation, where she is scheduled to get a new computer? It is imperative that IT is aware of preservation orders that may affect current or separating employees so that a proper plan can be implemented regarding how to handle employees' data during the normal course of business. Simply transferring a current employee's data to a new computer without proper consideration during a litigation hold can lead to charges of spoliation if the data is not handled correctly.

Figure 6.1 Jane in the Enterprise

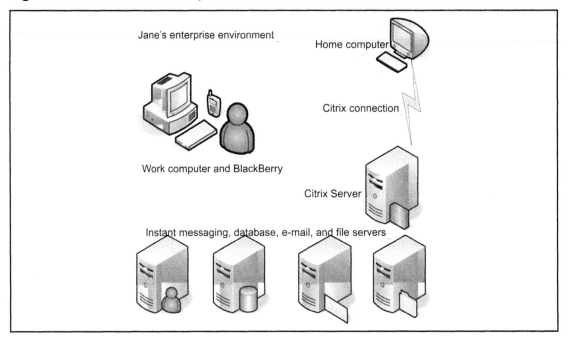

The enterprise comprises any number of these components. Depending on the nature of the environment, it can include other components that store ESI. Personal items, such as a personal home computer or personal e-mail, are, strictly speaking, not part of the enterprise, as they are commonly not maintained as part of the corporate infrastructure. However, they should not be immediately excluded as potential sources of relevant information because people can easily transfer data between systems and telecommuting is a frequent reality in the workplace. How do we begin to collect this ESI? And more importantly, how do we do so defensibly? Now that we have defined common types of data within an enterprise, what do we even mean by "defensible data collection"?

Tɪᴘ

Do you feel baffled at times by the technical terms bandied about these days in regard to e-discovery? A common vocabulary is one of the most important tools people have for communicating as long as there is some agreement as to what the words mean. The Sedona Conference (www.thesedonaconference.org/) has put together a glossary on e-discovery and digital information management. The glossary is available in the Publications section of the Web site.

What Does Defensible Mean?

Quite simply, if something is defensible it can be defended. Typical parties who might challenge your collection will depend on the type of matter and may include:

- The opposing party in a litigation
- External auditors
- Regulatory bodies such as the U.S. Securities and Exchange Commission (SEC), Department of Justice (DOJ), and Federal Trade Commission (FTC)
- Grand jury members
- Third-party litigants, such as in a shareholder suit
- Tech-savvy judges or e-discovery masters

What does that mean when it comes to data collection in the enterprise? As not all cases are created equal, what will be defensible in one situation will not always be defensible in another, depending on the facts and circumstances involved. We cannot offer you a magic solution that would be considered defensible in all situations. What we will explain are items you need to be aware of to ensure that your collections are performed to the highest and most defensible standards possible.

Standards

On December 1, 2006, amendments to the Federal Rules of Civil Procedure went into effect, which specifically address the handling of ESI. Prior to this, the existing rules were interpreted to adapt to the emerging role of ESI in litigation. The Federal Rules of Civil Procedure apply to all cases filed in federal court. Nonfederal cases may be subject to guidelines on e-discovery that are unique to the locality involved, although many follow the Federal Rules of Civil Procedure in large measure. Whether the Federal Rules or local rules apply, the emphasis is on collecting data in a defensible manner. Rule 26, "Duty to Disclose; General Provisions Governing Discovery," pertains most directly to how your discovery will be conducted.

The Electronic Discovery Reference Model (EDRM) Group has created a reference model for e-discovery which explains the steps involved in the process, including collection. The EDRM Project was launched in 2005 in an effort to address the need for standards and guidelines in the rapidly expanding e-discovery market as identified in the Socha-Gelbmann Electronic Discovery surveys of previous years. The need for these standards was expressed by both the consumers and the providers of these services. The Evergreen Project specifically endeavors to keep the EDRM model relevant and enhance its usability by providing guidelines for use of the model. It also aims to teach people involved with e-discovery how to effectively use the model to enhance the standards of e-discovery. Numerous e-discovery service providers and vendors are involved with this project. You can find more information online at http://edrm.net. Their guidelines begin to provide a framework that you can use to develop a defensible standard. In the next few sections, we will discuss the important areas to keep in mind when creating your standards to maintain defensibility.

Documentation

The importance of good documentation for your data collection cannot be overemphasized. Everything from the data collection protocol to the mechanics and output of the collection itself should be documented.

The creation of a written collection protocol presents an invaluable planning opportunity for your team members to discuss all facets of the collection as well as their roles and responsibilities in the collection. Documentation of the process that leads to certain decisions (which custodians are being collected, how certain data is being collected) also provides an invaluable record as time passes and personnel on the project potentially change. This document should be sufficiently detailed to provide structure on how the collection should proceed, but it should be flexible enough to change as needed within the parameters of the collection. Once the collection is completed, it should provide an accurate record of what transpired and provide a road map of how to proceed if additional custodians are identified or if follow-on collections are required. At a minimum, our collection protocol will contain the following information and can be further customized based on the scope of a project or as requirements dictate:

- Labeling convention to uniquely identify collected items

- Labeling convention for media on which the collected data will be stored

- Collection methods and software type for the data types to be collected

- Secondary data collection methods that will be employed as needed

- Technical escalation procedures for collections that fall outside anticipated parameters

- Types of data to be collected for each custodian

- Standard documentation methods to use

- Templates for standardized documents to use

- Proper documentation methods for exceptions

Our documentation also includes a method for tracking custodians and items collected, such as a spreadsheet or database, depending on the scope of the project, which serves as the basis for any number of reports typically requested during the collection phase of a project. This documentation includes information similar to that found in the Chain of Custody documentation and records other metrics for gauging progress.

CoC documentation is an essential element in your documentation. You should create CoC documentation for each piece of "evidence" collected. CoC documentation catalogs externally available information regarding the evidence to establish its integrity, track its location, and indicate whether it changes custody through the project's life cycle. The form should contain sufficient detail based on the context in which it is used, and you may have multiple formats based on how they are used. At its simplest, a CoC form will track the transfer of an item from one person to another with a simple description and unique attribution, as illustrated in Figure 6.2.

Figure 6.2 A Simple CoC Document

CHAIN OF CUSTODY RECORD

Matter: Libri   **Matter Number: 1008.001**

The evidence described herein has been transferred according to the below log.

DESCRIPTION OF EVIDENCE: RIM BlackBerry Curve 8310
SERIAL NUMBER: 7832xdfrhw2e3

RELEASED BY	RECEIVED BY
NAME: Veeral Gosalia **DATE:** June 2,2008 **TIME:** 20:05 **COMPANY:** Self **NOTES:** Personally owned cell phone. May contain call records for relevant time period related to company business. No longer activated.	**NAME:** Nicole Donnelly **DATE:** June 2, 2008 **TIME:** 20:05 **COMPANY:** NAD Consulting **NOTES:** Received phone in person from Mr. Gosalia on site.
NAME: **DATE:** **TIME:** **COMPANY:** **NOTES:**	**NAME:** **DATE:** **TIME:** **COMPANY:** **NOTES:**

Additional documentation of a more technical nature that adds to the defensibility of your collection includes catalogs and log files of data and data collection procedures for verification purposes. For example, the log file from running NTBackup to collect data, as shown in Figure 6.3, adds to the defensibility of how you performed your collection because it shows how many files were collected and whether errors occurred. Determining and documenting the MD5 hash value of the resultant file will further enhance the defensibility of your collection (see the "Accuracy" section).

Figure 6.3 NTBackup Log File

```
                                                    backup01.log
Backup Status
Operation: Backup
Active backup destination: File
Media name: "Backup.bkf created 7/6/2008 at 11:43 PM"

Backup (via shadow copy) of "C: FTI_BASE"
Backup set #1 on media #1
Backup description: "Set created 7/6/2008 at 11:43 PM"
Media name: "Backup.bkf created 7/6/2008 at 11:43 PM"

Backup Type: Copy

Backup started on 7/6/2008 at 11:44 PM.
Backup completed on 7/6/2008 at 11:44 PM.
Directories: 7
Files: 8
Bytes: 2,893,548
Time:  1 second

-----------------------

Verify Status
Operation: Verify After Backup
Active backup destination: File
Active backup destination: C:\Backup.bkf

Verify of "C:"
Backup set #1 on media #1
Backup description: "Set created 7/6/2008 at 11:43 PM"
Verify started on 7/6/2008 at 11:44 PM.
Verify completed on 7/6/2008 at 11:44 PM.
Directories: 7
Files: 8
Different: 0
Bytes: 2,893,548
Time:  1 second

-----------------------
```

Accuracy

Inaccurate or incomplete collection puts you are risk of data spoliation. Have all potential custodians and the possible locations of their ESI been accounted for? Did the tools you use preserve the metadata of the files you collected? Do you have a way to verify that you collected everything at issue?

A common way to establish the accuracy of a collection is through the use of hash values. Typically, MD5 hash values are utilized. A *hash value* is a unique value generated via an algorithm run against the contents of a file. If one bit within a file changes, the hash value will change. If hash values are determined at the point of collection and documented, the accuracy of a file can always be verified.

Auditability and Reproducibility

The protocol used for data collection should be auditable and reproducible to be defensible. Documentation, as outlined earlier, is a large factor in the audibility of a production. Although collection of data from a live system will not be reproducible because data is constantly changing, the methods to collect it should be reproducible by anyone with proper experience following the steps outlined in your documentation and collection protocol.

Collection Methods

Collection methods are the most varied aspect of a defensible protocol. The methods used will vary based on the scope of the collection, the format of the available data, the burden of collecting the data, and numerous other factors. Data collection methods need to address the ability to preserve metadata with the associated data type as well as preserve the content of the files being collected. However, it may not be possible to preserve metadata in every case.

Protocols, Tools, and People

The four areas outlined under standards are the sound basis for creation of a protocol, the selection of tools for data copy, and the selection of people to execute a defensible collection. All of these aspects are interdependent to create the overall level of defensibility. Weakness in one area will begin to degrade the defensibility and integrity of the overall collection.

The information to follow will give you the points to consider when designing a collection strategy for defensibility.

The Defensible Protocol: Considerations in Planning

Although the task of creating a protocol may seem overwhelming at first, if it is broken down into these smaller segments the task becomes more manageable. An e-discovery consultant can often prove invaluable. Among other things, the consultant can assist with developing a collection protocol based on past experience and general knowledge of corporate infrastructures.

With or without an outside consultant, developing an effective collection strategy is a collaborative and potentially iterative process. Ideally, a steering board or working group should be formed that includes, among others, the legal team and IT, to tailor the protocol to the environment and requirements of the collection. Another key to the success of the protocol is ownership. Each member of the team should understand the scope of her responsibility, deliverables, and timetable. As the collection progresses, the protocol should be sufficiently flexible and scalable to account for changes in scope or other factors that may change.

What questions should you ask when developing your protocol? Remember the five Ws and one H: Who, What, Where, When, Why, and How. They are commonly considered the fundamental elements for research papers, and journalists often use them to write stories. These questions can also help to ensure that all aspects of a defensible collection strategy have been considered. Some of them include:

Who

- Who should be enlisted to devise and implement the collection strategy?
- Who will be the main point of contact for each group on the collection team?
- Who are the document and/or data custodians?
- Who has responsibilities for creating and maintaining documentation?

- Who is responsible for tracking media assets within the company?

- Who maintains the servers and databases that store the ESI?

- Who will be responsible for obtaining budget approval for the collection costs?

- Who are the most knowledgeable individuals for each system you plan to collect?

What

- What ESI will be collected?

- Based on the ESI, what metadata needs to be preserved?

- What type of collection is warranted in the situation (forensic, logical, etc.)?

- What documentation will be created and kept for this collection?

- What mechanisms for auditability exist in the final protocol?

- What, if any, risks are associated with the chosen collection strategy?

- What data retention and/or destruction policies are in place?

- What type of inventory system exists for tracking media assets?

- What backup procedures are used for employee data when an employee leaves the company or receives a new computer?

Where

- Where will collections take place?

- Where: are multiple locations involved?

- Where: are international locations involved?

- Where does the ESI reside within the enterprise?

- Where is potentially relevant data stored off-site?

- Where are potentially relevant corporate documents maintained by third party agents?

- Where do employees dispose of unwanted media?

When

- When will the collections take place (overall time frame)?

- When will the collectors have access to the ESI that requires collection?

- When will each custodian and/or custodian's computer be available (for interview and individual computer collection)?

- When do collections need to be completed by?

- When was the last time any media asset inventories were updated?

- When is the relevant time period for which you are collecting?

Why

- Why is this collection occurring?

- Why has any potentially relevant data been destroyed (such as through the operation of route deletion activities)?

- Why is certain potentially relevant data inaccessible or too burdensome to collect or restore (such as through the operation of routine deletion activities)?

- Why are computers swapped out for new ones?

How

- How will the custodians be identified?

- How will the custodians be notified of their preservation and collection obligations?

- How will collection interview activities be scheduled with individual employees?

- How will the data be collected?

- How will the accuracy of the collected data be verified?

- How will individual items be tracked?

- How will data sources collected by others be tracked and accounted for?

- How will deviations be accounted for?

- How can this process be scaled if necessary?

Defensible Tools: How Will You Collect?

Depending on the collection strategy employed, a variety of commercial tools exist. Rarely is only one tool appropriate for the job, and you will find that preferred tools for certain collection types vary among service providers.

Forensic Images versus Logical Collections

First, what is computer forensics and what role does it play in e-discovery? As a discipline, computer forensics involves the preservation, identification, extraction, documentation, and interpretation of computer data (www.developer.com/java/other/article.php/3308361). As a forensic discipline, there is a focus on reproducible methodologies and handling techniques for admissibility as evidence in a court of law. Traditionally, computer forensic specialists have been found working for law enforcement and for government intelligence agencies. As the paper office has been replaced with the electronic one, opportunities have expanded for forensic practitioners to leave their traditional roles and enter the private sector in the ever-growing consulting and litigation support realm. Consulting firms with people from this background may offer traditional computer forensic services such as investigations on the use of individual computers for cases such as intellectual property theft. In addition to this, the skills of computer forensic practitioners have been used in the ever-expanding role of collecting and processing ESI in e-discovery cases. When ESI is collected in a forensically sound manner, it is easier to defend against spoliation claims.

Some computer forensic terminology and techniques are found in the world of e-discovery. The "forensic image" is considered the gold standard of collection for legal proceedings. A *forensic image* is a bit-for-bit copy of data. The purpose is to capture everything—every bit of data—and allow for the recovery of active and deleted data, residual data, and unallocated space. Due to the use of the word *image* for other purposes in e-discovery, The Sedona Conference refers to this as a *bitstream backup* or *forensic copy*. You may also hear it referred to as a *mirror image*. When created properly, a forensic image is considered the best evidence in court and it can be used in lieu of the actual item as evidence. Depending on your requirements, it is often desirable to create a forensic image of a custodian computer, particularly in the case of important custodians, high-risk matters, or in circumstances where recovery of deleted files may become necessary, as a forensic image is the only means for potentially capturing deleted files. In many situations it can be quicker to create a forensic image, depending on the size of the hard drive in the computer, than to attempt to identify all potentially responsive data through a custodian interview and then collect only those pieces. Additionally, a forensic image mitigates the risk of missing data. As an example, forensically imaging, verifying, and creating a backup image of a 60GB hard drive can often be accomplished in two to three hours depending on the techniques employed, and multiple hard drives can be forensically imaged simultaneously. Forensic images preserve all metadata, and if any questions arise in the future about collection or spoliation, all the available data has been preserved.

Tools & Traps...

What about Macs?

For someone who is well versed in forensic imaging, a hard drive is a hard drive is a hard drive, at least when it comes to capturing forensic images. Therefore, imaging a Macintosh in a forensically sound manner is not any more complex than imaging a hard drive from a computer running a Windows operating system. You can use a variety of tools and techniques, ranging from attaching the Macintosh to another Macintosh, to attaching the Macintosh to a Windows machine, to removing the hard drive (this is not always advisable depending on the Macintosh model), to booting the Macintosh from an external USB devise or from a CD. Some of the tool names may be familiar if you have been around collection operations before (EnCase, AccessData FTK Imager, and Helix), or some might be new to you because they are geared toward the Macintosh (BlackBag MacQuisition, SubRosaSoft MacForensicsLab, and Raptor).

Continued

Even though acquisition of a Macintosh image is typically straightforward, you should still take certain things into consideration during planning. First, OS X allows users to encrypt their data with a built-in program called FileVault. If FileVault is enabled when a Macintosh drive is enabled, you will collect encrypted data. There are ways to decrypt it after the fact *if* you have the proper equipment, the username and password, and the time to do it. You can have the users decrypt FileVault prior to acquisition of the machine, but again, there are special considerations that a knowledgeable consultant can lead you through.

Once you have your Macintosh, how will the data from it be handled? Programs written for both Windows and the Macintosh do not always use the same file formats. This is especially true if you are dealing with older Macintosh systems. If the data is going into an online review environment, ask whether Macintosh data has ever been put into that online review environment before. Does it require a lot of conversion? Will the review platform handle the e-mail type you are dealing with? One major difference between Macintosh and Windows in a corporate environment for e-discovery is that there is no Outlook in the world of Macintosh. The Microsoft e-mail client, Entourage, uses a completely different file format on Macintoshes than Outlook uses on Windows.

Despite these warnings, Macintoshes and the data from them can be handled. Make sure to ask your vendor or service provider if they have experience with Macintoshes and explore their planned approach.

Logical collection involves collecting only the active files of interest without additional deleted, residual, and unallocated space. The simplest way to do this in Windows is via a "drag and drop" copy from one location to another in Windows Explorer. This will not preserve the metadata of the files and will present problems if well-meaning custodians or uneducated IT employees attempt to help by consolidating all of their data in one location. Many tools exist to perform logical file copies and some offer the ability to preserve the metadata of the file being copied. Occasionally, logical file copies are performed on custodian computers, but more frequently they are performed on servers in the enterprise environment.

Forensic images are not frequently performed on servers given the data volumes associated with the typical corporate server. Servers are the workhorses in corporate infrastructure, and they often have substantial hard-drive space. Unless there is a compelling motivation, such as a court order or a reason to suspect active sabotage through data deletion, copying an entire server is rarely necessary for e-discovery purposes. Not only is the process expensive and time consuming, but also it may increase the risk that the company will be compelled to filter or review a much larger data pool, most of which may be irrelevant to the inquiry.

Additionally, servers are generally multiuser environments. As a result, high usage demands are put on the file system, with a much higher number of writes to the disk space. Therefore, potentially recoverable deleted information is overwritten faster on a network share server than on a single-user system such as a PC. Moreover, if deleted data is recovered, attribution of the data to a specific user can be more difficult and may not even be possible.

Many servers have specialty functions. Others, such as a Microsoft Exchange Server, have a single function. But with such systems, there is not likely to be deleted data of interest to recover unless you are investigating deliberate sabotage of the entire system environment.

Ultimately, the decision to use forensic or logical collection must be made by counsel, taking into consideration such items as the nature of the case, the burden involved with each level of collection, and other factors specific to the case.

Collection Tools for Specific ESI Types

Tools themselves could probably be the subject of an entire book. The information in the following sections is meant to highlight various tools for specific collection challenges in the environment. The list is not meant to be exhaustive, nor is it an endorsement of any one tool over another. To investigate some of these tools and their functionality we will look at them in the context of the enterprise we defined earlier.

PCs

Forensic images are a typical collection technique for PCs regardless of the operating system (Windows, Macintosh, Linux) they use. You can create them either with software or with specialized hardware devices.

EnCase is one of the most common image file formats created in forensic imaging. An EnCase image is a proprietary file type created by Guidance Software's EnCase software for use with its software packages. EnCase images are byte-level images created with built-in cyclical redundancy checks (CRCs) and the EnCase software will detect when any part of the image file has been changed. Depending on the version of EnCase used (Forensic Edition, Enterprise Edition) and the options selected (physical disk, logical volume, logical files), it can create a variety of permutations to produce images. In addition to its own image files, EnCase can read dd image files.

"dd" is a Unix-based copy program that also copies data at the byte level. Many variations of the dd program have been developed, including forensic implementations that automatically produce hash values of the image files and log any errors. Many forensic practitioners run dd via Helix, a "Live" Linux CD—a self-contained operating system on a CD. Helix is a forensic implementation of Linux that ensures that all drives attached to a machine the CD is used on will be write-protected until the user indicates otherwise.

Access Data's Forensic Imager has the ability to create dd- and EnCase-formatted images, and its Forensic Toolkit will read certain versions of EnCase image files as well as dd.

Norton Ghost images are often provided to consultants with the representation that an image of the data was created. Ghost is a tool initially created for IT professionals to quickly clone data across numerous drives (such as a base "image" for a corporate hard-drive setup). By default, Ghost performs only logical volume copies. You can use Ghost to capture a sector-level image of a drive, but to fully capture all sectors of a hard drive the user must change the default operation of the program. You must use a third-party application to determine the hash value of the Ghost image files created.

A variety of handheld hardware devices can also create forensic hard-drive images. From an e-discovery perspective, the end result is the same: the production of a forensic image. Although handheld devices may offer slight advantages in speed and portability, their use is a matter of preference because their functionality is limited.

Logical file captures of PC data may also be appropriate based on the circumstances of the collection. We will discuss logical file collection tools in the next section, as you can use the tools for both forms of ESI.

File Servers: Group Network Shares and Personal Network Shares

You can use any of the forensic imaging tools discussed previously to capture file server data, including handheld hardware devices. But some of these methodologies may prove problematic when dealing with servers that use Redundant Array of Independent Disk (RAID) technology. This means multiple hard drives are configured in a way to increase a system's speed and/or redundancy. It is critical to inquire at the outset how the RAID is implemented so that it can be reconfigured later for data extraction. It is also possible to image the RAID in the volume configuration in which it presents itself via the operating system as opposed to imaging each individual hard drive in the RAID configuration. But this method is time-consuming due to the large amount of space on servers, and large amounts of hard-drive space will be required to contain the resultant image. As a result, logical collection of file server data is the more typical approach.

When you are dealing with Windows operating system servers, NTBackup (also referred to as Windows Backup) is frequently used as a way to logically capture files, for a number of reasons. First, it has the ability to preserve the metadata of the files it copies. Second, it is built into the operating system, so it is readily available. Third, it logs any errors during the copying process. And last but not least, it *containerizes* the copied files (copies all the single files into one larger file), so there is no chance you will inadvertently modify the metadata of original files after they are collected. NTBackup has the added advantage of having a command-line version, so multiple collections can be scripted to run at one time. The major disadvantage of this approach is that working with the data after collection requires restoration of all the files. If the collection is large, this can be time-consuming.

Additional command-line tools are available for command-line copying in the Windows environment. Robocopy is a Windows Resource Kit tool that copies files individually and preserves their metadata. XXCOPY is a shareware tool with similar capabilities and multiple options which allow for the preservation of all metadata.

File servers can also frequently be a variety of UNIX or Linux. Utilities exist within the operating system to handle the majority of logical file system copy operation requirements without the need for additional tools. These tools can almost always be used on Macintosh systems running any variety of OS X because the OS X family of operating systems is based on a variant of UNIX. The same metadata does not get tracked in UNIX and Linux operating systems as is tracked in Windows. In addition, transferring data among file systems utilized by different operating system requires special handling.

E-mail

The most common type of e-mail server we encounter in corporate environments is Microsoft Exchange. The collection method depends on the size of the custodian mailboxes and the version of exchange server at issue. Frequently, the collection technique involves extracting custodian data from the Exchange server in the form of a Microsoft personal storage file or "PST" format. Microsoft provides a tool to facilitate this process (in some circumstances), called ExMerge. If the data collection is sufficiently large, an alternative method is commonly used to collect the data, such as shutting down the server and copying the entire Exchange database or running a special tape backup to collect some or all of the server data.

Lotus Notes and GroupWise are also found in the corporate environment, although less frequently. These may present different collection considerations based on the version of the mail server and configuration of the server environment. When collecting Lotus Notes data, for example, it is important to request the user ID and password as Lotus Notes e-mail databases may be encrypted.

BlackBerry and Treo Devices

BlackBerry and Treo devices contain potential ESI as well and are fairly prevalent in corporate environments. Typically, the data is replicated with the corporate Exchange server, so separate collection from the handheld devices themselves is usually unnecessary. However, in limited circumstances, the data may become out of sync. In such cases, the extracted data may not easily lend itself to online review environments. Oftentimes, a BlackBerry or Treo will be collected in the interest of completeness and referred to later if a question arises.

Paraben and CelleBrite are two packages that you can use to capture the contents of BlackBerry, Treo, and other mobile devices. Paraben's software product has minimal additional accessories. CelleBrite offers its package as a separate portable kit.

BlackBerry and Treo devices can also be backed up with desktop and Web-based software, which can be used to capture data on the device if other methods fail. In the case of these devices, the third-party software is performing the equivalent of a physical image on these devices, where the vendor-provided backup software is providing the equivalent of a logical backup. One additional benefit provided by such backup software is that the computer used to sync the data may become a redundant source of data if the device fails or it may provide the only source of data should the device itself become inaccessible.

TIP

Each update to the Apple iPhone changes the ability to download information from it using software designed to capture data from mobile devices. However, because of the way the iPhone was created, how it stores information, and how its sync procedures work, it is typically more productive to collect data from the computer an iPhone was synched with rather than attempt to retrieve data from the iPhone itself. The sync data stored on the computer can then be examined for ESI, including deleted data.

Paraben's Device Seizure is one software package that you can use to create an image of a BlackBerry device to be viewed later. As shown in the following figures, you can browse the contents of the device within the Device Seizure interface. Figure 6.4 illustrates some of the numerous databases used to store data in a BlackBerry.

Figure 6.4 An Acquired BlackBerry in Paraben's Device Seizure

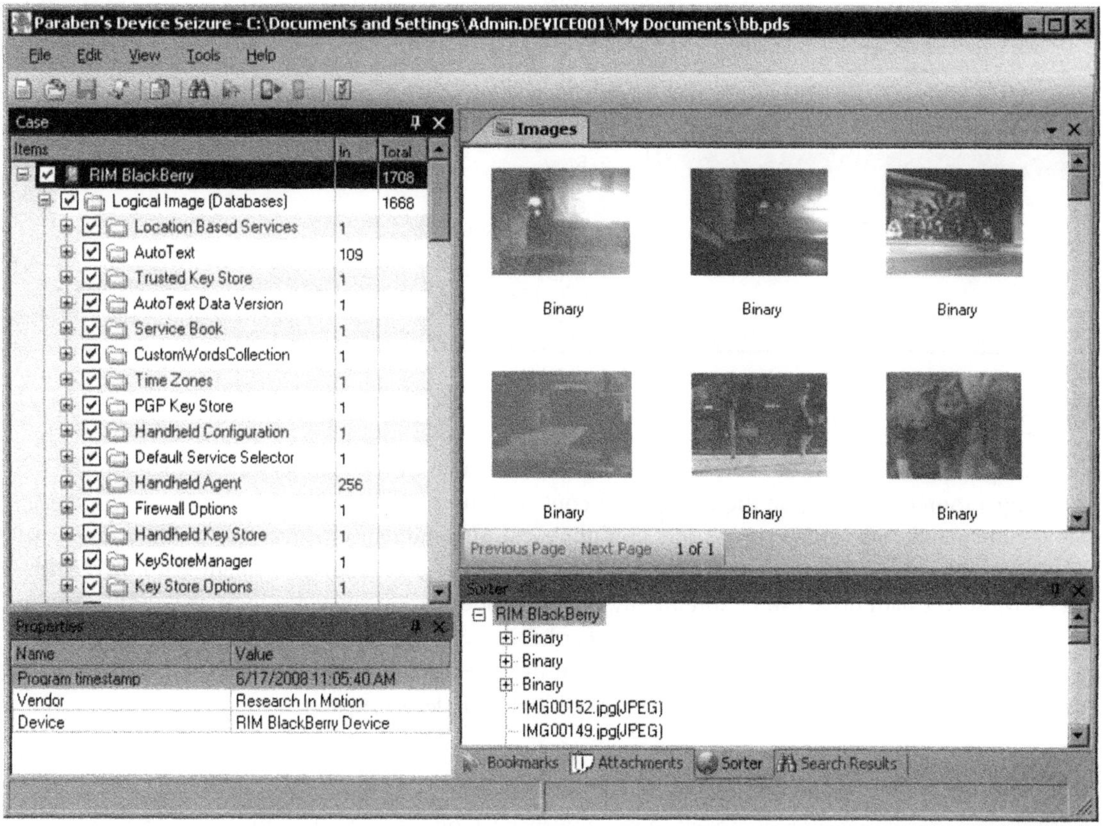

In Figure 6.5, we see the Paraben Device Seizure view of the captured BlackBerry device's address book.

Figure 6.5 Address Book of a Captured BlackBerry in Paraben Device Seizure

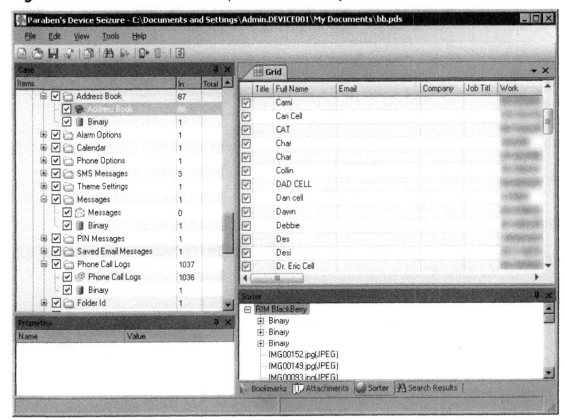

Voice-Mail Servers

Depending on the scope of discovery and the nature of a matter, voice-mail servers are increasingly becoming a source of interest in the e-discovery context. This is particularly true of voice-mail servers that are integrated with e-mail servers and configured to store and deliver messages via employee e-mail. Newer voicemail servers run on computer hardware just as file servers do. As with any hard drive, the voice-mail server hard drive can be forensically imaged. Older systems may not look like computers, but they typically still contain storage media such as hard drives. Such servers are frequently found in the same room as the telephone routing equipment. You may need to consult the telephone support engineer if the voice-mail server is maintained outside the IT department.

IM Servers

IM servers are becoming more prevalent in the enterprise. Consult IT to determine whether and where logging is enabled. Most IM servers have logging options on the server and client end. If logging is not enabled on the server, determine whether instant messages may have been logged on the employee's computer, assuming the feature is engaged.

Backup Tapes

Backup tapes are created in nearly every corporate network. How much data is available will depend both on the corporation's data retention policies and whether they are being followed. Tape backups are frequently stored off-site and older tapes may even be stored without an adequate tape inventory or labeling, so it may require significant time and expense to assess the tapes and bring back those with potentially relevant data. Tapes frequently hold substantial amounts of data, and they can be costly and time-consuming to restore. However, if tapes are managed properly and smartly, targeted tape restoration can be less painful than it sounds, should it become necessary.

Depending on the circumstances of a collection, you can use backup tapes as a source of ESI. In some cases, collecting substantial amounts of network data from the live server can negatively impact system performance, so a backup tape may be a better alternative. In other circumstances, restoring data for the last tape backup or a tape proximate to the relevant time period may prove more efficient or appropriate. In some cases, creating a custom backup tape as a method of preservation should future processing become necessary may be the best answer. You should thoroughly analyze the utility of using tapes for collection, if they are not the only location to collect relevant ESI.

If tapes exist solely for disaster recovery purposes and have not been created for business archival purposes, the tapes may be legally deemed "inaccessible" in the e-discovery context under the FRCP absent compelling circumstances. Counsel should be thoroughly apprised of the situation concerning the tapes before decisions are made to proceed with data collection. Restoring and searching data contained on backup tapes may be shifted to the opposing side in the appropriate circumstances.

Technology relating to the search and restoration of tape data has been advancing recently. In the past, data would need to be restored in order to search the contents of the files. In many cases, this is still done. The tapes are either restored "natively" by using the software that created them in the first place, or by using proprietary software created by companies to restore the data regardless of how it was written to the tape. Various levels of scans can be performed on tapes to provide information on their contents, including what server(s) were backed up onto the tape, when the tape was created, and even the names of the files on the tapes. Newer technology includes the ability to index the contents of the files on tapes, search them, and selectively restore individual files from the tapes. Index Engines' Tape Engine has automated this offline tape discovery process via a network appliance. Instead of restoring tapes to find specific content, tapes can be searched and responsive data can be extracted quickly and easily without ever using the backup software. Unordered tapes are loaded into a tape drive or tape library and scanned to generate a catalog and full text index. Boolean and metadata searches allow you to cull through millions of files to find all responsive documents and e-mail. Once this data is found, it can be easily extracted from tape, keeping all metadata intact, without the original backup software. Automated tape discovery saves significant time and resources.

The following steps walk you through the software screens that you would encounter during the typical tape discovery process using Index Engines' Tape Engine.

1. Plug the tape library or tape drive into the Tape Engine. Insert the tapes into the drives. Tapes are catalogued to provide a high-level view of the tape contents (see Figure 6.6).

Figure 6.6 Inserting Tapes into the Tape Engine

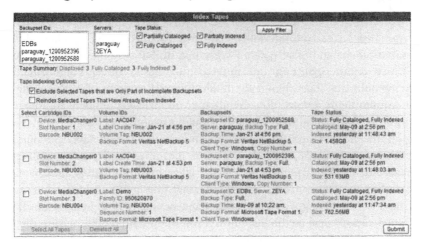

2. Select specific tapes for indexing. Scanning occurs at tape speed and all text and metadata are indexed. The software displays real-time progress of the tape indexing (see Figure 6.7).

Figure 6.7 Scanning a Tape with the Tape Engine

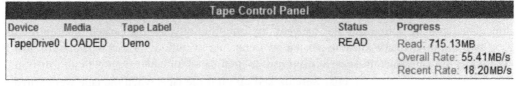

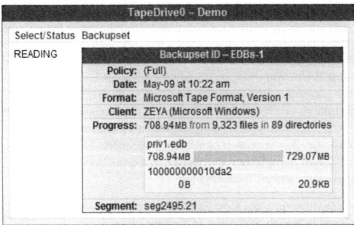

3. A report is generated detailing the file and e-mail contents of the tape and the indexing status (see Figure 6.8).

Figure 6.8 An Index Segment Report

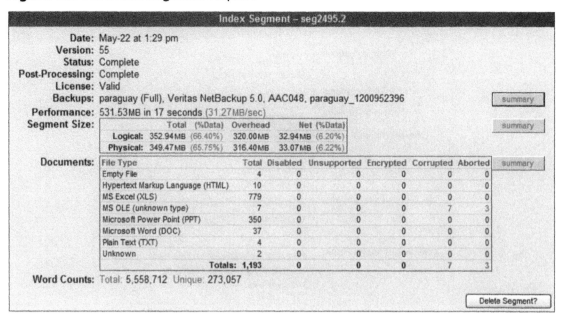

4. Perform a full-text Boolean search and metadata search on the tape contents to find all responsive data (see Figure 6.9).

Figure 6.9 Finding Responsive Data

5. Specify how duplicate files are managed—by content, message ID, and so on. When you query data you will be assured that only unique files are reviewed (see Figure 6.10).

Figure 6.10 Specifying How Duplicate Files Are Managed

	Preferences
Display Options	20 ▾ Results Per Page
	☐ Backup Information
CSV File Options	☐ Include Document Essence
Search Timeout	(no timeout) ▾
Results Deduplication	☑ By Path
	☑ By Content
	☐ By Occurrence
	☐ By Message ID
Search Only these Fields	☐ Author / From ☐ To ☐ Cc ☐ Bcc
	☐ Title / Subject ☐ Content / Message
	☐ Path
Attachment Search Mode	○ Searched Separately from Messages
	◉ Searched Together with Messages
	○ Not Searched
	Save Preferences

6. Execute the query to deliver a full list of the relevant content (see Figure 6.11).

Figure 6.11 A List of the Relevant Content

7. Select the file and e-mail to be extracted from the tape using the tagging feature (see Figure 6.12).

Figure 6.12 Using the Tagging Feature to Flag Items

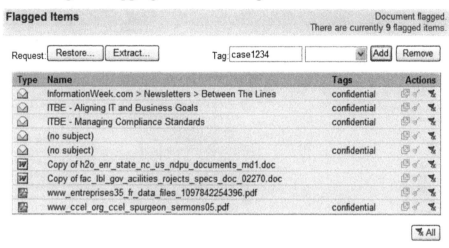

8. An extraction job is then executed for these files (see Figure 6.13).

Figure 6.13 Extraction Request

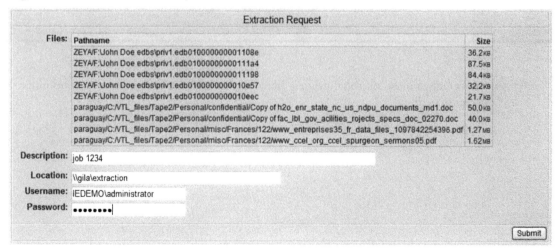

9. The files are ripped from tape to an online repository, keeping all metadata intact (see Figure 6.14).

Figure 6.14 Online Repository

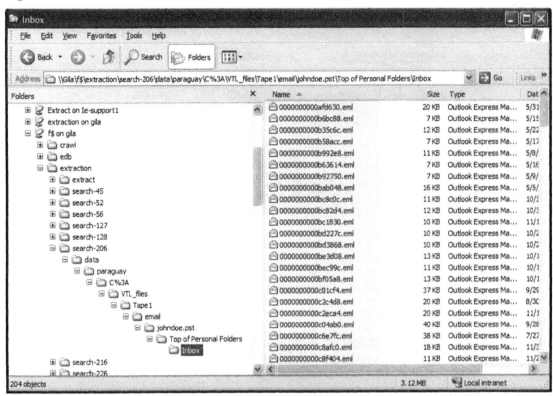

10. At this point, you can examine original files and e-mail or place them on litigation hold (see Figure 6.15).

Figure 6.15 Sample E-mail Result Stored in the Online Repository

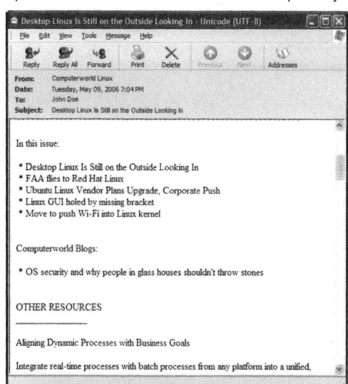

External Media

Custodians frequently have the ability to burn data to CDs or DVDs. Additionally they may have the ability to utilize external hard drives or smaller USB storage devices known as *thumb drives* or *pen drives*. Even MP3 players can be configured to act as external hard drives and can store files of interest. These devices can be collected forensically or logically and should not be overlooked when collecting data.

Collecting Data from Database or Other Structured Systems

The first concept that usually pops into people's minds when they hear about ESI collection is e-mail and loose e-documents such as Word or Excel files. The typical data storage sources mentioned earlier may include the custodian's hard drive, the e-mail server, and the file server, but a sometimes-overlooked source of data can be found in a company's database or otherwise structured data systems. These systems may manage data for the company's finances, the payroll, cash disbursements, expense reimbursements, inventory, sales, document management systems, and many other business-critical functions. Further, many of the current commonly used document review systems do not provide a facility to handle data from these types of systems natively.

Some common examples of these systems and platforms may include:

- Microsoft Access databases

- Microsoft SQL Server

- Microsoft Great Plains/Dynamics

- Oracle

- Hyperion

- SAP

- PeopleSoft

- Lotus Notes

- Quicken

The necessity to collect information from these systems will depend on the nature of your issue. For example, if your matter concerns an FCPA investigation of bribery, you may consider collecting data from the company's expense reimbursement system or cash disbursements system. If you are producing data in response to a Second Request for a pending merger, you may need to collect data from the company's sales system. Finally, if you're investigating a possible accounting or financial fraud, the company's general ledger or accounting system may be of huge value.

The first step to collecting structured data is to gather information regarding how this information is stored and how the company makes use of it. Simply copying the database files or imaging the server on which the database resides will get you only the data, which can be meaningless without the context in which the data is used. A typical structured data platform will have a few components which may not all be self-contained on the database server. For example, a document management system may store document attributes in a database, store the actual documents on a file server, and interact with employees using an application which is installed on their computers. Gathering this information will require that you have a discussion with both the IT person in charge of maintaining the system and an end-user of the system. You may consider having the end-user give you a walk through of a typical transaction so that you can understand which components and fields he utilizes.

The next step is to gather the technical documents or blueprints behind the system along with any technical documentation the company may have. Most structured data systems will store data into tables that contain rows of information. These systems will minimize redundant data to reduce data storage requirements. For example, in a cash disbursements system, there may be a table that identifies vendor information such as name, address, point of contact, and unique vendor identification code. There may also be a separate table that provides a record of each disbursement that contains a vendor ID, date of disbursement, and amount. To determine which vendors were paid in the past 90 days, you would need to "join" the Vendors table with the Disbursement table using the vendor ID. You do this to avoid storing the name and address of the vendor each time the vendor is paid. For someone to under-stand how to query this data, you may consider requesting a copy of the system's Entity Relationship Diagram (ERD). The ERD is a diagram of each table and how it relates to the other tables in the database. You may also consider requesting a Data Dictionary which provides you with an index of each field in the system and a description of what data is stored in that field along with some other technical information.

Last, you will need to consider how to collect this information for analysis. As we mentioned earlier, simply imaging the server on which the data is held or copying the files may not be helpful. Here are some items to consider:

- Do you have the same or equivalent software available to examine the data? For example, if the databases are stored in Microsoft Access, do you have a copy of that software?

- If this system was created by the company or is a heavily customized version, can the company provide you with the software?

- Does the system have any export capabilities?

- Are you able to run reports against the system to mirror the query you are seeking? What reports are run a regular basis?

- Has any data been purged from the active system that will require you to restore backups?

- Are you able to copy (sometimes called *transforming* the data) from its existing system to one that's more familiar?

Once you have the data in a format that you can utilize, you should consider interrogating it to ensure that it is what it seems and your understanding of how the business logic is applied to query the data is accurate. One way to do this is to ask for *control totals*. For example, have a company employee confirm for you how many disbursements were made in a certain period. Compare that amount to your own query. You may also request historical reports that were run from the system. Another method is to compare your data set with an external source. You may consider requesting bank statements for which you can trace activity through the company's system. You could also reconcile your data set to the company's externally audited financials.

Defensible People: Consultants, IT, and Custodians, Oh My!

Once you have a defensible protocol in place and the appropriate tools for the job, who will perform your collection? A defensible process requires the use of defensible people. How do you know who they are and settle on what are they supposed to do?

Third-Party Independence versus Internal Collection

Many people are tempted to use internal resources to collect responsive data to save money and time. Usually these tasks fall on the IT staff. In some environments, companies have developed internal e-discovery teams to respond to ongoing litigation requests. In these cases, the people responsible for data collection have typically had additional training beyond the functions performed by IT. However, if your company does not have an internal e-discovery staff for such collections, should you use internal resources?

When an ESI collection begins in response to an e-discovery request, it can be the first time corporate counsel, IT, and corporate security have all sat down at a table together. It may also be outside counsel's first experience with anyone inside the company other than general counsel. IT is knowledgeable and highly proficient at supporting the corporate infrastructure for hundreds, thousands, or even hundreds of thousands of employees. However, locating all potentially responsive ESI in a corporation, particularly a larger company that may be composed of multiple and potentially international locations, can be daunting in the best of circumstances. IT departments tend to fully utilize their personnel resources at all times and proper ESI collection and documentation is very time-consuming. Moreover, defensible ESI collection is a concept that many IT professionals have never encountered, much less experienced, and it is fraught with legal risk for the company.

WARNING

A full discussion on the legal issues surrounding international collection of ESI is beyond the scope of this chapter. You do need to be aware, though, that European Union (E.U.) laws concerning collection of computers or data used by custodians are more restrictive than those in the United States. When you know the scope of data collection will involve data located on servers and individual computers in international locations, or where the custodian involved is a citizen of another country that works for the company outside the United States, you should consult counsel familiar with the laws of that country as early as possible.

When using a third party for any facet of the e-discovery process involving international collection and review of data, whether the company has received Safe Harbor certification may be important for your data-handling concerns. Safe Harbor certification is a program run by the U.S. Department of Commerce that allows the data-handling practices of a business to be certified in compliance with the stricter privacy control practices of the European Union.

Preservation of metadata and an adequate CoC during collection can be challenging even for IT professionals. The risks increase dramatically where custodians are directed to self-collect data. Custodians are one of your best sources for identifying a majority of responsive data because they produced and/or manage it. But if IT does not have a full understanding of the tools used to correctly collect and preserve ESI, it is unreasonable to expect IT to undertake the collection without providing adequate consultation resources. It is even less likely that a custodian can be relied upon to self-collect in a defensible and documented fashion. Among other things, at the beginning of a matter, you may not yet know the full scope of the issues, so the collection may need to be repeated down the line if the collection was too narrow. In addition, preserving the metadata associated with the ESI is so complex that it may be virtually impossible for employees to perform the necessary tasks, absent the rollout of enterprise ESI record management and data collection software that permits the employee to drag and drop files in a documented manner. If you ask a custodian to self-collect, it also provides the custodian an opportunity to destroy or remove data before you have the opportunity to look at it, which increases the risk of data spoliation.

Notes from the Underground...

When Custodians Go Bad...

How and when custodians are approached regarding data preservation and collection should be carefully considered. A search through some court cases shows numerous examples of people destroying data by using "scrubbing" software or by attempting to physically destroy the item, such as the hard drive on which the data resides.

Whether data is removed maliciously or through some misguided belief that there is a compelling reason to remove data of a personal nature before turning over a business computer for forensic imaging, the presence and/or evidence of use of disk scrubbing software can be very detrimental. *Disk scrubbing software*, also referred to as *wiping software*, is software that allows a user to overwrite data that exists on a system so that it cannot be recovered. However, virtually all of these programs leave traces that are obvious to an experienced computer forensic practitioner. What have some people attempted to do and what were the results of their actions?

In *Ameriwood Industries, Inc. v. Liberman*, 2007 WL 5110313 (E.D. Mo. July 3, 2007), the defendant was found to have used the disk scrubbing software Window Washer days prior to turning the computer over to a forensic expert. The defendant was also shown to have performed "mass deletions" of data. The plaintiff was awarded numerous costs and fees and the jury trial proceeded on the issue of damages.

In *Anderson v. Crossroads Capital Partners, LLC*, 2004 WL 256512 (D. Minn. February 10, 2004), the plaintiff agreed not to remove data from her drive and then used CyberScrub software to do so. Based on additional misrepresentation, an adverse inference instruction was issued.

In *APC Filtration, Inc. v. Becker*, 2007 WL 3046233 (N.D. Ill. October 12, 2007), the defendant disposed of his hard drive in a construction dumpster 20 miles away after receiving notice of the lawsuit. The defendant was ordered to pay certain fees and costs and certain facts were deemed conclusively proven.

Counsel has many issues to focus on during a matter and the collection of ESI is just one aspect of the many balls to be juggled. Counsel understands the legal requirements for the collection of data, but does not always have the technical background or experience to understand the "how" behind the collection.

One last but vitally important consideration in deciding whether to handle the collection with in-house resources is the benefits offered by third-party certification. When the company is required to describe its collection methodology or defend the manner in which preservation and collection were undertaken, do you really want to put an employee on the stand? The weight accorded to the judgment of third-party professionals in developing and executing the collection protocol can often head off challenges to the collection that can drive up costs through needless overcollection, overprocessing, and excessive data review.

A third-party service provider can bring something to the table that typically does not exist in companies that lack an effective internal e-discovery team: they can bridge the gap between IT and the legal department to help make the team run smoothly. A good e-discovery consultant is familiar with and knowledgeable of both the legal and the IT issues surrounding data collection and has expertise on how to collect the ESI properly. Such a consultant is able to facilitate requests from legal and translate technical information back from IT so that counsel understands what ESI exists and where it is. The consultant works closely with IT and utilizes their intimate knowledge of the enterprise to devise a data collection strategy that is complete and performed to the best standards possible for ultimate defensibility.

Roles and Responsibilities

Once you decide who will be performing your electronic discovery collection, what roles and responsibilities need to be filled to ensure that your process is successful? The size and scope of the matter will determine the number of people involved to handle each role.

Each team will have several components. If multiple people are on each team component, someone should be designated as the focal point for communications. During a collection on a short timeline, it is easy for items to be over looked if they are not properly tracked.

Outside counsel typically takes the lead in coordinating the collection. They will work with in-house counsel to define the scope of the discovery and to draw up a custodian list. Outside counsel will assist in-house counsel with selection of third-party consultants and will often guide the collection work.

In-house counsel typically takes responsibility for coordinating the in-house team, including corporate IT. They will also coordinate the scheduling of custodians for interviews and imaging, or partially delegate this task to corporate IT.

Third-party consultants need to be prepared to talk to corporate IT and get a sense of the corporate infrastructure and where the custodians are likely to store data. They need to assess probable data size per custodian based on information provided by IT and provide strategic advice on the scope of collection, including sources and likely duplication among them. They also commonly deal with issues such as potential encryption and various levels [define or delete reference] of password protection of data. They will be expected to provide recommendations to counsel on a sound collection scenario, revise the scenario as requested by counsel to meet considerations such as timelines and impact to daily operations, and provide a time and cost estimate for the collection.

Once on-site, all four groups and any additional parties that may have been involved (project or case managers from counsel's office, paralegals, outside vendors for specialty processing such as paper collection, and the like) will need to meet to scope out the tasks, protocols, and timelines. The active involvement of IT will be crucial to facilitate access to the data. During this time, counsel will typically perform custodian interviews, often with assistance from consultants on technical questions. Counsel should use care to avoid discussing the substance of the case under investigation in the presence of third-party consultants, given the risk that legally privileged information could lose its protection if disclosed in the presence of a third party. The actual collection is generally performed by the consultants in partnership with IT.

Qualifications: Certifications, Experience, and Training

As with any industry, people list certifications that read like a veritable alphabet soup if you are not familiar with them. A majority of the certifications you are likely to run into are more likely to be held by people with a computer forensic background. E-discovery certifications do not yet exist in the same numbers. Certifications, experience, and training all play a role in the defensibility of the people performing your data collection.

NOTE

Do you want to help shape what certification and professional standards should look like in the different disciplines of e-discovery? Get involved in one of the groups out there that are actively working to establish standards. The Association of Litigation Support Professionals (www.alsponline.com) is working to establish a certification examination program. The Electronic Discovery Reference Model (EDRM; http://edrm.net) has a project addressing the creation of a code of conduct for e-discovery professionals and e-discovery clients.

In computer forensics, you see two major certification types: vendor-specific and vendor-neutral. Vendor-specific certifications typically certify that someone passed a general knowledge test and then performed a forensic examination using the vendor's software. Non-vendor-specific certifications can vary. Some follow a similar setup: a written test followed by a series of practical exams. Some are written tests only or may have follow-on exercises for different levels of certification. Depending on the certification, some certifications require documented prior forensic experience. Others may require a background check and/or agreement to an ethical standard. Some require none of these. Additionally, colleges and universities have begun to offer degree and certificate programs in computer forensics.

In the vendor arena, Guidance Software has offered its EnCase Certified Examiner (EnCE) certification for a number of years. Access Data also offers a certification that covers three of its software packages, called the Access Data Certified Examiner (ACE).

The International Association of Computer Investigative Specialists (IASCIS) and the International Society of Forensic Computer Examiners (ISFCE) offer popular vendor-neutral forensic certifications. The Certified Forensic Computer Examiner (CFCE) certification from IASCIS is open only to law enforcement personnel. The Certified Computer Examiner (CCE) certification from ISFCE is open to people who meet certain training or experience requirements and pass the background check.

SANS Institute, a large provider of information security training and research, offers certification through an affiliation with Global Information Assurance Certification (GIAC). It offers a forensic certification with a heavy Linux focus, called the GIAC Certified Forensics Analyst (GCFA).

The realm of e-discovery certification programs looks fairly bleak when compared to that of computer forensics. They simply do not exist in the same numbers as computer forensic certification programs. Kroll Ontrack, an e-discovery service provider, has a two-day e-discovery certification course that leads to a Certified Electronic Discovery Specialist designation. The intent of the certification is to provide attendees with knowledge to manage e-discovery and make decisions in ESI investigations. Additionally, many consultants are beginning to offer specialized training in a similar vein.

The Association of Information and Image Management (AIIM) offers a variety of certifications that do not strictly pertain to e-discovery, but lend themselves to the focus of the industry. AIIM offers six different certificates to allow you to better understand and manage business information. Among these certifications are enterprise content, electronic records, and e-mail.

Based on the current state of commercially offered training and certification, on-the-job experience and internal training make up a bulk of the background which people in the e-discovery realm bring to the table. More opportunities are beginning to present themselves as traditionally forensic-oriented conferences expand to cover more e-discovery topics. Additionally, litigation support groups are starting to expand to provide more information on e-discovery.

TIP

To find out about new and upcoming training opportunities or to find potential instructors that can offer courses at your place of employment, begin networking with professionals that have similar career backgrounds. LinkedIn (www.linkedin.com) has multiple e-discovery groups you can request to be affiliated with. Also, Women in eDiscovery (www.womeninediscovery.com) offers monthly meetings internationally that provide opportunities for networking paired with a lunchtime seminar on a topical subject of interest.

Summary

Daubert v. Merrell Dow Pharmaceuticals, 509 U.S. 579 (1993) was decided by the Supreme Court and set the legal precedent for admitting expert testimony in federal legal proceedings, holding the testimony must be relevant and reliable. A litmus test to consider whether your collection procedures would survive, a Daubert challenge, could include the following items:

- Is your collection process well documented?

- Is the collection process or methodology generally accepted by your peers?

- Has your collection methodology been tested and results documented on other similar matters?

- If someone were to undergo the same collection exercise on the same data set, would he have the same results as you?

- Does the collection process potentially alter any of the data being collected?

- Can you put the people who collected your data on the stand to testify?

If you do not feel that you can confidently answer each of those questions with a "yes," you should assess the weaknesses in your. And, it is always important to remember because of a large number of different sources of evidence (as well as types of media) that the collection process typically takes more than one person – ultimately enabling you to build a defensible and admissible collection protocol.

As technology changes, the defensible process will evolve. As mentioned in Chapters 2 and 3, companies are employing litigation-ready enterprise content management systems as part of their enterprise. These systems provide for a single point of search and collection, which will eventually provide a single-point and streamlined collection methodology. Additionally, third-party consultants are also starting to deploy data cataloging and mapping devices (as mentioned in Chapter 5) on client networks to inventory files prior to collection. This too will benefit the overall collection process by identifying sources and volumes of electronically stored information throughout the enterprise. Regardless of the technology, tactics or personnel, the key of your program is to ensure that your evidence is defensible and admissible.

Solutions Fast Track

"A Day in the Life": Defining the Enterprise

- ☑ The enterprise environment is composed of a vast array of technological devices in the corporate infrastructure.

- ☑ Storage and backup procedures in the corporate environment make custodian data available on devices other than an individual computer, such as on network servers or backup tapes.

- ☑ Even though it is not an official part of the corporate enterprise, an employee's home computer should not be eliminated as containing responsive data because corporate data is accessible outside the office environment.

What Does Defensible Mean?

☑ Defensible data collection is data collection that can be defended from any one of a number of parties that may be involved in your matter.

☑ A defensible collection is created from a set of standards and may vary from case to case.

☑ For a collection to be defensible, you need to develop a defensible protocol, use defensible tools, and utilize defensible people.

The Defensible Protocol: Considerations in Planning

☑ Considering the 5 Ws and one H will assist in planning your protocol: Who, What, Where, When, Why, and How.

☑ A defensible collection protocol should be sufficiently flexible and scalable to account for changes that may need to be made as the e-discovery process progresses.

☑ Creating a defensible collection protocol is an iterative process typically combining input from all members of the e-discovery team.

Defensible Tools: How Will You Collect?

☑ Forensic imaging and logical file collections are two of the options available when collecting ESI in an e-discovery matter.

☑ A variety of options exist for forensic imaging and logical file copy.

☑ BlackBerry devices, instant messages, voicemail servers, and backup tapes are all sources to consider for potential ESI.

Collecting Data from Database or Other Structured Systems

☑ Databases and other structured systems contain potential ESI that needs to be considered when planning collections.

☑ Collection techniques will vary based on the type of system and required data.

☑ As with any ESI collections, steps need to be taken to verify the integrity of the data collection and that the desired results are achieved.

Defensible People: Consultants, IT, and Custodians, Oh My!

☑ Numerous factors lead to the decision to use third-party or internal consultants for collection.

☑ Roles and responsibilities of members on the collection team need to be outlined and understood ahead of time.

☑ The people performing your collection need to be knowledgeable, credible, and trustworthy on the stand should they have to testify.

Frequently Asked Questions

Q: What are potential sources of ESI that can be deemed responsive or relevant?

A: Any item that has the potential to store data, including but not limited to laptop and desktop computers; servers such as e-mail servers, IM servers, and database servers; voice mail; personal data devices such as BlackBerry or Treo devices; and external computer media such as CDs and USB drives.

Q: Where can I find a glossary of e-discovery terms?

A: The Sedona Conference (www.thesedonaconference.org/) has put together a glossary on e-discovery and digital information management.

Q: Are there any special concerns when providing employees new computers if they are potentially part of a litigation hold or data preservation request?

A: Yes! You must properly address the transfer of their data to a new system if their data has not been preserved yet or you risk spoliation issues. Additionally, prior to disposing of an old computer you need to make sure you have all data you need from it.

Q: Where can I find step-by-step instructions on how to conduct defensible collection for e-discovery?

A: There is no "one size fits all" method for defensible collection. You can find guidelines for defensible collection in places such as the Federal Rules for Civil Procedure and the EDRM Project.

Q: What is the purpose of Chain of Custody documentation?

A: To establish the integrity of an item and track its location during the life cycle of a project.

Q: Why is a protocol important?

A: A protocol outlines what needs to be done, how it will be done, and ultimately how it was done. It defines roles and procedures so that everything is performed accurately, completely, and in a reproducible manner.

Q: How do I even begin to plan a defensible collection?

A: Focus on the 5 Ws and 1 H: Who, What, Where, When, Why, and How. All of those questions should be answered in planning.

Q: My collection scope changed and now exceeds my protocol. What should I do?

A: A protocol should be a scalable and flexible procedure. Reevaluate how your protocol cannot accommodate your new requirements and fix it accordingly. Look critically at the entire document to see whether any additional adjustments need to be made.

Q: What is a physical image?

A: A forensic (bit-for-bit) copy of data on a device such as a hard drive.

Q: I have a Ghost image of the drive. Can it give me all the deleted files that were on the drive?

A: It depends on how the Ghost file was created. Although it can be possible with Ghost to capture the required information to do so, it is not a default setting nor is it the recommended way to go about retrieving deleted data.

Q: I would like to retrieve only those files that meet certain keyword criteria from a tape. Is that possible?

A: Yes. Index engines can index and search a large number of file formats located on tapes without restoring the data.

Q: Can I capture data from a BlackBerry/iPhone/cell phone?

A: Yes. The method and what can be viewed will vary based on the model.

Q: Do I need to collect data from an Oracle/PeopleSoft/SAP database system?

A: Database systems should be evaluated for potential relevant data and use by identified custodians.

Q: Can I just run reports to retrieve the data from a database system?

A: Database systems can be quite large and span a large period of time. It is possible that reports exist in the system that will mirror the query for data you intend to run. You will need to evaluate which reports are run on a regular basis to ensure an understanding of which data is being retrieved from the system.

Q: Why can't I just review the Oracle database in Concordance?

A: Large databases represent complex relationships between data. In most situations, they will not be able to be natively viewed in an online review platform.

Q: What is Safe Harbor certification?

A: Safe Harbor certification is a program run by the U.S. Department of Commerce that allows the data-handling practices of a U.S. business to be certified in compliance with the stricter privacy control practices of the European Union.

Q: What can an e-discovery consultant bring to my team? I want to run everything internally.

A: Although an e-discovery consultant may not know your particular system, he or she has expertise on a variety of tools and a depth of knowledge gained from working on a variety of e-discovery-related matters.

Chapter 7

Data Structures and the Anatomy of a File

Solutions in this chapter:

- Structured versus Unstructured Data
- Components of a File
- File Integrity

☑ Summary

☑ Solutions Fast Track

☑ Frequently Asked Questions

Introduction

In most cases, it is helpful for all e-discovery team members (legal and technical) to understand what types of data they are considering preserving, collecting, and analyzing. Toward that end, this chapter outlines and describes data structures and associated file components. Understanding data structures and the anatomy of a file can provide you with insight regarding the types of questions you should ask consultants or vendors during the e-discovery process, and it can provide guidance to your team when they are preserving, collecting, processing, or producing data. You also can use your knowledge of data structures and file components when arguing an opposing party's preservation efforts.

Structured versus Unstructured Data

A critical distinction to make when analyzing files is whether the data contained in the files is in a structured or unstructured format. In a *structured* data file, a container or template defines how the data within the file is arranged so that a computer can use it efficiently. Typical examples of structured files are database files and delimited files. An *unstructured* data file lacks this container or template and, thus, this efficient organization of data. Examples of unstructured data files include word processing documents, spreadsheets, presentations, and individual e-mail messages. Such files, though not visibly unstructured or unorganized to the user, are not easy for a computer to read. Although it is common to analyze information residing within a database to determine whether information there has been altered or removed, ultimately the focus of e-discovery is on unstructured data.

The Basics of Unstructured Files

For the purposes of this chapter, a *file* is a group of binary digits that are ordered in such a way as to represent some form of information. This information can be text, numbers, pictures, music, or any number of other items. Each file type has a specific file format. When you place information into one of these formats, the computer can understand it using a specific program or group of programs to allow an end-user to view the output of the information on a screen or in print.

Because most technical managers, vendors, and consultants provide advice to counsel, your ability to interpret the functionality of a file is critical. Your primary role/responsibility is to prove that the information collected, reviewed, and produced is of the highest quality and meets certain standards. If you fail to address those standards, results could range from spoliation of evidence to sanctions for your company or client. Therefore, utilizing your understanding of what files are and how to maintain their integrity provides a safety net for your case.

Components of a File

To understand the breadth of information which can be relevant during e-discovery, it is necessary to examine a file from a holistic point of view. Therefore, it is important that you clearly understand how this information interrelates with other information in your case.

The interrelationship of information is helpful for you to collate it to a common point of reference. For example, a library contains a collection of books and other materials designed to be accessed by library cardholders. Therefore, when a visitor is looking for specific information on a subject, two methods are available: The visitor can wander through the library and look at each book on each shelf until he or she finds something related to the subject of interest, or the visitor can browse the card catalog. The card catalog provides the exact location of the book within the library. It also provides a lot of data about the book, such as its author, title, date of publication, publisher, edition, and other important information. The card does not contain actual information from the book. This information is contained only within the book itself.

Each book is located in a specific area of the library, and all of the books are grouped into like categories, whereby the color of the card describes its contents. For example, all the books containing text only have a white card in the catalog. All the picture books have a blue card in the catalog. Books containing sheet music have a red card in the catalog. Furthermore, only the item number is located on the outside of the book. It doesn't have any other information.

Say that as a visitor to this library you want to find a book on the Apostle Luke. You look up the information that is specifically related to this subject within the card catalog, and you find an interesting work called *A Biography of Luke the Apostle*. You notice that the card in the card catalog lists the specific floor, section, aisle, shelf, and item number for this book. It is a book full of text, so its cover is white. You search through the library to locate the correct floor, section, aisle, and shelf. You find the book by locating its item number.

Now say you want to find some pictures of the Apostle Luke. You go back to the card catalog, and this time you find information on a book called *Pictures of Saint Luke*. The card in the card catalog lists the floor, section, aisle, and shelf where the book is located. It also lists the item number. You find the book, and you see that the cover is blue, indicating that this is a picture book. You follow this same process to locate a book of church music.

With all three books in hand, you go to the front desk. The librarian looks at the books you want to check out. She then notes today's date and time on each book's card, indicating when each book was checked out of the library. You notice that the card also includes the date and time that each book was placed onto its respective shelf.

You are excited about the books you just checked out of the library. You take them home, and explain to friends that you checked out three different types of books: a book with only text, a book with only pictures, and a book with only music. When you open the books, however, you notice that you have two books with text and one with pictures. This means someone switched the book covers around either on purpose or by accident.

We can use this example as we explore the information that relates to computer files. For instance, in our library example we had two different types of information regarding the books: the cards in the catalog and the actual books. Each book was placed in a certain location and on a certain shelf within the library. That shelf is akin to a file folder. A file folder holds files and other folders. In our analogy, no two books on the same shelf can have the same name. The same is true of a file. There can be two files with the same name in different folders; however, no two files with the same name can reside within the same file folder.

Files contain two types of information which might be critical in the e-discovery process:

- External data (the card catalog)
- Internal data (the book itself)

The information within each category is not necessary readily apparent. Our analogy does not really hold up entirely; however, it serves as a useful aid in understanding the relationship between a file and the data the file system maintains regarding the file.

File Integrity

This thorough understanding of the environment in which electronic information exists is a critical first step toward ensuring that *file integrity* (the preservation of data, and any structure, within a file) is maintained. For example, consider a large e-mail environment, with all of the support servers operating in clusters. Your task is to ensure that e-mail messages, including such forensic information as the date and time each e-mail was received, the original sender and recipient, the size, and any attachments, are preserved in their original states without any later modifications. The cluster environment complicates the task of maintaining file integrity as the computer systems are using sophisticated file sharing and updating procedures and protocols. For instance, is one version of a critical e-mail stored on one machine and another version, different in size and time, stored on another member of the cluster? What about backups that might be available? What if a member of the cluster goes offline and thus some contents of its data store are inaccessible?

Then, you must add the variables of employees and technicians that may be working in, on, and modifying the environment. A technician might inadvertently back up and then restore data in such a manner that changes key forensic information, such as the date and time of original receipt. Perhaps changes are made to the e-mail environment as a whole that, say, strip out attachments that are received (some messaging antivirus systems by default quarantine messages with certain file types as message attachments). You can begin to see how file integrity, although important to maintain for evidentiary purposes, is difficult in complex environments.

When certain accounts were created might be a chief concern within the e-discovery process. Also, when a system is upgraded, updated, or patched could provide some valuable information as to the type of file that was changed and the integrity of other files. These processes could be of paramount importance if there have been significant changes before or during the e-discovery process. It might also be helpful for you to interview numerous individuals, including policy makers, end-users, and others outside the traditional system administrator role. If an organization is routinely involved in e-discovery, a document or collection of documents may be assembled for the purpose of providing you an understanding of the computing environment.

External Data

A computer's file system and operating system provide a comprehensive list of its contents. The operating system locates information and displays it in a usable form on your computer screen. In this way, operating system controls access to the computer's files and provides information on their location, their name, and other property information. We will explore this type of data in the following sections to obtain greater insight into the information that can be gleaned.

Different operating systems provide and collect different information about every file on the system. The specifics of the information that is collected and the extent to which this information is usable depend on the operating system. Some general information is common to most of them. This file information can also be called an *attribute*. These attributes provide valuable information about the file and its contents. The attributes can include items such as the following:

- Filename
- File extension
- Modified, Accessed, and Created (MAC) date (discussed shortly)

The file attributes are set to a great extent by the operating system where the file resides. For example, a Microsoft Windows XP system contains certain attributes, whereas an Apple system might not. Within the Microsoft operating system a file is expressed in two ways: by its filename and by its extension. The filename is the most ubiquitous file attribute.

Filename

On electronic information, it is necessary to use a character or series of characters to identify a particular file in a given location. This is commonly referred to as the *filename*. This name is a unique string of characters provided by the user or the system; alternatively, it can be the first few digitals of the contents of the file. Each operating system has its own specific parameters and requirements regarding its filenames. In the early Microsoft days, a filename had to follow a specific naming scheme called *eight dot three*. This referred to the number of characters allowed within the filename. Eight was the maximum number of unique characters within the filename. As the Windows operating system became more sophisticated, it allowed for use of a greater number of characters, resulting in the ability to better describe the information contained within the file. The filename was followed by a dot (.), which was followed by three more letters.

File Extension

A *file extension* is generally referred to as the three or more characters to the right of the dot (.) within a filename. These characters tell the computer what program to use to read the contents of the file. For example, the *.txt* file extension generally refers to a plain text file. The *.rtf* file extension stands for *rich text format*. This text file has specific formatting information which is not available within *.txt* files. Some computer programs allow you to access and/or edit a variety of different types of files. For example, Microsoft Word will allow you to access/edit files having file extensions such as *.doc, .txt, .rtf*, and many more. Although each of these files is generally text-based, various features are exclusive of that extension. For example, a *.txt* file can't display a picture within the file; however, a *.doc* file extension can. The file extension allows you as the user the flexibility of determining what program to use to access/edit a specific file.

File Dates/Timestamps

Most operating systems keep track of the date/timestamps for files within their respective file systems. This basic tracking information is useful to the operating system. In some operating systems, this combination is referred to as the Modified, Accessed, and Created (MAC) date/timestamps. The MAC stamps provide information regarding each file on the hard drive and within some operating systems on the file folders as well. This information can be important in some e-discovery cases. This information becomes much more complex as there is a wide range of reasons for some of these date/timestamps to be updated. In fact, not all of them are stored in the same area or even in the same format. These facts can complicate the e-discovery process significantly.

NOTE

Computer systems keep track of date/timestamp information via an internal clock. The computer uses this clock for a large number of its functions. This information is stored on the computer's motherboard within the complementary metal-oxide semiconductor (CMOS) chip. This chip is powered by a battery that is connected directly to the motherboard. On some computers, this battery looks much like a watch battery. In addition to the computer date/time, the CMOS chip also stores a whole host of other important information, such as system settings, hard-drive information, random access memory (RAM) information. This information is generally set at the manufacturer, but you can change it by pressing certain key(s) as the computer is powering up. Although the CMOS information is stored on a chip, it is also interpreted by the operating system, which can maintain a separate set of date/time settings.

To further complicate this process, most operating systems allow the computer to keep track of the date/time via the time zone. Because the world is divided into different time zones, it is necessary for your computer to identify in which time zone it is located. When computers were more stationary and were not connected to a network, this was much less important. However, with computers being moved all around the globe and the sheer number of systems that routinely connect to the Internet, it is important that the time zone of the computer is taken into consideration.

WARNING

Just because a computer is set for a particular time zone does not mean this setting is correct. In fact, it is common for computers to be moved from one time zone to another. The computer does not have a magic sensor to tell it what time zone it is really located in. It relies on the user to provide this information. As with all user-provided information, this information may or may not be correct. When conducting an e-discovery production it is important that this information is cross-checked and verified by the individual who is collecting the information. For example, if a computer was forensically imaged on the East Coast and then analyzed on the West Coast, will the date and timestamps be accurate? The answer is, only if the individual conducting the analysis has taken into account the time difference. Many e-discovery platforms as well as forensic analysis platforms do just that. They allow the examiner to adjust his or her software to account for time differences.

Another consideration with date/timestamps is the adjustment for daylight saving time. If the computer was set to adjust for daylight saving time and it was moved to an area which does not recognize daylight saving time, it could create problem. All of these factors must be considered as the three most common date/timestamps are examined.

Creation Date/Time

A file's creation date/timestamp can be important. Because Microsoft Windows is the most ubiquitous operating system, we will examine this information from this perspective.

Some people believe that the Creation Date/Time timestamp shows the original date/time the file was complied. This is not true. The file creation stamps show the first time the file was placed into its current location. Each file within a particular folder must have its own unique filename. Two files with the same filename cannot reside within the same folder. This is also considering that the file extension is part of the filename. This means that when a file is copied from one folder to another the creation time for the new file will be set to the current date/time. It does not change the original file. In our analogy of the library, the creation date/time information was kept within the card catalog. This entry within the card catalog would be changed when the book was placed onto a different shelf within the library. It would also be updated if the book was copied and placed on another shelf. This concept is confusing to many people; however, as long as you keep in mind that Creation Date/Time refers to the file's current location, it will be much easier to understand.

Last Accessed Date/Time

Last Accessed Date/Time is the date/timestamp which changes the most often. This does not necessarily mean the file was changed or even updated. The information in the file could have remained exactly the same. In addition, some programs can cause this timestamp to change. In our library analogy, this means that if someone picked up a book and looked at it, and then put it back into its original spot, the Last Accessed Date/Time would still be updated within the card catalog.

Modified Date/Time

Modified Date/Time refers to the last time a file's actual contents changed. In other words, a file was opened, changed, and then saved. However, this does not necessarily mean the change was intentional. For example, let's assume you use an older version of Microsoft Word to create a document for work. This document is created on your home computer. Because it is a work document, you save it onto your thumb drive to take into the office. When you arrive at your office you put your thumb drive into your work computer and open the Word document. What you don't realize is that your original document was created with Microsoft Office 97. Your work computer has Microsoft Office 2003. You review the contents; however, you don't edit or change the actual document. When you click on the button to close the document the program prompts you to save changes. You might think this is quite odd; however, you click on the Save button nonetheless. You have now changed the actual document.

You may be confused by this because you did not add or delete any content from the document. So, why is the program asking you to save changes? This is because Microsoft Word keeps a large amount of metadata within these documents. (*Metadata* is data about data, and we will discuss it in a later section of this chapter.) When the document is opened using a different version of Word, the program will automatically begin by updating the metadata. This will frequently cause the size of the document to change because of the changes within the metadata. If the user chooses not to save changes, only the document's Last Accessed Date/Time will be changed; however, if the user chooses to save changes, the Modified Date/Time as well as the Last Accessed Date/Time will be changed.

All of the issues surrounding date/timestamps become much more complex because information can be stored in different formats by various operating systems. Also, different programs may store their timestamps in different formats. If a programmer is creating a new program, it is up to him or her to decide to implement date/time information within the application. Due to the global connectivity caused by the Internet and the ease of program creation, the situation has become even more complex. It is common to find UNIX date/timestamps on Windows computers, and even Windows stores date/timestamps differently from the core of the operating system, to the Windows Registry, Internet history, and so on. This is one of the many reasons why it is critical to employ the skills of a digital forensic professional. These individuals have specific training and knowledge to assist with these sorts of challenging issues.

NOTE

All date/timestamps are not created equally. Because the operating system is just a program designed to run your computer, the programmer(s) can choose to implement date/timestamps in any manner he or she sees fit. For example, UNIX uses a 32-bit value for its date/timestamps. This value represents the total number of seconds that have elapsed since January 1, 1970. This can also be referred to as *epoch* or *Coordinated Universal Time (UTC)*. On the other hand, Windows XP uses a 64-bit date/timestamp. This value represents the total number of 100-nanosecond intervals since January 1, 1601. Due to the limitations in the way each numbering scheme calculates information, at some point neither one will be able to calculate time. For the 32-bit date/timestamp of UNIX, this is approximately 60 years after 1970. For the 64-bit date/timestamp of Windows, this is roughly 58,000 years after 1601.

Another reason to employ highly qualified professionals is that date/timestamp information is the most fragile of all computer information. It can be changed by the user or computer either intentionally or accidentally. For example, the act of booting up just the Windows XP operating system changes an enormous number of the date/timestamps as well as many other logs on the system. This information may be critical to a particular aspect of your case, or it may pertain to your allegation/defense. To ensure that this information is preserved, it is necessary to employ highly specialized tools and techniques.

On traditional desktop, laptop, and removable media, this process is simple:

1. Gain direct access to the computer system or media.

2. Thoroughly document its state and condition.

3. Connect each media item to a write blocker separately.

4. Create a forensic image of the data.

Numerous tools are available for media write protection. These devices are made by various vendors, including Digital Intelligence, Tableau, and Intelligent Computer Solutions. By following the procedures and protocols used in such tools, you ensure that your date/timestamps remain intact and unaltered.

The next step is to create a forensic image of the media. This is sometimes referred to as a *physical forensic image*. Although some people might argue that the forensic imaging process is not necessary, it remains the most secure way of ensuring that the data is unaltered. Because date/timestamp information is so fragile, it is, in most cases, the most prudent way to secure digital media. Numerous tools are available for forensic imaging. The most ubiquitous tool is EnCase, by Guidance Software. This program was one of the early pioneers in digital forensics and sets a high standard for others to follow. Another popular solution is FTK Imager, by Access Data (see Figure 7.1). In addition to being a robust forensic imaging tool, it can also be used to perform most rudimentary analyses.

Figure 7.1 FTK Imager, by Access Data

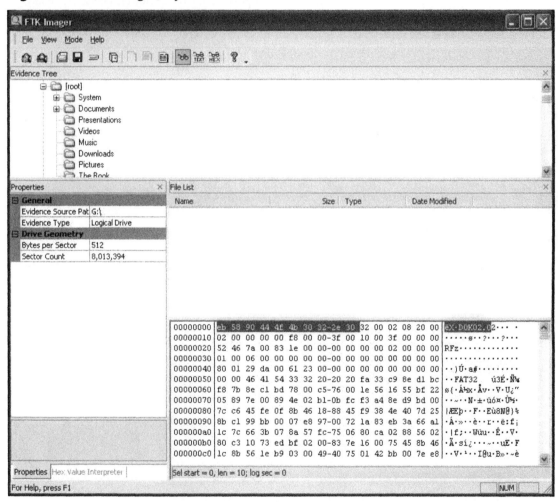

The real problem is created by files which reside on devices other than removable media, laptops, and desktop computers. These devices include mission-critical production servers, enormous file servers, instant-on communication devices, and a broad array of mobile devices. Due to the unique nature of these systems, it is difficult to provide simple, easy-to-follow instructions for securing this information. One tool for capturing specific data is called the *logical evidence file*. This is the terminology Guidance Software uses. This process forgoes imaging of the entire hard drive and drills down to only certain information. Because this tool is forensically aware, it can capture all of the necessary information, including date/timestamps, attributes, and various other items, to make the file as valuable as possible to the reviewer. For mission-critical production servers, some people have opted to take their redundant failover servers offline to create a full physical forensic image or logical evidence file. Other techniques are also available, such as loading an agent on a computer system. This agent is designed to operate at a low level within the system and essentially provide access for the forensic processing to occur. The goal of all of these advanced tools and techniques is to collect data in such a way as to provide as much information as possible for the reviewer. This is especially true of such fragile items as date/timestamps. As computer technology continues to evolve, innovations in digital forensic tools and techniques will continue to evolve as well.

Tools & Traps...

Robocopy, the Big Kid on the Block

When it became apparent that standard copy tools were not sufficient for administrators' needs, Microsoft quickly developed a tool to allow users to copy large amounts of data from one place to another. This tool is called Robocopy, which stands for Robust File Copy Utility. This command-line tool has a wide variety of switches and logging capability, which makes it a good choice for the digital forensic professional. You can download it for free from the Windows Server 2003 Resource Kit, at: www.microsoft.com/downloads/details.aspx?familyid=9d467a69-57ff-4ae7-96ee-b18c4790cffd&displaylang=en

Many computer forensic professionals rely on this tool. Although it is not a forensic tool per se, it does provide some useful features. Here is an example of a forensic use of the Robocopy command

```
Robocopy x:\location\of\original\data j:\location\of\output /e /np /tee
/r:3 /w:15 /log: j:\location\of\output_log.txt /TS /FP /COPY:DAT
```

The following is an explanation of the preceding command. Note that each option is separated by a single space.

- **Robocopy** The name of the program. You will need to have this program within the external command path.
- **x...** Used to identify the location of the original source information.

Continued

- **j...** Used to identify the location where you would like the information to be copied to.
- **/e** A switch that means to copy all of the folders and subfolders, including empty ones.
- **/np** A switch that disables the percentage copied display.
- **/tee** A switch that displays what is happening on the screen as well as in the log file.
- **/r:3** A switch that means the copy failed to retry three times. This is important because the default is 1 million.
- **/w:15** A switch that means the amount of time to wait between retries in seconds. This command would cause the program to wait 15 seconds before attempting to copy the file again, if the original copy failed.
- **/log:...** A switch that indicates the path to the log file.
- **/TS** A switch that puts the date/timestamps from your source file into the date/time of your output file(s).
- **/FP** A switch that tells the program to include the entire file path in the output file(s).
- **/COPY:DAT** A switch that tells the program to copy all of the data, all of the file attributes, and all of the timestamp information.

Internal Data

Generally, folks work on a computer to manipulate the information on the computer or to create some electronic product—in most cases, the result is the file, and in many of those cases the information is stored in binary format. Inside some of these files are instructions for the operating system, with a header, some metadata that describes the other data contained in the file, the data area, and then the footer. Not every file will have all of these parts, but most of them generally will have them in that order. Operating systems can display file contents to the user as hexadecimal (hex) values. Hexadecimal is a common way to display binary information. Each hex character represents 16 values. These values are illustrated with the symbols 0–9 and a–f. The hexadecimal system is basically computer shorthand.

File Headers

A *file header* is a series of hex characters at the beginning of the file. This header provides some information about the contents of the file. It serves as a check to ensure that the information associated with the file extension is actually contained with the file itself. The goal is to ensure that the correct type of information can be opened by the operating system. Just like the title page is usually near the front of a book, the file header is the first few bytes of the file. This is mostly because file headers are not standardized. When a programmer creates a new application, he or she is not required to send it to a particular board for approval. The programmer does not have to apply for a building permit and any other standards control board to create his or her application.

It is largely left up to the programmer to determine what header and file extension to use. As you can imagine, this could and has created some confusion. Due to these factors, two organizations are attempting to sort out this mess. They are the International Telecommunications Union–Telecommunications Standardization Sector (ITU-TSS) and the International Organization for Standardization (ISO).

Table 7.1 is a list of some of the most common file headers.

Table 7.1 Examples of File Headers

Extension	File Headers in Hex							
.doc	7F	FE	34	0A				
.doc	31	BE	00	00	00	AB	00	00
.rtf	7B	5C	72	74	66			
.dbx	CF	AD	12	FE	C5	FD		
.jpeg	FF	D8	FF	E0				

File Data

For a file to be useful, it must have some information of value.

Other Data

Just like the writer of a book can determine what will be inside, a programmer can also determine whether it makes sense to put other types of information inside a file. This information can provide additional information about the file. Perhaps it could contain a disclaimer, a copyright notice, and some other information that the programmer wants to put in there. This information may or may not be used by the program. It is entirely up to the creator of the program. Certain applications are recognized as generally having some additional information. A detailed applications examination is beyond the scope of this book; however, there are two that deserve mention.

Metadata

Metadata is often defined as data about data. This means the information contained within metadata has specific information. This data may have useful information regarding the file. For example, Microsoft Word is widely recognized as having lots of metadata. This information can provide an enormous amount of information about the document. The following figures illustrate the amount of information stored in a Microsoft Word document.

Word Metadata

Word metadata can be automatically collected by the application and placed inside the file without the user even knowing it is there. This data could include additional information about the file, such as all the changes made to it. Authorship information can be stored here as well as a wide range of other items. This information can be valuable during the e-discovery process. It can provide insight and conclusions that might not be otherwise possible (see Figures 7.2 and 7.3).

Figure 7.2 An Example of Word Metadata

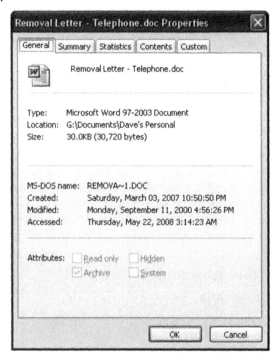

Figure 7.3 A Summary of the Properties of a Word File

Tools & Traps…

Removing Word Metadata

There are lots of ways to remove metadata from a Word document. The easiest method is to cut and paste the actual text from Word into Notepad or another text editor. This converts the document into a plain text file. However, this option is not elegant, and the author loses the ability to place sounds or images within the document as well as the ability to perform some advanced editing options. After all, why use Word if you have to save the data into Notepad or some other similar utility?

The second option is to manually remove the data. In Word 2003, there are two ways to accomplish this:

- File | Save As | Tools | Security Options
- Tools | Options | Security

Both methods provide you the option to "Remove personal information from file properties on saves."

Although this way works for a single document, it is rather limited. So, our friends at Microsoft have provided a solution. It is called rhdtool.exe, also known as the Remove Hidden Data Tool. It was first released in 2004, and you can download the tool from:

www.microsoft.com/downloads/details.aspx?familyid=144e54ed-d43e-42ca-bc7b-5446d34e5360&displaylang=en

When you download and install this application, the default install location is C:\Program Files\Microsoft Office\Remove Hidden Data Tool\. This tool has a command-line option. The great part of using this tool's command feature is the amount of control that it provides. For example, to use this tool you will need to open each document individually and run the *Remove Hidden Data* command. You can find it on the File menu, assuming that you have enabled Microsoft as a trusted publisher. If not, you will need to refer to the specific instructions provided within the rhdtool help file. Rhdtool's real command-line power comes from the ability to change multiple documents, create a log of the process, and either overwrite the existing file or put files in a separate location altogether. Another powerful option is the ability to generate a comprehensive report of all the metadata within a file or files.

EXIF

Another source of information is called EXIF data. This is data that a digital camera saves when it takes a photo. This information can be helpful to someone who wants to edit the photo later. It can include such things as the camera's make, model, and serial number, the specific setting used when creating the picture, and numerous other data. It can also include a date/timestamp for when the picture was created. Numerous programs are commercially available for extracting and viewing this data. It is also possible to view some of this information by using Notepad to open a picture. Not all cameras will produce digital pictures with EXIF data in it. It depends on the camera make, model, and manufacturer.

File Signatures

You use a file signature analysis to compare and contrast the information contained within the header of a file against a list of known file headers and file extensions. Although this process may sound rather complex, it is not.

Here are the steps necessary to perform this analysis:

1. Identify a file or group of files.

2. Examine the file extension on the file in question.

3. Determine the appropriate file header for this file extension.

4. Compare the known file header to the file header within the questioned file.

Windows

For example, in Windows, when a program attempts to open a file called *windows.doc* it does not look to the file header to determine which program to use to open the file. Microsoft determines which program will attempt to open a file by looking at the file extension. It does this because Windows provides an interface to allow the end-user to examine what program should be used to open a file. Because the user is the one who will be installing and placing the program on the system, it is assumed that the user will have some level of understanding of how a file should be opened. For example, let's assume that you have installed an application in Windows XP, and this application is used for word processing. How does the computer know what program to use to open the file? In Windows XP, this is presented to the user when he or she highlights the file, right-clicks on the mouse, and then selects **Properties**. The user then sees the dialog box shown in Figure 7.4. This dialog box allows the user to determine what application will be used to open that file.

Figure 7.4 Windows File Property Display

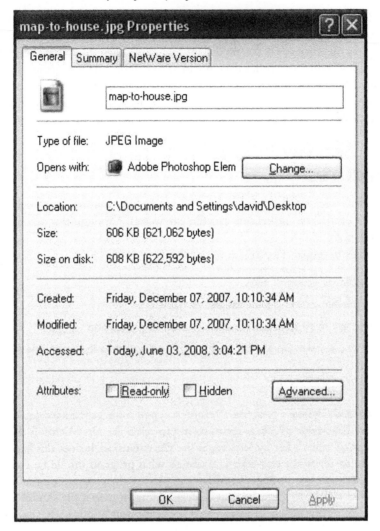

The "Opens with" option allows the user to determine what program Windows will use to open a particular file.

An Experiment

Let's try a little experiment to discover how Windows keeps track of the connection between a file and your operating system. For this experiment, you will need a computer running Windows XP. You will also need to download and install Adobe Reader onto your computer (you can download it from www.adobe.com).

Adobe Reader comes installed on many computers because it is a common format for information exchange among technology professionals as well as many others.

Next, you will need to download a PDF file from the Internet. It really does not matter what file you use. For example, I downloaded a file from www.forensicexams.org, called *test.pdf*; I created this file and placed it onto my Web site. Place the file onto your Windows XP desktop. Double-click on the file and it will be displayed within Adobe Reader. Now close this application, and let's begin our experiment.

Highlight the *test.pdf* file and right-click on it. Next, click on the **Properties** button. Look in the dialog box and you will see a button labeled Change. This button has nothing to do with the file, but more to do with how the operating system will treat all files with this file extension. Click the **Change** button and you will see the box shown in Figure 7.5.

Figure 7.5 The Open With Dialog Box

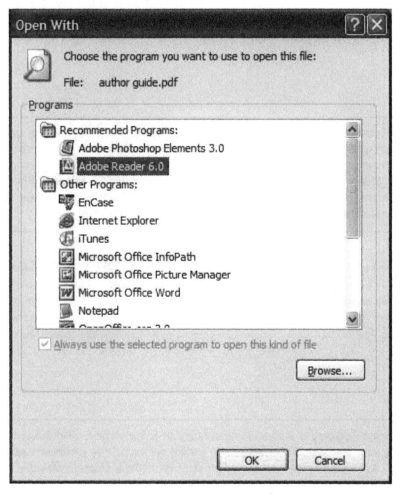

This box displays many of the applications currently installed on the system. Adobe Reader should be listed. You'll note that Windows evens attempts to help you by listing some recommended programs.

Look for an application called Notepad. Notepad is a default installation application within the Windows XP family. Highlight this application and click **OK**.

Now go back to your desktop and double-click on the same file you were just viewing. Notepad will launch; however, you will get an error message indicating that there was an error when Notepad attempted to open the *test.pdf* file. You can click on any *.pdf* file on your computer. Your computer dutifully launches Notepad and attempts to open it.

First, let's change the setting back, and then we'll explore what the operating system was doing. Highlight the same file on your desktop, right-click, and select **Properties**. Now click on the **Change** button and locate the Adobe Reader application within the file listing. Select **Adobe Reader** from the list and click **OK**, and then close the dialog box.

As you noticed, it was easy to change the way your Windows XP computer attempted to open a *.pdf* file. This is because your computer keeps a chart with a list of the file extensions and the application it should use to open them. This information is kept in a special location within Windows XP, called the Registry.

NOTE

In the early days of Windows and DOS, all configuration information was stored within configuration files. As operating system demands increased, Microsoft created a new repository for this information, called the Registry. As Windows has continued to evolve, the importance of the Registry has continued to expand. The Registry can contain information such as file associations, the Control Panel, system settings, policies, installed hardware/software, and other components.

This listing is kept in a file called *ntuser.dat*. Inside this file are various keys or information listings. You can find the specific key for file listings within *\Software\Microsoft\Windows\CurrentVersion\Explorer\FileExts*. Every file extension located on your computer will probably have an entry in this special chart. In our earlier example, you changed the way the computer opens all files with the *.pdf* extension. You used a dialog box to make this change. The operating system actually makes the change to the Registry.

WARNING

The Windows Registry is a special repository of information. A change within this repository can dramatically change the entire system. Only experienced computer users with advanced system knowledge should make a change directly in the Registry. Even when such users make changes it is highly recommended that they always make a full backup of the Windows Registry beforehand. Entering a single character in the wrong place can cause the entire operating system to stop functioning.

Why is this important? For a long time, people have been looking for ways to hide information. The prevalence to hide potentially sensitive information increases with the importance of the information. A simple way to accomplish this is by changing the file extension. Another way is to use encryption, a topic we will discuss later in this chapter.

The Apple Platform

Although Microsoft is by far the most dominant force in the computer office space, Apple has finally begun to make some serious progress. In the early years of computing, Apple created the point-and-click environment. This and other Apple innovations quickly found their way into Microsoft software. As these changes were occurring, IBM gained ground in the office space market. However, after a series of good strategic moves, including moving onto Intel-based platforms and reliance on Free BSD as the core of its operating system in 2007, Apple began to finally make significant gains in market share.

For years, Apple was regarded as *the* graphics platform, which meant that if you wanted to create high-end computer graphics you used an Apple computer. However, with the release of the Tiger and then Leopard operating systems, many corporate executives began at ask their support teams to give Apple a try, hence their relevance to the discussion of file anatomies in e-discovery.

The core Apple operating system is nothing like the core of Windows, although both operating systems use file associations to help determine file type. Apple uses a series of rules the first three of which follow:

- Apple allows the user to identify which application to use when opening a file. Again, it is assumed that the user is going to know what application he or she wants to use with a particular file or file type.

- When there is no user-defined way to open the program, the operating system looks at the "creator code." In older Apple OS versions, this was a 4-byte code that described the application. In newer versions of the Apple OS, it is best described as allowing the application that created a file to open the file.

- If all else fails, the file extension is used. In early Apple operating systems, the file extension was not necessary. However, as various operating systems have begun to work together more closely, the file extension has become increasingly necessary. File extensions have become an even greater necessity as many people are using multiple computers and sometimes even running Apple and Windows operating systems on the same computer.

Hashing

Hashing has evolved into a widely used function with numerous applications in the computer industry, including databases, passwords, encryptions, and many others. In the digital forensic and e-discovery field, hashing is most commonly used as a means for file identification. *Hashing* is the application of a mathematical formula to uniquely identify the contents of a specific file. It is possible to create a forensic hash of a file, of a series of files, or of an entire hard drive. A hash value is often referred to as a file's *DNA* or *digital fingerprint*.

We will focus primarily on two different hash types: MD5 and SHA1. *MD5* is an acronym for Message Digest Algorithm 5. As the name suggests, this algorithm is in its fifth reincarnation.

MD5 was developed by Ron Rivest, who is a professor at the Massachusetts Institute of Technology. This hash algorithm produces a unique 128-bit value of data. This value is displayed as 32 hexadecimal characters. You will notice, as with all information presented in hex, that the numbers 0–9 and the letters a–f are used. An example of an MD5 hash is 1CFC968CAAB8084683B688BFEA357F91.

The algorithm is called *SHA1*. This stands for Secure Hash Algorithm, and it was developed by the National Security Agency. This hash algorithm produces a unique 160-bit value, and it is displayed as 40 hexadecimal characters. Many people believe SHA1 will replace MD5 at some point. As with anything else, there is the slight possibility of two files producing the same hash. Further discussion of hash collisions is beyond the scope of this book.

In the forensic and e-discovery context, a hash value has many purposes. For one, it is used to validate that a file has not been changed. A variety of forensic and e-discovery applications have built-in hash verification. The hash value is also used to eliminate duplicate files. On your computer, you may be surprise to find how many duplicate files exist. These files can even reside in the same folder as long as the filename is different. The hash value has nothing to do with the actual filename, but it has everything to do with the actual contents of the file. As we mentioned earlier in this chapter, much of a file's information resides outside the actual file. A file can also be changed without the user making any intentional changes. Because of unique identification and removal of duplicate files, this function is important to our profession.

Compression

If you have been using the Internet for longer than a month, you have undoubtedly come across files to download that use the ZIP compression method. Or perhaps a computer you were using was running out of free (available) disk space and you chose to compress the files that were present on the computer to increase your usable space. Such techniques alter files and their integrity, although not always in ways that can't be reversed. Here is how compression works.

Much of the data within a computer file is redundant, meaning that the sequence of individual bits and bytes appears many times within the same file. Although the overall placement of those bits and bytes is important, their repetition is wasted space when a file is not being actively used. Compression programs work to identify strings of these repetitive data sequences and replace all but one of them with a simple, small "pointer" to the only remaining instance of that string.

In many languages on Earth, certain letters and words often appear together in the same pattern consistently. Text files, which, as you know, are simply human-readable words, compress well because of this. However, they tend not to be the largest files in the first place, so although the efficiency of the compression algorithm is relatively high (a reduction of 50 percent or more is typical for a good-size text file), the practical reasons for saving a few kilobytes, in these days of massive half-terabyte drives, are few. Most source code files from programming languages are also redundant because they use a relatively small collection of commands, which frequently go together in a set pattern. Of those types of files that don't benefit much from compression, graphics or MP3 files top the list because the unique images and sounds these files contain don't repeat a lot of the same data sequences.

Encryption

Encryption is the idea that data itself can be converted into a form, known as *ciphertext*, which cannot be interpreted without specialized knowledge of the way that data was transformed. That interpretation process, which usually requires some key piece of information, is called *decryption*, which means reversing the encryption process and converting the data back to its original form.

Encryption has been around since the time ideas were first exchanged, and it is an ultimate provider of privacy and protector of sensitive information. In wartime, a cipher can be employed by one side to keep the other from getting a usable understanding of the contents of transmissions. Simple ciphers include the substitution of letters for numbers, the rotation of letters in the alphabet, and the mangling of voice signals by inverting sideband frequencies. Today, most ciphers use hardened and sophisticated computer algorithms that digitize data bits into seemingly random signals.

To recover the contents of an encrypted signal, the correct decryption key is required unless you are attempting to use brute force to decrypt an object. The key is an algorithm that reverses the work of the encryption algorithm. A simple rule of thumb is that the more complex the encryption algorithm, the more difficult it becomes to listen in on the communication without knowing the key.

Windows includes the following mechanisms to encrypt single files or entire volumes, which render them difficult to use in discovery without the associated decryption file or key:

- **The Encrypting File System, or EFS** EFS allows files to be transparently encrypted on NTFS file systems to protect confidential data from attackers with physical access to the computer. EFS uses a symmetric encryption algorithm to encrypt files. The key to decrypt the files is ultimately based on the encrypting user's account password, meaning strong passwords secure the encrypted file more than weaker, shorter passwords.

- **BitLocker** New to Windows Vista and Windows Server 2008, BitLocker is a full disk encryption feature designed to encrypt entire volumes. By default, it uses the AES encryption algorithm along with a strong 128-bit key, combined with the *Elephant* diffuser for additional disk–encryption-specific security not provided by AES. BitLocker is difficult to break and sometimes even relies on a further encrypted trusted platform module, a hardware component in many business systems designed specifically to securely store decryption keys.

File Integrity

Before you can fully appreciate a file's anatomy, you must ensure that the file is protected. This means you must ensure the integrity of every file under your care.

File integrity ensures that your data remains in an unblemished state. File integrity must be the highest priority throughout the discovery process. If you minimize or ignore the role of file integrity, the anatomy of your file could change. Although change is not an automatic discriminator, it certainly calls into question a great number of things. If changes go undocumented and are the result of careless or reckless behavior, the anatomy of your files can change. Some changes may not be disastrous, whereas others may be unrecoverable.

For instance, when two companies are involved in a lawsuit they must exchange information. When a company wants to receive documents, it sends a Request for Production of Documents (RPD). This process allows the company to obtain during documents during discovery. As it relates to e-discovery, here are some of the initial questions in an RPD:

- What documents are we going to collect and search?

- Are these documents the right ones?

If an employee has a moderate to high computer aptitude, is it reasonable to suspect that some of the file extensions were changed? This could have happened inadvertently. For example, an employee may have installed an application, used it to edit a document, and in the process of saving the document changed the file extension. Or perhaps there is an attempt to hide a user's information from prying eyes. If these simple efforts were made to obscure the documents, does that change the requirement to produce "any and all documents" related to a certain matter? In addition, many computer applications such as Microsoft Word and Excel produce a large number of temporary files as part of their routine processes. Are these documents going to be discoverable also? If you are only searching for information based on file extension, you will never know if these documents are discoverable. Although some people may rely on file extensions to be correct, have you really exercised due diligence by just producing information based on file extensions? These seemingly innocent questions could be the Achilles' heel of your e-discovery production.

Summary

By understanding the anatomy of files, their attributes, some methods under which they are stored, and their e-discovery role, you are better prepared to address the various challenges presented during electronic discovery. The aspects of this process can be critical to correctly responding to legal inquiries. Your role as an e-discovery professional is to assist legal counsel in producing files. You accomplish this role by locating information through a process of searching, reviewing, and producing additional information. Understanding the various components of a file is at the heart of the electronic discovery process.

By ensuring that a file's integrity remains intact, you reduce the avenues for others to attack your work. Always keep in mind that your goal is to answer a request for information. By understanding the basic principles of file signatures and hashing, encryption, and compression, you are armed with the information necessary to begin working through these complex situations.

Solutions Fast Track

Structured versus Unstructured Data

☑ Digital files must be understood within the context of their environment.

☑ Workflow diagrams allow you to understand how information is utilized within an organization.

☑ A thorough, well–thought-out, reasoned, and comprehensive electronic information preservation plan protects your digital information from spoliation.

Components of a File

☑ Date/timestamps are the most fragile pieces of electronic evidence.

☑ In Windows, files are opened by programs based on their file extension.

☑ A file hash is similar to a digital fingerprint.

File Integrity

☑ Before you can fully appreciate a file's anatomy, you must ensure that it is protected.

☑ File integrity ensures that your data remains in an unblemished state.

☑ File integrity must be the highest priority throughout the discovery process.

Frequently Asked Questions

Q: Does the Windows file creation date indicate the first time the file was created?

A: No, the Windows file creation date indicates when a file was saved in a particular location. Frequently, a file's last modification date is earlier than its file creation date. This indicates that the file was created in another location and was then moved into its current location.

Q: Can you hide the contents of a file by changing its file header?

A: No. Changing a file header could corrupt a file's data. It could also cause a program to attempt to open a file when it may not have the ability to. This would result in an error message.

Q: Within Windows, is a file's modification date the most commonly changed date/timestamp?

A: Within Windows, Last Accessed Date/Time is the most frequently changed timestamp. A file's modification date is changed when a file is opened, edited, and saved. If you simply open a file and don't change anything without saving the file, only Last Accessed Date/Time would be updated.

Q: How many characters are in an MD5 128-bit hash?

A: There are 32 hexadecimal characters in an MD5 128-bit hash.

Chapter 8

Data Identification and Search Techniques

Solutions in this chapter:

- Search and Identification in Compliance with the Federal Rules

- Determining Where the Data Lives

- Search and Identification Techniques

- An Overview of Search and Identification Tools

☑ Summary

☑ Solutions Fast Track

☑ Frequently Asked Questions

Introduction

Data search and identification is one of the most important phases of the e-discovery process. To meet the duty to preserve potentially relevant data, you must be able to effectively search for and identify this data.

The duty to preserve is not a new duty; it existed long before the December 2006 amendments to the Federal Rules of Civil Procedure became effective, and it is well established in case law in virtually every jurisdiction. The duty requires you to preserve any potentially relevant information/ data when litigation or investigation is reasonably anticipated or presents itself. In light of the proliferation of data, demonstrating that you have made a good-faith effort to preserve potentially relevant data often requires the use of effective search and identification technology.

The first step in meeting the duty to preserve is determining where your data lives. This may sound easy, but with a distributed enterprise and information technology (IT) infrastructure, along with a mobile workforce, it becomes a daunting proposition. Reasonable efforts to locate the data are necessary, often requiring a variety of techniques to locate all potential sources of data.

Once you determine where your data lives, you must identify the potentially relevant data. To best determine what data may be potentially relevant, you must be able to search the data. The challenge here is to determine the best technique for identification purposes among the many different techniques and search strategies available.

Finally, in today's world of multinational organizations, it is important to be aware of the differing regulations on employee privacy and how electronic data is handled across the globe. Although this chapter won't go into great detail on this topic, be aware that there are thorny challenges to sending data across international borders, so you should closely examine this issue based on the jurisdictions involved.

DISCLAIMER

This chapter is provided for informational purposes only and should not be construed as representing legal advice. The reader should consult his or her own counsel regarding application of the concepts, ideas, and theories discussed in this chapter and should not rely upon any information contained herein for any purpose without seeking legal advice from a duly licensed attorney competent to practice law in the applicable jurisdiction.

Search and Identification in Compliance with the Federal Rules

As noted earlier, the duty to preserve provides the foundation for this chapter. Although you may be asking "isn't this the search and identification chapter?" and wondering why we are covering the duty to preserve here, the answer is simple: The search for and identification of potentially relevant data is inexorably linked with the duty to preserve. In short, you cannot effectively preserve potentially relevant data—without preserving the entire universe of data, which would be inordinately expensive—if you are not able to search for and identify the relevant data. So, let's start with the rules that serve as the underpinnings of the duty.

The Federal Rules of Civil Procedure

The Federal Rules of Civil Procedure (FRCP or Federal Rules, for short) were amended effective December 1, 2006. The amendments represent the most sweeping changes to the rules in the past 30 years, but they did not alter or change the duty to preserve. The *Zubulake* cases drove home the importance of preservation and set the stage for the amendments to the FRCP. Although the concept of electronic data was nothing new to the FRCP and the rules had recognized electronic data for more than 30 years, they did not offer any guidance to deal with the challenges that the enormous volume of electronically stored information (ESI) presents today. The main changes to the FRCP centered on new practices and procedures for dealing with electronic discovery, creating a newfound emphasis on ESI in recognition of the explosion of electronic data across the enterprise.

The December 2006 amendments were designed to provide clarity and guidance to litigating parties on how the identification, preservation, collection, and production of ESI should be handled. In the interest of brevity, we will summarize the amendments at a high level. It is easy to think of the FRCP amendments as falling into two basic categories: the "early attention" requirements and the "systemized process" requirements.

The amendments that can be classified as those necessitating "early attention" require both plaintiffs and defendants to address the issue of ESI early in the case, with the goal being to deal with the potentially challenging e-discovery issues as early as possible. The Pretrial Conference in Rule 16(b) and the Discovery Planning Conference in Rule 26(f) highlight the need for you to be prepared early, understand the nature and extent of your ESI, and understand what type of potentially relevant data may be available. The Pretrial Conference offers provisions for disclosure or discovery of ESI and provides an opportunity for the parties to disclose any agreements they may have reached to handle claims of privilege which may attach to potentially relevant material. The Discovery Planning Conference includes a mandate that the parties discuss issues relating to the preservation of discoverable information, as well as any issues relating to disclosure or discovery of ESI and the ultimate form of production. The amendments also introduced requirements regarding the form of production of ESI (Rules 33 and 34), evidencing a preference for forensically sound native file production or fully text-searchable image production with the metadata preserved.

TIP

It pays to be able to search for and identify potentially relevant data early in the case. With the proper technology, you will be better prepared for the Pretrial Conference and Discovery Planning Conference by having the ability to complete an early case assessment. Such an assessment may help you to determine whether there is a viable cause of action, what type of evidence exists, and whether it is in your best interest to settle early or fight on. Tools such as Aungate Legal Hold and Aungate Investigator Early Case Assessment, Kroll Ontrack Firstview, FTI Ringtail, and Guidance Software EnCase eDiscovery can be helpful in giving you an early view into the available data and allowing you to make an early case assessment so that you can enter the Pretrial Conference prepared.

The FRCP amendments that can be classified as necessitating a "systemized process" essentially require that the organization have processes and procedures in place for handling ESI. Rule 26(b) offers both the "clawback" provision, for inadvertent production/disclosure of privileged data, and the "reasonably accessible data" provision, offering a modicum of protection from the need to access and search what might otherwise be inaccessible data sources. The "safe harbor" provision in Rule 37(f) offers some protection for inadvertently deleted data when the deletion is due to the "routine, good-faith operation of an electronic information system." These amendments can be called the "systemized process" amendments because they essentially require that an organization adopt a systemized, repeatable, and defensible process for handling, searching for, and identifying ESI to benefit from the rules' protections.

The FRCP amendments may have dramatically changed the requirements for managing and preserving ESI for litigation, and The Judicial Conference Commentary on the Amendments further reinforces this idea by noting that "[t]he proposed amendments to Rule 16, Rule 26(a) and (f) and Form 35 present a framework for the parties and the court to give early attention to issues relating to electronic discovery, including the frequently recurring problems of the preservation of the evidence....," but the duty to preserve remains, surprisingly, unchanged. Nevertheless, you still must approach the duty in a systemized, repeatable, and defensible manner to show a good-faith effort and effectively meet the early attention requirements.

The Duty to Preserve

As noted previously, the duty to preserve potentially relevant data requires that you make a good-faith and reasonable effort to preserve potentially relevant data when faced with litigation or when you reasonably anticipate litigation.

NOTE

Although the duty to preserve encompassed by the FRCP extends only to potentially relevant information in the context of litigation, the duty to preserve in the face of an investigation is similar, although it may pose notable differences. Whether it is an internal investigation, government or agency investigation, or otherwise, you should clarify what types of data you need to preserve early on, as this could dramatically alter your search and identification requirements and present additional challenges. It is also important to verify that your preservation efforts meet statutory requirements, local laws, agency rules, and any other requirements that may govern the investigation.

For litigation purposes, the duty to preserve extends to only potentially relevant information; in other words, you must preserve evidence that is relevant and material to the cause of action or claims at issue. As has been stated by the courts, "[t]he duty to preserve evidence, once it attaches, does not extend beyond evidence that is relevant and material to the claims at issue in the litigation."[1]

The duty extends *only* to potentially relevant information—nothing more, nothing less. As the *Zubulake* court noted: "[c]learly [there is no duty to] preserve every shred of paper, every e-mail or electronic document, and every backup tape...Such a rule would cripple large corporations."[2]

NOTE

The duty to preserve extends only to potentially relevant data. Once you are aware of pending litigation, reasonably anticipated litigation, or an investigation, the duty to preserve begins and counsel must make an initial determination as to the potential custodians and potential scope of information subject to the preservation obligation, and then must search for, identify, and preserve that data.

Enterprise search technology does not expand the duty to preserve potentially relevant ESI. The deployment of search technology, such as Autonomy's IDOL platform, Guidance Software's EnCase eDiscovery, or other enterprise search offerings from Kazeon, StoredIQ, or ZyLAB, does not alter this duty. The deployment of technology does not mean you must search *every* source and *every* potential custodian for each case. Rather, these technologies facilitate the ready identification of important data sources, help delineate key from peripheral custodians, and enhance your ability to exclude pools of data and employees altogether.

A key concept to keep in mind is that the legal team must determine the potential custodians and data based on the cause of action and the facts available to them; ultimately, this is a risk management analysis that is fact-specific and we will not cover it in this chapter. However, the *Zubulake* court discussed one defensible process:

> "To the extent that it may not be feasible for counsel to speak with every key player, given the size of a company or the scope of the lawsuit, counsel must be more creative. **It may be possible to run a system-wide keyword search; counsel could then preserve a copy of each 'hit.'** Although this sounds burdensome, it need not be. Counsel does not necessarily have to review these documents, but only see that they are retained. For example, counsel could create a broad list of search terms, run a search for a limited time frame, and then segregate responsive documents..."[3]

It might be advisable to solicit a list of search terms from the opposing party for this purpose so that it cannot later complain about which terms were used.

TIP

You may find it useful to complete a test run of potential keywords prior to the Pretrial Conference and Discovery Planning Conference. By testing keywords early in the case and performing the early case assessment, you can be prepared for the conferences, know what data is available, and understand what keywords will produce what documents. This can also assist you by helping to prevent the introduction of an overly burdensome keyword list that could increase your costs and risks and could require an extensive review process. Additionally, you will benefit from a more targeted review and production at the back end of the case.

The *Zubulake* court went on to say the following regarding the duty and the requirement that you search for and identify potentially relevant information:

"In short, it is not sufficient to notify all employees of a litigation hold and expect that the party will then retain and produce all relevant information. Counsel must take affirmative steps to monitor compliance so that all sources of discoverable information are identified and searched. This is not to say that counsel will necessarily succeed in locating all such sources, or that the later discovery of new sources is evidence of a lack of effort. But counsel and client must take some reasonable steps to see that sources of relevant information are located."[4] Note that the *Zubulake* court views the duty to preserve as encompassing several elements, including reasonable steps to see that sources of information are located, and affirmative steps to ensure that all sources of discoverable information are searched. Simply put, this requires that you have a reasonable process to search for and identify potentially relevant data.

The Real World: What Is Reasonable?

The preservation obligation is frequently a topic that arises in the course of litigation. The courts have been quick to act when a party doesn't meet its preservation obligation. A key point to understand regarding the duty is that reasonable steps must be taken to preserve potentially relevant information. However, this does not mean you have to find every shred of evidence and search everywhere; you merely need to make a reasonable effort to search for and identify potentially relevant data based on a reasonable interpretation of the issues, timelines, and custodians in the case.

However, what is a reasonable effort is a topic of much discussion in the courts. A reasonable effort could consist of a good-faith effort to search for and identify potentially relevant data and then preserving that data in a forensically sound manner. The method of preservation can vary, but the FRCP and case law require that the data be preserved in a forensically sound manner with the metadata preserved.

NOTE

Metadata is data about the data or the document. There are two types of metadata: file metadata and system metadata. File metadata typically contains information about the attributes of the document, such as the author, creation date, last modified date, last accessed date, and so on. System metadata contains information that the operating or computer system uses to access the data, such as file type, file path, location, and so forth. As a general rule, metadata is not typically viewed from within the document.

The bar of what is reasonable is constantly evolving, and this chapter will examine techniques and technologies that are available to help ensure that you can effectively search for and identify potentially relevant data.

Determining Where the Data Lives

Searching for potentially relevant data can be daunting. Across the enterprise, the volume of data is exploding. Often, multiple copies of documents are stored in multiple locations, including, for example, copies of e-mails stored on an Exchange server, on BlackBerry devices, and in custodian PSTs on laptop and desktops. With the advent of unified messaging services, which enable voice messages to be delivered via e-mail, custodians may also have audio files embedded in e-mails. And these are but a few examples of the proliferation of data faced increasingly in the litigation context. The challenges include widespread distribution, volume, variety of electronic data, legacy systems, backup tapes, and paper, among other things.

NOTE

Although this chapter focuses on ESI, it is important that you not forget that potentially relevant information may be found in hard-copy paper documents. The amendments to the FRCP may have focused on ESI, but the duty to preserve extends to paper documents. Unfortunately, searching for and identifying potentially relevant paper documents can require substantially different techniques, which can include manual searching of mountains of paper, accessing documents in archives or storage facilities, or searching the file cabinets and desks of the potential custodians. Interviewing potential custodians is a key.

Many organizations today manage to treat paper documents, once reasonably sorted, in a similar fashion to electronic documents. They simply scan, code, and OCR paper documents so that they may be reviewed in the same manner as electronic documents. Although the scan, code, and OCR process can be costly, an electronic review of documents makes it easier to track the search and identification uniformly.

Distribution of Data: Building a Data Map

One of the great challenges of searching for ESI comes from the fact that we live in a world of multinational corporations, with a global workforce, connected 24 hours a day. In addition to the traditional locations in which to store electronic data—personal computers, file servers, and e-mail servers—data is increasingly stored in archives, content management systems, and multitiered data storage systems. Potentially relevant data can be anywhere and everywhere, as employees increasingly work around the clock, in their homes, on airplanes, and in hotel rooms, just to name a few places, all over the globe. These activities implicate laptops, workstations, file shares, BlackBerry devices, thumb drives, portable hard drives, iPods, smart phones, and more. An additional challenge arises when employees also work on their home computers, sending documents to a personal e-mail account or transferring them via thumb drive so that they may work on them from their homes. The list of potential ESI sources can be dizzying, but it is not impossible to manage if approached methodically.

Tools & Traps...

Employees' Home Computers

The duty to preserve doesn't end with the machines and data sources your organization owns or controls. You should search for and identify potentially relevant ESI wherever it may reside, even if it is on an employee's home computer. It is not uncommon for employees to take work home with them and then bring the completed work product back to the office. It is important to remember that this at-home work may be completed on the employee's own computer, not on an enterprise-owned system. Even though the completed document is returned to the company-owned machine, do not forget that the copy on the home computer is potentially relevant data that must be preserved. This means it is imperative that you interview the custodian to determine whether he or she uses a home computer to complete work projects or documents when you are determining potential sources to search for ESI. Although this can add significant time, cost, and effort to the search and identification process, it is critically important that you ascertain any data source a custodian may have used that could contain potentially relevant data. In many cases, the documents stored on home computers may be duplicative, as files are typically returned to workplace servers after an employee works on the file at home. Provided you feel reasonably confident following interviews that data stored on home computers is likely duplicative, the notion of excluding such computers from collection, search, and possibly even preservation can become a topic for negotiation with the opposing party to reduce the burden associated with potentially duplicative data.

Building a data map can be a daunting task, but it is the most effective means to search for and identify potentially relevant data in a methodical and sound manner. There are several approaches to building a data map, from completely manual processes that require extensive time and research to more automated solutions that utilize software and connectors to data sources.

The traditional method is an extremely time-consuming manual process. The company's IT data stewards must be interviewed to determine the nature and extent of the enterprise systems; the HR department must be interviewed to assess whether employee records are up-to-date, including their business divisions and assigned computers; and employee/custodian interviews are required to determine what computers the employees actually use and where they store their data. This is a time-consuming process that can also be quite challenging. However, absent a more automated way to build the data map, this effort may be necessary to gain an accurate picture of the different sources of and locations for enterprise data.

Another approach is more automated, but it still requires some degree of manual effort as there is unfortunately no fully automated data mapping software available that can accurately and efficiently identify all potential data sources across today's varied enterprise environments. A semiautomated solution can rely on spider technologies or connector technology that enables you to scan across the enterprise and access and examine most, if not all, data sources. Although the use of this technology does not supplant the need to interview individuals within your organization to determine where data may be stored, a more automated technology will eliminate some of the manual effort.

The Challenges of Building a Data Map

Data mapping is not an easy task, even though you may think it would be simple to locate your data across the enterprise. The structure of today's enterprise can be challenging. Many companies grow by acquisition, so they may have disparate IT departments and systems that utilize different operating systems or enterprise content management (ECM)/archive systems, or even separate legal departments. Others have high employee turnover in the IT department, so few employees have historical knowledge of the evolution of systems, backup processes, databases, and legacy systems. In the absence of an effective inventory, the challenge of identifying all potential data sources in an enterprise can be daunting. Additionally, most global organizations also face the challenge of a distributed workforce that spans continents and time zones. Additional challenges can arise if your organization's IT infrastructure and networks are not integrated, as you will have to involve more people in the process to understand the different organizational data systems. Additionally, if the IT infrastructure and network are not integrated, the process of building the data map will be significantly more manual as the automated solutions will be unable to reach, examine, and analyze data sources that are not part of the network.

Managing individual custodian data sources can be just as challenging as managing enterprise-wide data sources. As already discussed, employees may have a workstation or desktop PC in the office, a laptop for travel, a personal computer for work at home, thumb drives, portable hard drives, BlackBerry devices, and other data sources that include, but are not limited to, iPods, digital cameras, and cell phones. All of these devices can store potentially relevant data, so you must take them into account when you build your data map.

Notes from the Underground...

Searching for and Identifying Data on Laptops, Desktops, and PDAs

Today's workforce is more mobile than ever, relying on laptops, Blackberry devices, thumb drives, and other technologies to carry data with them wherever they go. Although this mobility is essential in the business world, the more mobile the workforce,

Continued

the more challenging it is to search and identify potentially relevant data. One of the more common methods for searching and identifying these potentially relevant data sources can also carry the most risk: custodian self-collection.

The pitfalls of custodian self-collection are many, and courts frequently order sanctions for organizations that choose self-collection and fail to execute it in a defensible manner. Because sanctions for lost data can include an adverse inference against the company—an assumption that the evidence would have favored the opposing party—the outcome of a case can turn on whether self-collection was conducted effectively. Custodians are generally not e-discovery experts and may not be able to accurately judge relevance. Additionally, the resultant search may exclude inculpatory evidence, either inadvertently or intentionally. If inculpatory evidence is missed and those documents are produced by the opposing party, the risk of sanctions and adverse inference instructions rises substantially.

It is also dangerous to assume that employees know the limitations of electronic search tools. By way of example, many users don't realize that the search functionality in Outlook does not search the contents of attachments, and this could cause many potentially relevant documents to be overlooked in a custodian-run search.

Although custodian self-collection can be effective in some cases, it is more prudent to rely on this method only when absolutely necessary, preferably only for second-tier custodians and smaller matters. In any case, self-collection should be undertaken methodically and with written instructions that provide the technical guidance needed to shore up the collection and encourage consistency. It is also recommended that counsel take steps to verify the accuracy and completeness of any custodian self-collection, to ensure that all potentially relevant data has been preserved and collected.

Finally, the multitude of file types, including not only Microsoft Office documents, e-mails, electronic faxes, and TIFF and PDF files, but also voice, video, instant messages, database records, and the like, all present different challenges. Add in the disparate systems on which these different file types are stored, from databases, to content management systems, to file servers, and archives, and the challenges are many. Nevertheless, a careful, thoughtful, and well-planned approach can help ensure that your data map is complete and that you are well prepared for the search and identification phase.

Search and Identification Techniques

Search and identification are an integral part of the duty to preserve. Early detection of all forms of ESI has become critical as the presence of audio, image, video, and foreign language files in discovery has grown markedly. The information explosion, multinational workforces, and the proliferation of data storage devices have made the search and identification process more challenging than ever. Although traditional methods of search and identification, such as hard-drive imaging, can still be effective in this process, traditional methods can be time-consuming, manual, and expensive. Newer, more advanced search and identification techniques are available which can give lawyers and investigators a more comprehensive methodology to identify files that are often buried in data sources and collections. Although it is not required that you use advanced technology in the search and identification phase, this technology can reduce the amount of manual effort, time, and expense involved in searching for and identifying potentially relevant ESI.

There are a wide variety of methods to search for and identify potentially relevant data, and this section will examine several different techniques and products, while discussing some of their benefits and shortcomings.

One of the first challenges in the search and identification phase is being able to access and analyze ESI across the enterprise. The FRCP amendments clearly defined ESI as "including writings, drawings, graphs, charts, photographs, sound recordings, images phonorecords, and other data or data compilations stored in any medium from which information can be obtained—translated, if necessary, by the respondent through detection devices into reasonably usable form."[5] Although it is not essential that you search all of these data sources, the rules define ESI broadly, including audio and video sources, and preservation of potentially relevant ESI is required under the rules.

Though preservation of all potentially relevant ESI, including audio and video, is required under the rules, the *Zubulake* court noted "[a]lthough this sounds burdensome, it need not be. Counsel does not have to review these documents, only see that they are retained." Whereas you can negotiate the scope of discovery with opposing counsel in the Pretrial Conference and the Discovery Planning Conference to limit the scope of the discovery and exclude data types such as voice and video, it is important that this data be preserved should your processes and procedures ever be challenged. One argument that can be made is that it is expensive and time-consuming to search audio and video data, and whether or not these data sources are searched can be negotiated among the parties and possibly be subject to cost-sharing. However, technology is rapidly evolving, and the ability to automate the search and identification process for audio and video is rapidly advancing.

NOTE

There are several misconceptions regarding what the FRCP requires you to search and identify for ESI preservation. The rules make it clear that all data sources are covered in the definition of ESI. Two common misconceptions in the e-discovery process are that you only need to preserve e-mail, and that audio and video files do not need to be preserved or searched. Although you can negotiate what needs to be searched and produced with your opponent, nothing in the FRCP or case law suggests that either of these misconceptions is correct.

Once you are able to search all data types across the enterprise, the next challenge is to determine what technique will be used to search and identify the different data sources and meet the preservation obligation. We can divide the search and identification techniques into the categories of basic and advanced. Basic search and identification techniques include custodian self-collection, hard-drive imaging and subsequent searches, keyword and Boolean searches, metadata searches, and e-mail conversation threading. Advanced search and identification techniques include advanced analytic technology such as clustering and categorization, and concept and contextual search (see Figure 8.1).

The basic search technologies have been used for many years and tend to be viewed as the standard bearer for search and identification techniques. However, recent research challenges the notion that these technologies are effective at identifying potentially relevant data. The advanced techniques have been the topic of only limited discussion in court cases to date, but they are beginning to be recognized as effective methods to cull down data to the potentially relevant data in a more effective and efficient manner.

Figure 8.1 Advanced Data Search and Identification Techniques

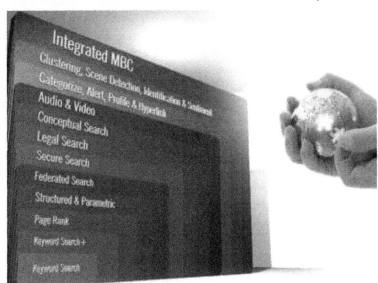

Before diving into the different search technologies available today, you should be aware that it is of utmost importance that you are able to search your data effectively and accurately. As the court in *Peskoff v. Farber*, noted:

> "The producing party has the obligation to search available electronic systems for the information demanded...The new Federal Rule of Civil Procedure pertaining to electronically stored information makes this explicit."[6]

Despite arguments that it may take time and effort to search for potentially relevant data, the court went on to say that "accessible data must be produced at the cost of the producing party..." and that "[i]t cannot be argued that a party should ever be relieved of its obligation to produce accessible data merely because it may take time and effort to find what is necessary."[7] Thus, you should determine the range of potential custodians, effect a litigation hold, interview the custodians to determine where they may have potentially relevant ESI, and then make a good-faith effort to search for and identify potentially relevant ESI for preservation and collection purposes.

Although the FRCP and U.S. case law govern the duty to preserve data and how that data must be handled, if you are part of a multinational organization you must be cognizant of the rules and regulations in other countries. Keep in mind that the United Kingdom, European Union, and many other jurisdictions have strict privacy regulations that can limit how and when you can search for data on employee computers. Be sure to check with regional counsel prior to searching for, identifying, and collecting ESI from other countries.

This does not mean, however, that you must search the entire enterprise every time you receive a request for potentially relevant data. The courts typically require only that search and identification efforts be reasonable. "Preservation efforts can become unduly burdensome and unreasonably costly unless those efforts are targeted to those documents reasonably likely to be relevant or lead to the discovery of relevant evidence related to the issues in this matter."[8]

A word of caution on keyword searching: Although the courts suggest that limiting a search to keywords, dates, and custodians is acceptable, this does not supersede the duty to identify and preserve potentially relevant ESI. Be aware that as you approach the search and identification phase of your e-discovery process, different techniques and methods can produce wildly different results. Additionally, many traditional keyword search engines are unable to search data sources such as voice and video. As such, the range of material subject to the preservation obligation may often be broader than the results of keyword searching. All data that is likely to contain relevant material should be preserved, even if it is not searched in the first instance, to ensure that it remains available in the event the court requires broader keyword searching or the review of non-standard file types.

Legacy Search and Identification Techniques

Legacy search and identification techniques include custodian self-collection, hard-drive imaging, and subsequent searching, keyword, and Boolean searches, metadata searches, and conversation threading. These techniques do not typically rely on advanced technology or mathematical algorithms. They are well accepted and understood by most courts, and they have been the standard bearers for search and identification for many years. That being said, recent court cases and studies have examined the limitations of keyword searching, and a recent NIST-TREC study showed that keyword searching can miss up to 78 percent of potentially relevant data. Accordingly, search terms are often a topic of negotiation and agreement among the parties, court, and/or regulator involved.

Custodian Self-Collection

Custodian self-collection may seem like an obvious method to include in this chapter, but to collect data, custodians must first search for and identify potentially relevant data. Although custodian self-collection may not be recommended in complicated legal matters or for key custodians, there may be circumstances where custodian self-collection is an efficient and acceptable method of complying with a discovery request.

Custodian self-collection is fairly straightforward. After receiving a legal hold notice that alerts the custodian of the duty to preserve potentially relevant ESI, the custodian can be guided to search for, identify, and collect the potentially relevant data the custodian has in his or her possession. At first blush, this seems like a logical way to handle the search and identification process as individual custodians should be in the best position to locate their potentially relevant ESI. But this process is fraught with risk.

For one thing, custodians may not be in the best position to judge relevance, as they generally lack the legal or technical expertise to fully comply with discovery obligations. Even with proper instruction and training, employee self-collection can be error-prone and subjective, so the output may vary widely among custodians. Some employees may simply not understand how to properly search for data, or they may not understand the limitations of search technology used for various electronic files, such as e-mail attachments.

Another reason custodian self-collection is inherently risky is because it is rarely conducted in the systemized, repeatable, and defensible manner required by the FRCP. First, self-collection is not systemized, as each custodian will likely use different criteria and search techniques in the same case. Second, it is not repeatable, as individual custodians must use their best judgment for preservation, leading to inconsistent results. Third, it is difficult to establish that self-collection is defensible and to have confidence in the accuracy and thoroughness of the process. Counsel cannot definitively rule out employee bad acts, such as omitting documents that may reflect badly on the employee or that may place the employee at risk of reprimand.

Prior to the 2006 amendments to the FRCP, courts were beginning to address the concept of custodian self-collection and challenge the adequacy of such an approach. For example, the *Zubulake* court stated that "it is not sufficient to notify all employees of a legal hold and expect that the party will then retain and produce all relevant information. Counsel must take affirmative steps to monitor compliance so that all sources of discoverable information are identified and searched."[9] The *Zubulake* court saw the potential for errors and spoliation when custodians were relied on to search for, identify, and preserve potentially relevant data.

Once the FRCP amendments became effective, the courts were quick to judge custodian self-collection. The court in *Samsung v. Rambus* held that "[i]t is not sufficient … for a company merely to tell employees to 'save relevant documents.' "The court further remarked that "this sort of token effort will hardly ever suffice" and criticized "the lack of specificity in defining what documents would be relevant to litigation."[10] In yet another case, *Cache La Poudre Feeds, LLC v. Land O'Lakes, Inc.*, 244 F.R.D. 614 (D.Colo. 2007), the court faulted the defendant for directing employees to produce relevant information while relying on those same employees to exercise their discretion to determine what ESI was relevant. What you realize from these cases is that the courts have not looked kindly on organizations that rely on individual custodians to search for and identify potentially relevant ESI. Although these cases do not discuss what technology or methods should be used, it is clear that custodian self-collection is fraught with risk.

The court in *Wachtel v. Health Net* further examined the challenges of custodian self-collection, highlighting not only the importance of issuing a proper legal hold, but also the importance of monitoring employee compliance to preservation orders. "Health Net relied on the specified business people within the company to search and turn over whatever documents they thought were responsive, without verifying that the searches were sufficient." The court deemed the process "utterly inadequate," as it was "one of looking for selected specific documents by a specific person rather than all responsive documents from all Health Net employees who had such documents." This case also highlighted the inherent risk of custodian self-collection in that "employee-conducted searches managed to exclude inculpatory documents that were highly germane to Plaintiffs' requests."[11]

WARNING

In a case highlighting the potential consequences of self-collection, a principal witness in the lawsuit received a legal hold notice, agreed to comply with the notice, and subsequently intentionally deleted relevant evidence. Despite issuing a proper hold notification and following up with the custodian, the company was held to have facilitated the misconduct even though it was the custodian that acted in bad faith. An adverse inference instruction was issued against the company because it "simply told [the custodian] to preserve all evidence and trusted him to comply," rather than taking reasonable steps to prevent spoliation.[12]

WARNING

E-mail attachments can be particularly challenging when relying on custodian self-collection. Many e-mail applications, including Microsoft Outlook, do not enable keyword searching of attachments. Therefore, any custodian e-mail search that relies solely on automated search features will, by its nature, overlook attachments. In many cases, attachments could hold potentially relevant ESI subject to the preservation duty. Be aware of this limitation as you plan your search and identification strategy.

For laptops and desktops, the most traditional method is to take a bit-by-bit image (or copy) of the hard drive and then do a subsequent search and identification on the image to find potentially relevant ESI. This method typically relies on forensic software such as Guidance Software's EnCase Forensic and AccessData's Forensic ToolKit (FTK); other methods such as Symantec Ghost and Robocopy exist for imaging, but they are not the predominant methods. Hard-drive imaging is one of the methods used to gather data so that you can search for and identify potentially relevant ESI because this technology was one of the few options available at the dawn of the e-discovery age; there were not many options.

We will not address hard-drive images in detail in this chapter. What is important to note, however, is that once the drive is imaged, the data must be searched to identify the potentially relevant ESI via the other techniques and methods discussed in this chapter.

As a general rule, hard-drive imaging is an extremely inefficient method to search for and identify potentially relevant ESI as it frequently results in a gross over-collection and over-preservation of data that is not relevant. Hard-drive imaging may often be needed for preservation purposes, and may be needed for searching, particularly when dealing with key custodians, or in the case of white-collar crime or government investigations, where the consequences of and potential for spoliation can be much greater. In other circumstances, full hard-drive imaging is not required as a matter of course. See *Diepenhorst v. City Of Battle Creek*, 2006 WL 1851243 (W.D.Mich. June 30, 2006).

TIP

Although hard-drive imaging is not always necessary or advisable, it is essential when you may need to search for deleted files, ensure preservation of all of a custodian's data, or conduct a high-risk investigation. A forensic, bit-by-bit image will enable you to search for deleted documents that may remain on the hard drive. The employee's act of deleting a document simply breaks the link between the document and the user (the path and filename of the document are removed from the computer's index and moved). It does not actually overwrite the hard-drive space unless the employee takes additional steps to wipe the disk or the computer overwrites the space when new files are created. A forensic recovery consultant is vitally important if reconstruction of deleted files or verification of the use of wiping programs becomes necessary.

Keyword and Boolean Searches

Keyword and Boolean search methods are among the most widely used and vetted methodologies available. They should be considered as part of any comprehensive search and identification undertaking when searching for potentially relevant ESI. However, as recent cases and studies have shown, there are pitfalls to using this technique as it often fails to uncover a large portion of potentially relevant data.

Keyword searches have been defined as a method of searching for documents which possess keywords specified by a user, a search using a full text search filter whereby a search term list is applied to a full text index to find responsive files, and a search for documents containing one or more words that are specified by a user.[13]

A keyword search is exactly that. If you have a keyword such as *e-discovery*, the search would be for that term and only that term. If it is a straight keyword search, you would only pick up *e-discovery* and not *electronic discovery*, *eDiscovery*, or *E Discovery*. There are limitations with basic keyword searches, as they can fail to uncover variants of a word. Furthermore, if there is a typo or a misspelled word such as *edisocvery*, or an abbreviation such as *eDisco*, basic keyword search technology will miss these search terms.

You can eliminate some of the limitations of keyword searches through the use of wildcards that will allow you to search for different forms of a particular word. The typical wildcard symbol is "*" or "!" and this will enable you to search for multiple variations of a word. For example, let's assume you were dealing with a sexual harassment case and you had to search for documents and e-mails that were related to that topic to determine whether others in the organization had knowledge of the potential harassment. You could search for words such as *sex, sexual, sexuality, sexist,* and *sexism* with the search term *sex** as that wildcard search would allow you to search for any word containing *sex*.

Although wildcard searches allow you to search for variations on a word, they do have limits. If a word is misspelled or there is an abbreviation, the wildcard search may miss the word. In the preceding example, if someone used *sxy* or *sxist*, due to either a typo or an abbreviation, the wildcard phrase *sex** would miss those spellings. The search could be altered to take into account misspellings, abbreviations, and typos, but after a certain point, the search term will become so overly broad that it would result in a gross over-collection and not be helpful in determining whether the search was, in fact, accurate.

Using a keyword search can be risky, and the recent federal case *Victor Stanley, Inc. v. Creative Pipe, Inc.* highlights how the use of keyword searches to identify documents, in this case privileged documents, can be risky. In this case, the defendants claimed inadvertent production of privileged documents because of a failure of the extensive keyword-based privilege cull of text-searchable ESI and a manual review of non-text documents and an added burden of too much data to review in the time allotted. The plaintiffs countered that the privilege review was faulty. In his opinion, U.S. Judge Magistrate Paul Grimm wrote that "all keyword searches are not created equal; and there is a growing body of literature that highlights the risks associated with conducting an unreliable or inadequate keyword search or relying exclusively on such searches for privilege review." He determined that the defendant waived privilege in large part due to "faulty privilege review of the text-searchable files and by failing to detect the presence of the 165 documents" in the production.[14] This highlights the challenges with keyword searching alone.

Boolean searches add an additional dimension to keyword searches, allowing you to search for multiple keywords together, or exclusive of each other, or within a certain distance from each other. The term *Boolean* refers to a system of logic developed by an early computer pioneer, George Boole. Boolean searching of text is based on the underlying logic functions of various true/false statements and uses standard operators to interlink search terms. The standard operators can include *and, or, not, within, near,* and more. This method of searching allows multiple keywords or search terms to be linked together to improve the relevancy of the documents identified by this methodology.

Using Boolean search techniques, the *and* operator between two words results in a search for documents containing both of the words. Therefore, a search term, using the earlier sexual harassment case, for *sex** and *harass** would turn up documents with *sexual harassment* in them while also turning up documents where the words *sex* and *harass* were anywhere within the document. By way of example, an e-mail discussing how a sex education class gave students ample opportunity to harass the teacher would also come back as relevant, even though it has little relevance to a sexual harassment case.

Other Boolean operators operate in a similar method. The *or* operator serves to find documents which have one term or the other, so *cat or dog* would turn up any document with the word *cat* or *dog* in it. In contrast, the *not* operator for *cat not dog* would turn up documents that mention *cat* and have no reference to *dog*. The *within* or *near* operator allows you to search for terms within a certain distance, in either words or characters, from each other or near each other; *cat w/5 dog* would turn up documents that mentioned *cat* within five words of *dog* for a search where *w/#* was configured to find terms within a certain number of words from other terms. In a similar fashion, *w/s* will turn up search terms in the same sentence as each other, and *w/p* will turn up search terms within the same sentence as each other. Other Boolean search operators include phonic searching which can find words that sound alike, such as *Smythe* and *Smith*, and stemming to find variations on endings, such as *applies*, *applied*, and *applying* in a search for *apply*.

Fuzzy Search

One of the challenges with traditional keyword-based searches is the potential that typos or misspelled words will be overlooked. Fuzzy search technology is a method that has been developed to find terms that may be misspelled, and it is particularly helpful when there is a need to compensate for errors due to OCR of paper or imaged documents. Fuzzy search algorithms apply the concept of wildcard searches to individual characters in the search term. For example, fuzzy logic would enable you to find both *harass* and *harras* if these were two variations on the search terms. Additionally, most fuzzy search engines allow you to adjust the search parameters or accuracy of the search so that you can fine-tune the search to account for a certain level of typographical or OCR errors in the search.

Although fuzzy search can help uncover potentially relevant data, it does not necessarily offer increased recall or accuracy, as it is still subject to the limitations of a keyword search.

WARNING

Though it is not always necessary to search all forms of potentially relevant data in every case, you must take stock of the potential sources of discoverable data for the purposes of disclosure, including voice and video data. The amended FRCP Rule 26(a) "demand(s) an exhaustive search for and identification of sources of discoverable electronically stored information, regardless of form, including email and voice content for disclosure." Voice recordings are a growing form of critical digital evidence from call centers in consumer product liability cases to call recordings in regulated industries. For example, in a dispute between two large banks, the defendant's "failure to retain audio recordings of its traders' telephone calls was sanctionable." In the judge's opinion, the "appropriate sanction was adverse inference jury instruction;" and damages were in excess of $600 million. E-mail and voice communication files are more critical and complex than ever before and legal technology consumers require scalability and analytical tools to more effectively understand and manage them.[15]

Metadata Searches

Another common search technique involves searching for and identifying files based on their metadata. This method of searching is typically combined with keyword or other advanced techniques to further narrow down relevance. Metadata is data about the document or ESI source and includes information such as the file creation date, author, last accessed date, and so on. Typically speaking, metadata for e-discovery purposes can be divided into three different categories: document metadata, file system metadata, and e-mail metadata.

Document metadata includes data about the file, stored as part of the file. Document metadata is not part of the content of the file and is generally not accessible from within the document. This type of metadata is typically viewed when viewing the file properties. Document metadata usually includes information such as the author, company information, creation and revision dates, last accessed dates, and last user, among others. However, it is important to understand that this data can be inaccurate, especially when searching the author of the document.

File system metadata includes the information about the file contained in either the file or the operating system. File system metadata includes the name, size, location, and usage of the file. It is not contained within the document and can be extracted from the file or operating system. This information is more important when you are relying on the operating system to search and identify your ESI.

E-mail has its own set of metadata. E-mail metadata is stored as part of the e-mail, but the information is not typically viewable from the client application that created the message. E-mail metadata can include such vital information as BCC addresses, sent, received, and opened dates, attachment information, and conversation thread information. Although e-mail metadata can be vital to your search and identification efforts, the quantity and quality of metadata available will depend on the system used to send the e-mail.

Though searching metadata alone will not typically be the only means of identifying potentially relevant ESI, searching metadata can be useful to narrow down date ranges, file types, authors, recipients, and other information that may be contained in the metadata. Additionally, you should ensure that your search techniques do not alter the metadata, as the FRCP and case law require that metadata be preserved and maintained.

TIP

All metadata is not created equal. You should be wary of searching by the author metadata tag to determine who created a document. This information can be set when you are installing a program, such as Microsoft Word, and in many organizations the owner of the program may be an IT director or the company itself. Metadata could also identify a custodian's administrative assistant as the document's author. Further, if you are creating a new document from within another document, this may also cause the author metadata to be inaccurate.

E-mail or Conversation Threading

Another method for searching relates specifically to e-mails. E-mail threads or conversation threads allow you to search for e-mails that follow or build on an original message, but they may not always be relevant. Typically, an e-mail thread will link together a series of e-mail responses and/or forwards that are created from an original message, but like metadata, their completeness will depend on the system used to create and send the message.

E-mail or conversation threads can be useful if a particular topic is potentially relevant, as responses and forwards of that original e-mail can also contain potentially relevant data and also offer up additional custodians.

Where e-mail threads fall down, however, is when a response to an e-mail changes the topic or adds an additional topic. When relying on e-mail threads, you should be careful to realize that you may inadvertently exclude potentially relevant data or include non-relevant data. This occurs when a new topic is added to an e-mail thread. If the initial e-mail is deemed not relevant, and you assume all e-mails in that thread are not relevant, you can exclude relevant data if the correspondence changes to a new relevant topic. Though not as risky, you can just as easily include non-relevant data when the topic of a relevant e-mail is changed to a non-relevant topic.

This method can be useful, but you should use this approach only in conjunction with other methods to search for and identify potentially relevant data. Additionally, not all e-mail clients are created equal when it comes to tracking e-mail threads, and if the reply to an e-mail does not contain the body of the original e-mail, the thread could be broken.

Advanced Search and Identification Techniques

Although legacy search techniques have been the standard bearer for e-discovery search and identification to date, newer, advanced search and identification techniques should not be ignored. These advanced techniques include federated or pan-enterprise search technologies, clustering and advanced e-mail threading, and concept and contextual search. These techniques are considered advanced because they offer additional capability that legacy techniques cannot offer and some of the techniques rely on mathematical or syntax-based algorithms. Although the legal community has been slow to embrace these techniques, a growing body of evidence and case law point to the fact that these advanced techniques have advantages over legacy methods: They can search for and identify potentially relevant ESI more accurately and effectively, and they can reduce the number of false positives significantly.

Conceptual and Contextual Searches

Conceptual and contextual search techniques offer capabilities beyond legacy methods. Up until now, they have not received much attention in case law or legal circles, but that is beginning to change. Conceptual and contextual analyses offer you the ability to search the context in which a term appears and to also search for similar terms or concepts. These techniques, when combined with legacy methods such as keyword, metadata, and Boolean searches, offer you the best chance of finding potentially relevant ESI. By way of example, concept searching considers both the word and the context in which it appears to differentiate how the term is used—for example, Madonna (singer) and Madonna (religious figure).

Until recently, few, if any, court cases addressed using concept searching as a way to search through electronic documents. Although e-discovery and search vendors touted their conceptual search capabilities, there was no case law to analyze their claims. This changed in June 2007. U.S. Magistrate Judge John Facciola required the parties in the *Disabilities Rights Counsel of Greater WDC v. WDC MTA* case to meet and confer and to present him with an agreed search protocol for ESI.

In discussing the need to effectively search a large volume of ESI, Judge Facciola wrote "how will they be searched to reduce the electronically stored information to information that is potentially relevant? In this context, I bring to the parties' attention recent scholarship that argues that concept searching, as opposed to keyword searching, is more efficient and more likely to produce the most comprehensive results."[16]

Conceptual searches consider the search term or terms and the context in which they appear to determine relevance. There are two techniques for concept searching and conceptual analysis: the first relies on a manually constructed thesaurus and relates certain words to others. The second approach uses fully automated methods to show associations among words based on mathematical or statistical analyses of the occurrence or proximity of certain words to others.

Thesaurus-based concept searching relies on a thesaurus of terms and relates the search terms to related terms in the thesaurus. The "concepts" are based on the search terms and the related terms in the thesaurus that are used as part of the search engine. A thesaurus-based concept search engine can help increase both precision and recall, but as a general rule it is more limited than the fully automated methods based on mathematical or statistical analyses. The thesaurus-based approach is limited by the size and comprehensiveness of the thesaurus and language.

NOTE

The dtSearch product offers, among other things, a thesaurus-based approach to conceptual search. The dtSearch engine output is limited to the language of the thesaurus, which highlights some of the challenges with concept searching using this approach. Although dtSearch can perform fuzzy, keyword, Boolean, and proximity searches on Unicode-based languages, the conceptual analysis is limited based on language. These limitations are not limited to dtSearch, but are also indicative of any concept search engine using this type of process.

The first limitation is based on the size and complexity of the thesaurus used. If the concept engine lexicon does not contain the search term or does not conceptually or contextually relate the term to other terms, the search will be incomplete and will overlook potentially relevant terms or concepts. The shortcoming of the lexicon can be overcome through manual processes that require users to build out the lexicon, but it is still a shortcoming nonetheless. The second shortcoming of this approach is language specificity. Because the thesaurus is tied to a specific language—say, English or Spanish, for example—a different thesaurus would be required for another language. Additionally, language barriers in this approach are more complex because translating the thesaurus into another language is typically not effective, as words, concepts, and synonyms differ from language to language.

The second type of concept searching uses statistical and mathematical analyses to determine the meaning and relevance of the documents being sought, and there are several types of this conceptual analysis. One of them is based on the concept of latent semantic analysis and the other on computational pattern recognition (non-linear adaptive digital signal processing) and contextual linguistic analysis. These types of conceptual search offer advantages over thesaurus-based search as you are not limited by either the depth of the thesaurus or the language.

One benefit of the statistical and mathematical models is that that they do not rely on a thesaurus or words, but rather on a mathematical relationship between the words. This functionality gives them an increased ability to analyze the meaning behind the documents independent of a thesaurus, looking at the patterns, usage, and frequency of terms that correspond to a specific concept. The mathematical/statistical approach to concept search technology enables the technology to avoid the limitations of other techniques, ranging from language dependence to susceptibility to misspellings and/or slang or code word usage.

NOTE

Autonomy IDOL is a search engine that relies on mathematical and statistical analyses in the search and identification phase. Other solutions on the market also use similar technology, but Autonomy's technology is widely accepted as a leader in the field and many other vendors in the e-discovery space rely on Autonomy technology for their e-discovery–related processes. Autonomy IDOL has found wide acceptance with the DoD, NSA, and other federal governments, and with many enterprise customers who have standardized on the search functionality of IDOL for managing enterprise data and knowledge. Other technologies in this space offer functionality similar to IDOL, but IDOL is viewed as a leading technology in this space.

Clustering or Categorization Technology

Another benefit to using advanced search technology such as conceptual searches is the ability to cluster or categorize similar and related documents together. As with conceptual search, there are many different methodologies and techniques for clustering, including the two techniques discussed in conceptual search: the thesaurus and statistical/mathematical techniques.

The key advantage to using clustering technology in the search and identification phase is that this technique can help you categorize data more quickly and group similar, potentially relevant ESI together. Additionally, when it comes time to review and analyze this data, you can perform a non-linear review and focus on ESI that may be most relevant upfront. Clustering and categorization also play a key role in the analysis phase, as defined by the EDRM.

Although there are different techniques for performing clustering operations, there are benefits to using a mathematically based clustering and categorization technique over using a thesaurus-based technique. A mathematical-based technique will look at the relationship between the terms independent of language or meaning. In contrast, the thesaurus-based technique will look at the relationship between the terms based on their definition and categorization in the thesaurus. By way of example, if you were searching for the concept of *dog running down the street* as it relates to the idea of a criminal (or your daughter's no-good boyfriend) being chased down the street, you would want to exclude documents that discuss someone chasing his pet down the street. A thesaurus-based clustering engine would rely on the relation of *dog*, *street*, and *running* to determine the relationship, and the cluster would contain documents relating to the *dog* as a pet and as a criminal (or ex-boyfriend), which would reduce your precision rate dramatically. In contrast, the precision rate of a mathematical/ statistical approach would be dramatically higher as it would look beyond the meaning of *dog*, *street*, and *running* to determine the manner in which the words were used and related; you would be able to fine-tune the results to increase the accuracy and precision with this technique in a way you could not when relying on a thesaurus-based approach When all is said and done, it is important to vet your technology to see what your searches are relying on.

Advanced E-mail Threading

Although discussed earlier as a legacy technique, e-mail threading can also be considered advanced technology when combined with conceptual search techniques. As a legacy method, e-mail threads rely on a user replying to a particular message and the functionality of the e-mail client that created and sent the message. However, advanced conceptual search techniques can uncover the meaning in an e-mail and help you determine true e-mail threads. There can be distinct advantages to this technique. First, by using conceptual search, you can eliminate messages which take on a different, non-relevant topic. Second, advanced techniques can also string together conversation threads when the "chain" of the conversation was broken, either by the e-mail client itself or by the user replying to the message and deleting the text of the original message.

Though it is not an advanced technology on its own, advanced e-mail threading can be of assistance when you are trying to group together like e-mail topics.

An Overview of Search and Identification Tools

Now that we have explored the duty to preserve, the requirements that you search for and identify all relevant information, and many of the techniques available to you for search and identification, you need to choose a tool for the search and identification process. There are myriad options with different strengths and weaknesses, so it is best to conduct some due diligence before you finalize your approach.

In any search and identification effort, the biggest challenge is to search for and identify potentially relevant data from the unstructured and unmanaged data across the enterprise. The most challenging of these sources are the most mobile ones, namely employee laptops; however, you should not neglect the challenge of searching for and identifying data on desktops, workstations, file servers, BlackBerry devices, and any other data source available to store ESI.

Accuracy of Search and Identification Techniques

When deciding between advanced and legacy search techniques, accuracy and effectiveness—that is, precision and recall—must be considered as key requirements. Legacy search methods such as keyword and Boolean search can have significant limitations and efficiencies in larger-scale, more complex cases. As data volumes continue to grow, it will become more important to look to conceptual analysis and search techniques.

One organization studying these techniques is TREC, the Text Retrieval Conference, which is co-sponsored by the National Institute of Standards and Technology (NIST). For more information on TREC, visit http://trec.nist.gov. TREC employs both vendor and academic researchers to determine the accuracy and effectiveness of information retrieval methods on large-scale electronic data collections, and it has recently focused on some of the challenges in the e-discovery space. See TREC 2006 Legal Discovery Track and TREC 2007 Legal Discovery Track for additional information, downloadable from http://trec.nist.gov/pubs.html.

NOTE

Precision and recall are important concepts when completing a search. As defined in this chapter, *precision* is the proportion of documents in a query result that are relevant and *recall* is a measure of a search result's ability to find *all* relevant documents. It is important in e-discovery to have a high level of both precision and recall, to ensure completeness of the search and to reduce the costs and risks associated with reviewing the documents.

When measuring the effectiveness of your search technique, you can examine the rate of precision and recall at which the technology performs. Precision measures the proportion of documents in a query result that are relevant, and relevance is a key in meeting the duty to preserve. A query result with perfect precision would consist of all returned documents that are relevant. Recall measures a search result's ability to find *all* relevant documents, also important in meeting the duty to preserve. Ideally, your search and identification techniques would achieve both high precision and high recall, and this would enable you to find all relevant documents without returning unrelated content along with them. Of course, search and identification techniques are not perfect.

It is important to keep in mind that studies have shown that traditional Boolean search performs woefully according to this metric. In one study, the average Boolean query located merely 22 percent of the relevant documents, meaning that 78 percent of the relevant documents were not found. Additionally, the precision rate averaged only 29 percent, meaning that 71 percent of your documents returned using this search methodology were not relevant (see "Overview of the TREC 2007 Legal Track," http://trec.nist.gov/). Such low recall and precision rates have two potentially profound results from both a risk and a cost standpoint. First, the risk component stems from the fact that legally a party is required to identify and preserve all data that is reasonably likely to contain relevant ESI. Failure to do so would open the party to potential sanctions and adverse evidentiary inferences.

Second, the time and cost for reviewing large collections of overwhelmingly irrelevant documents can be quite high. As the amount of ESI grows and the pool of potentially relevant documents jumps from thousands to millions, the unnecessary cost of reviewing predominantly irrelevant documents can be staggering.

WARNING

Be wary of shortcuts that your index technology may use, as these shortcuts almost guarantee that your search and identification techniques will not comply with the FRCP. "Jump out" technology will miss potentially relevant documents because this search technology will stop looking across an index for potentially relevant information once it estimates a document is unlikely to make the top section of the results list. "Partial indexing" technology chooses not to index the entire content of the document, but only the first X pages based on assumptions. For example, if a document contains 500 pages of information, the search engine may index only the first five pages. If information relevant to the case appears first on page 6, it will not have been indexed and the search engine may miss this document and others. When these shortcut techniques are applied over even a modest number of files the result is an arbitrary and incomplete set of documents.

Although it is important to note that the TREC studies did not endorse a single search technique as offering the highest recall and precision rates, it has become apparent that more advanced search techniques combined with legacy methods will enable you to achieve much higher levels of precision and recall. By way of example, one can imagine that if a litigator were to search for the phrase *paint the town red*, the Boolean search engine would return not only documents relating to possible engagement of inappropriate behavior, but also completely irrelevant information regarding art, color, and cities that the busy litigator must spend his or her costly time culling.

In general, when you are looking to achieve both risk and cost reduction while ensuring compliance to the FRCP and the duty to preserve, it is essential for the enterprise to adopt search technology that does not fall prey to the limitations of legacy methods, but performs effective search in a scalable manner. The most advanced conceptual search technology will allow you to find information based on both words and concepts, enabling you to find potentially relevant ESI based on information both contained in and absent from the document. By utilizing advanced techniques and legacy methods that can provide a higher recall rate and can limit the search to a predominantly relevant content, combined with advanced analytics that cluster the results into conceptual buckets, you can save enormous amounts of time and money.

Tools & Traps…

Beware of Incomplete Search and Identification

The duty to preserve potentially relevant ESI in the face of litigation or an investigation is clear-cut. You must make reasonable efforts to search the enterprise, including custodian laptops and desktops, for potentially relevant ESI. The search should be thorough and should cover all data types and reasonably accessible data that may be potentially relevant, based on the legal team's assessment of the case. However, you must be cautious of search and identification techniques that rely on partial index or jump out techniques under the guise of a complete search. Vendors using these techniques argue that the speed of the search and identification is worth the time and cost savings. However, the FRCP makes little allowance for shortcuts or partial searches that are not disclosed and negotiated among the parties. The preservation obligation requires a reasonable and defensible search of the data that is reasonably accessible. The documents potentially missed by shortcut solutions could include smoking gun or exculpatory documents, and you run the risk of evidentiary sanctions, fines, or further hampering your case if you fail to identify relevant evidence. Where possible, choose a search and identification solution that is able to offer a complete and accurate index of all your enterprise data. When vetting your search technology, ensure that your vendor or software takes no shortcuts in building the index. If there are limitations in your enterprise applications, make sure to employ other search techniques to address the data pools or documents that may be missed.

Built-in Search Tools

Many enterprise data sources have their own built-in search and identification solutions. Archives, such as Autonomy EAS, Symantec Enterprise Vault, and EMC EmailXtender, have built-in functionality that allows you to search the mail and documents stored in the archive. Likewise, ECM systems such as EMC Documentum, OpenText Livelink, and IBM FileNet all have built-in search capabilities. Corporate database applications, HR systems, and other purpose-built solutions may also have their own search functionality.

Many organizations rely on the built-in search and identification capabilities of these in-house solutions, and the myriad solutions and functionality available to each solution make it impracticable to review each one in this chapter. When relying on the built-in search functionality of these databases and applications you must realize that the search capabilities will vary greatly from solution to solution. Many of the search and identification techniques rely on legacy techniques including keyword, Boolean, and metadata searches, which could affect both precision and recall. Someone in the enterprise or a third-party consultant should be consulted to ensure that you are fully apprised of the operation and limitations of the search functionalities to be used.

Finally, the greater the number of data sources in the organization, the less scalable it becomes to use each solution's built-in search functionality. In such circumstances, the efficiencies of moving to an enterprise-wide search tool become more apparent.

Enterprise-Wide Search and Identification

The amendments to the FRCP suggest the need for a systemized, repeatable, and defensible process toward e-discovery and ESI preservation. Reasonable efforts must be made to search for, identify, and ultimately preserve and collect potentially relevant ESI. To meet the challenge of e-discovery today, organizations are increasingly turning to technology that can scale to search across the enterprise. These enterprise-class search technologies will allow you to deal with the challenges of searching for and identifying potentially relevant information in response to an e-discovery or investigation request.

However, when choosing the right technology or vendor, you must ensure that you choose a technology that can meet the demands and rigors of e-discovery search and identification. You can eliminate many of the risks associated with the inability to identify potentially relevant ESI by using technology that includes enterprise-wide, multifile-type search techniques. The enterprise search and collection solutions also bring an objectivity and defensibility to the process that custodian self-collection cannot. This objectivity and defensibility helps to eliminate the challenges of custodian self-collection while mitigating the risk of spoliation as well as enabling counsel to monitor the preservation process by providing extensive reporting features that allow tracking the progress of a preservation effort. Further, an added benefit of these enterprise search and collection solutions is that they can provide an organization with a repeatable, defensible, and systemized process in compliance with the FRCP.

One of the challenges with choosing the right solution is to ensure that your search and identification solution is able to search across all of your data sources, including e-mail, standard Office and word processing documents, and voice and video data. A full range of search capability and functionality may not be available in every solution. Additionally, many index-based engines will miss relevant information because of performance-enhancing shortcuts designed to improve the response time and relevancy of information access requests from employees; these performance-enhancing shortcuts include jump out and partial indexing.

The key is to choose a solution that will allow you to search the disparate data sources you have across the enterprise while also ensuring that your organization remains in compliance with the FRCP. There are several factors to keep in mind when choosing your search tool: the ability to reach all enterprise data sources, search techniques used to search for and identify potentially relevant ESI, and the ability to comply with the FRCP by searching all data sources and not altering metadata. To explore a few of the many technologies that are emerging and are being used for enterprise searching, we will look briefly at Google, Guidance Software EnCase eDiscovery, and Autonomy's IDOL technology.

Ensuring That the Index Doesn't Alter Your Data

One of the potential issues with different index technologies is that they have the potential to alter metadata. As discussed earlier, the FRCP requires that metadata be preserved. If you alter metadata, you risk challenges to the authenticity of your data.

When you provide information for legal or regulatory purposes, the burden is on you, as the producing organization, to adopt a legally defensible process that does not alter or modify the data.

If the authenticity of data is challenged, you must show that the information presented is accurately represented by providing a detailed audit trail from initial collection through production to clearly establish the Chain of Custody (CoC) of the information. Because of this, the preservation of contents and metadata during both indexing and collection is critically important. It is also important that you ensure that your choice of indexing technology does not alter the metadata and provides for an accurate CoC record.

NOTE

When choosing the right indexing solution, be sure you examine how the index works and whether the index alters the metadata of the original ESI. As the FRCP requires metadata preservation, it is important that the technology you use to search for and identify potentially relevant ESI does not alter the ESI in any way. One of the key things to look for in a solution is to ensure that the indexing technology does not alter the last accessed date. Although this piece of metadata may be insignificant in most cases, you want to ensure that it is preserved if and when it is an issue in the case.

A Warning about the E-discovery Space

A word of caution is necessary before discussing a few established companies that offer technology which you may think of when thinking about ESI search and identification. E-discovery is a hot topic today, and many companies have jumped into this space. Some are experienced and established companies that are adapting their technology to be of use in response to the increased awareness of e-discovery, but others have limited funding and/or limited experience in the field.

When you are seeking a vendor for e-discovery search and identification, or any other part of the process, you should be concerned about several aspects of the vendor you are working with. First, you want to make sure the technology works as advertised and can deliver the promises of the marketing materials. Second, you want to make sure the technology is reliable and will work in a systemized, repeatable, and defensible process as required under the FRCP. Third, and finally, you want to make sure the company will be there for the long haul. Be sure the company is well funded and has a business plan to ensure that it will be there to meet your needs beyond the immediate future.

WARNING

Technology in the e-discovery space evolves and changes at a rapid clip. Although much of the information contained in this chapter regarding specific technologies is current as of this writing, the information contained herein is constantly changing and can become rapidly outdated. You should complete your own research when examining the options you have available for search and identification technology.

Google

When many people think of search, they think of Google. Google is a public company with a strong financial position, and the Google Internet search engine is the most widely used and well known search tool available today. However, Google technology has not really extended into the enterprise and e-discovery space the way that most people would have expected.

Google has offered an enterprise search tool for many years. The Google Mini Search Appliance and Google Search Appliance are intended to help users find and locate information across the enterprise. However, the appliances are limited in functionality and have shortcomings that limit their usefulness in the e-discovery space. The Google appliances are able to search more than 220 file types with query expansion, word stemming, and automated synonyms. However, much like Google Web searches, the ranking of documents is based on popularity rather than relevance to the query. When searching for potentially relevant data for e-discovery purposes, popularity is not the key; relevance is. Additionally, the Google appliances are limited in the number of files types they can search and in the data sources they can reach.

Google does offer desktop search capability through Google Desktop, but the desktop search functionality has many shortcomings for e-discovery purposes, particularly its inability to preserve metadata, an important element in e-discovery.

Guidance Software EnCase eDiscovery

Guidance Software is a pioneer in the forensic space. It is a publicly traded company, and its EnCase forensic solution is the most widely used software for imaging hard drives and has been around for more than a decade. In the past several years, Guidance has moved into the enterprise and e-discovery search and identification space with EnCase eDiscovery.

EnCase eDiscovery allows you to search across the enterprise and target laptops, desktops, file servers, and e-mail servers to conduct a targeted search and identification for potentially relevant data. Additionally, EnCase eDiscovery is able to perform full-disk images across the network if required. As of this writing, Guidance has yet to release connectors to search an organization's ECM or archive solution, but it has discussed the development of connectors for solutions such as EMC Documentum and OpenText Livelink.

EnCase eDiscovery is well known in the e-discovery space for its ability to reach out to the unstructured and unmanaged data on laptops and desktops. It is able to scan out, under the operating system, and conduct a targeted search and collection on any enterprise data source to which it can connect. EnCase eDiscovery does not build an index that it can reuse with each search, so the length of time a search requires will depend on a number of factors, including the complexity of the search, the number of keywords, the date ranges, and the file types being searched for.

EnCase technology relies on legacy search methods. As it does not build an index for searching, it can perform keyword, metadata, file type, and Boolean searches using *and*, *or*, and *not*. Another key factor with EnCase software is that it requires specialized training to ensure that the queries are properly fashioned. Also, EnCase software utilizes Global Regular Expression and Print (GREP) commands to create search terms, and this is another area where Guidance Software's solutions will require training. GREP is a UNIX pattern-matching utility. Guidance offers certification for use of its software—the EnCase Certified Examiner (EnCE), which is a certification for the use of its computer forensic software (see www.guidancesoftware.com/training/EnCE_certification.aspx for more information). Given the complexities and importance of executing these searches correctly, you should rely on trained or certified individuals when using EnCase eDiscovery to ensure that your search has been properly constructed and can withstand scrutiny if challenged in court.

Autonomy IDOL

Autonomy is a software company that specializes in information access. Founded in 1996 and based on technology researched at Cambridge University, Autonomy is one of the leaders in the conceptual search market space. Autonomy's core technology is IDOL, the Intelligent Data Operating Layer. IDOL allows Autonomy's solutions to search across the enterprise, utilizing legacy and advanced techniques, and access more than 400 different data repositories, including laptops and desktops. It can search and analyze more than 1,000 file types, is language independent, and is compatible with all operating systems. With the purchase and integration of e-discovery market leader ZANTAZ in 2007, Autonomy is moving aggressively into the e-discovery space.

Autonomy IDOL is a mathematical and statistical-based conceptual and contextual analysis search platform based on the mathematical works of Thomas Bayes and Claude Shannon. The technology allows a variety of search methods, including legacy methods such as keyword search. Combined with conceptual search capabilities, IDOL is designed to identify potentially relevant data with greater precision and recall than solutions relying solely on legacy search techniques or thesaurus-based conceptual search engines. IDOL fully indexes data to ensure a complete, FRCP-compliant search without altering the metadata, ensuring forensically sound data. It can also search all ESI types, including voice and video sources.

IDOL is positioned as a "pan-enterprise" search technology that combines advanced search technology such as conceptual analysis with legacy methods such as keyword and Boolean searching. The technology is designed to access all of your data sources across the enterprise, allowing an FRCP-compliant search that will cover all data sources, from Microsoft Office documents, to e-mails, voice-mails, and videos, including an ability to search databases, ECM solutions, archives, and SharePoint environments. The IDOL platform gives you the ability to search for and identify data across the enterprise from a single search interface, reducing the time, risk, and manual processes that would typically be required.

In addition to the IDOL platform, Autonomy offers several other solutions in the e-discovery space, including Aungate Legal Hold, which offers legal hold management and preservation and collection capabilities, with the added benefit of the IDOL platform underneath to search for and identify potentially relevant ESI. Additionally, Autonomy has a strong role in the processing, analysis, review, and production space with its Introspect line of products.

The one fear that users may have with Autonomy's technology is that conceptual analysis does not yet have the court vetting and backing that keyword search has. Although this is true, it is also apparent that the courts are beginning to notice the availability of technology using conceptual analysis. Though it may be some time before conceptual search is a standard in court cases, this technology already has wide acceptance in the enterprise market, with many leading corporations relying on this type of search technology to manage enterprise data and knowledge management. Although it is proven and tested in the enterprise, the technology is still not fully vetted in the court systems, though it has been used in hundreds, perhaps even thousands, of cases.

Summary

Search and identification of potentially relevant ESI can be one of the most challenging phases of the e-discovery process due to the need to fully map, preserve, and potentially search all sources of ESI that are reasonably likely to contain relevant discoverable data. The FRCP was amended in December 2006 to specifically address the challenges of ESI. Though the need to search all ESI sources existed in the rules prior to the amendments, the amendments highlighted the need for you to have a process in place for searching for and identifying potentially relevant ESI across the enterprise. The legal preservation obligation was unchanged by the amendments, but the rules served to underscore the need to search for, identify, and preserve all potentially relevant data sources, including, potentially, voice and video data.

To meet your preservation obligation and show a good-faith effort in searching for and identifying potentially relevant information, you must know where your ESI lives across the organization. With multinational organizations, a mobile workforce, and a proliferation of mobile storage devices and media formats, managing your ESI sources has become more important than ever. The early attention requirements of the FRCP make it essential that you be able to locate potentially relevant data quickly and, in the best of all cases, complete an early assessment of that data. Although building a data map can be daunting, in the end the data map will help ease the challenges of searching for and identifying your data.

You must also carefully consider and select the right tools and techniques for search and identification. These may include legacy methods such as keyword and Boolean searches, or advanced methods such as mathematically based conceptual analysis. Although no one method of search and identification has proven to have the highest precision and recall, you will be best served by choosing a combination of advanced and legacy methods that will ensure compliance with the FRCP and be able to search all data sources and all data types across the enterprise. Using the right techniques and increasing the accuracy of your search will also help you reduce risks and costs and reduce your storage burden by targeting your preservation, and will substantially reduce the costs associated with unnecessary review.

Finally, you need to choose the right solution from the right vendor to ensure that you have a compliance search and identification procedure. Be aware that certain search techniques may be more accurate than others and that some may offer a higher level of precision and recall. Also be aware that the market is flooded with e-discovery vendors who claim to offer the best solution for search and identification, with many making claims that they can handle e-discovery from end to end. It is important that you vet each solution from many different angles: Ensure that the solution works as advertised and performs at the claimed levels. Also ensure that the level of precision and recall is high enough to work in the real world, and choose a proven, well-established vendor. It may be prudent to retain a consultant to help you vet the available alternatives, given the nature of the investment importance of these activities to the company.

Solutions Fast Track

Search and Identification in Compliance with the Federal Rules

☑ The FRCP requires that you search for and identify potentially relevant ESI from all data sources, including, potentially, voice and video data.

☑ The duty to preserve requires that you make a good-faith and reasonable effort to preserve potentially relevant data when faced with litigation or when you reasonably anticipate litigation.

☑ To ensure compliance with the FRCP and case law, you should have a systemized, repeatable, and defensible process for handling your e-discovery, including the search and identification process.

Determining Where the Data Lives

☑ When searching for data, remember that you must search all data sources reasonably likely to yield relevant information. Also remember that it is imperative that you make efforts to find all data sources, regardless of type or location.

☑ The FRCP early attention requirements require a fast response when litigation is filed, so having a data map will make it easier for you to search for and locate potentially relevant ESI.

☑ You should be aware that your employees may use assets not owned by the organization, such as thumb drives, home computers, and iPods, to store information. It is important to determine whether there is potentially relevant ESI on these and other data sources and to negotiate the range of your search obligations.

Search and Identification Techniques

☑ Although legacy methods such as keyword and Boolean searching are the standard bearers in the e-discovery space, you should also consider employing advanced technology such as conceptual search to help narrow down the scope of potentially relevant data and minimize the costs associated with unnecessary review of irrelevant material.

☑ Use a combination of techniques to help you search for and identify all data types that may have potentially relevant ESI.

☑ Automated search and identification techniques are frequently less risky and more defensible than custodian self-collection.

An Overview of Search and Identification Tools

☑ Vet your vendor carefully to ensure that it offers the right solution for your search and identification challenges. Also ensure that the precision and recall are at a level you will find acceptable.

☑ Test potential search identification solutions in your enterprise environment to ensure that they work as advertised and will function on your network.

☑ Ensure that your vendor is well funded and well established so that you do not invest in a platform or technology that will not be supported long-term. Consider retaining a consultant to help you assess the best platform for your company.

Frequently Asked Questions

Q: Are all search and identification solutions FRCP-compliant?

A: No. Many search and identification solutions complete only a partial index or "jump out" to increase the speed of the search, causing you to miss potentially relevant data. Additionally, many solutions will alter metadata when they index, and the FRCP and case law require that you preserve metadata.

Q: Isn't e-mail all that really matters for purposes of e-discovery?

A: No. The FRCP and duty to preserve require that you search all data and all data sources that are reasonably likely to contain potentially relevant ESI. Even though you may think your custodians send and receive all potentially relevant ESI in their e-mail, you should make an effort to search all custodian data sources for potentially relevant ESI, in the absence of an agreement with the opposing party limiting the scope of the data sets to be searched.

Q: Unified messaging and voicemails are sent to my employees via e-mail. Do I have to search voice messages for e-discovery purposes?

A: Yes. The FRCP defines ESI as containing voice data and recordings. Unless you are able to negotiate out voice data at the Pretrial Conference and the Discovery Planning Conference, the FRCP requires search and identification of this data.

Q: Are keyword and Boolean searches required for e-discovery?

A: Although keyword and Boolean search techniques are legacy methods that are commonly understood and found in case law, they are not mandated techniques. You are required, however, to make best efforts to search for and identify potentially relevant ESI.

Q: Isn't asking custodians to produce their own data the most effective way to collect potentially relevant ESI?

A: No. Although custodian self-collection may seem like a good idea, the courts have frequently found fault with discovery that relies on employees to determine which documents might be relevant. Custodians are typically not experts and are often self-interested, so they may fail to produce inculpatory documents. Relying solely on employee self-collection substantially increases the risk of spoliation from improper search, preservation, and collection.

Q: Are hard-drive images required under the FRCP?

A: No, the FRCP does not require that you image hard drives as part of the preservation obligation. Although imaging all potentially relevant employees' hard drives can result in the gross over-collection of non-relevant data, in certain cases, such as white-collar crime, fraud, or in the case of key litigation custodians, hard-drive imaging may be preferable. It also provides effective preservation and allows for the potential of searching for deleted documents, in the event it becomes necessary. For routine discovery, however, targeted search, identification, collection, and review are preferred.

Q: Has conceptual or contextual search been discussed in case law?

A: Yes, conceptual search has been identified in recent case law as a method to cull through large amounts of ESI in an effective manner.

Q: Should I rely on keyword searching as it is court-accepted?

A: Not necessarily. Recent case law has criticized a party's reliance on simple keyword searches alone and cited reliance on inadequate keyword searching as the reason the party lost its claim to privilege by inadvertently producing privileged documents to the opposing side.

Q: What is the most important thing to look for when choosing a search and identification solution?

A: Look for a solution that combines advanced and legacy techniques with the ability to search all data sources and all data types across the enterprise. Precision and recall are also extremely important.

Q: What should I look for in an indexing solution?

A: Look for an indexing solution that is able to search all data types and sources in an FRCP-compliant manner. Do not employ an index or enterprise search tool that alters metadata or fails to fully index the ESI. Shore up any deficiencies with a combination of preservation and search techniques in a documented, defensible manner.

Notes

1. *Hynix Semiconductor Inc. v. Rambus Inc.,* 2006 WL 565893 (N.D.Cal. Jan. 5, 2006) at *27.)

2. *Zubulake v. UBS Warburg LLC,* 220 F.R.D. 212, 217 (S.D.N.Y. 2004) ("*Zubulake IV*")

3. *Zubulake v. UBS Warburg LLC,* 2004 WL 1620866 at *8 (S.D.N.Y. Jul. 20, 2004)

4. *Zubulake v. UBS Warburg LLC,* 2004 WL 1620866 at *8 (S.D.N.Y. Jul. 20, 2004)

5. FRCP Rule 34(a).

6. *Peskoff v. Farber,* 2007 WL 530096 (Feb. 21, 2007 D.D.C.)

7. *Peskoff v. Farber,* 2007 WL 530096 (Feb. 21, 2007 D.D.C.)

8. In *re Genetically Modified Rice Litigation,* 2007 WL 1655757 (June 5, 2007 E.D.Mo.). See also *Flexys Americas v. Kumho Tire:* 2006 WL 3526794 (N.D. Ohio); where the court limited the search to specific custodians, time frames, and keywords.

9. *Zubulake v. UBS Warburg LLC,* 2004 WL 1620866 at *8 (S.D.N.Y. Jul. 20, 2004).

10. *Samsung Electronics Co., Ltd. v. Rambus, Inc.,* 439 F.Supp.2d 524, 565 (E.D.Va. 2006).

11. *Wachtel v. Health Net, Inc.,* 2006 WL 3538935 at *8 (D.N.J., Dec. 6, 2006).

12. In *re Hawaiian Airlines, Inc.,* 2007 WL 3172642 (Bkrtcy. D.Hawaii October 30, 2007).

13. The EDRM Glossary, www.edrm.net/wiki/index.php/Glossary, citing Vinson & Elkins LLP Practice Support, EDD Glossary; Ibis Consulting, Glossary; Kroll Ontrack, Glossary of Terms, www.krollontrack.com/glossaryterms)

14. *Victor Stanley, Inc. v. Creative Pipe,* Inc. D.Md.,2008. ---, 2008 WL 2221841 (D.Md.)) May 29, 2008.

15. See E*TRADE SECURITIES LLC v. DEUTSCHE BANK AG, Nos. 02–3711(RHK/AJB), 02–3682(RHK/AJB). April 18, 2005.

16. See George L. Paul & Jason R. Baron, "Information Inflation: Can the Legal System Adapt?" 13 Rich. J.L. & Tech. 10 (2007). Disability Rights Council of Greater Washington v. Washington Metropolitan Transit Authority, D.D.C., 2007. June 1, 2007, 242 F.R.D. 139, at 10.

Chapter 9

Bringing It Together in a Review Platform and Managing the Review

Solutions in this chapter:

- The Cost of Document Review

- Creating a Streamlined Document Review Workflow

- Key Points in Selecting a Review Platform

- Understanding User Roles and Responsibilities

- The Benefits of Using an Early Case Assessment (ECA) Strategy

- Technical Issues Regarding Document Review

- Advancements in the Review Process

☑ Summary

☑ Solutions Fast Track

☑ Frequently Asked Questions

Introduction

A continued theme throughout this book focuses on the substantial increase in lawsuits, regulatory and government investigations, and inquiries from concerned parties along with the need to have a sophisticated e-discovery program. Given this arguable reality of litigation and compliance, and the growth of electronic communications and computer usage in businesses worldwide, it should not be surprising that e-discovery is a necessary and growing requirement. Between meeting shareholder demands for reduced costs, assuaging judges by acknowledging and delivering results on court-imposed deadlines, and efficiently deploying internal resources so as not to jeopardize current revenue-generating activities, effectively installing and deploying a successful e-discovery program is of crucial importance to companies today.

Overall e-discovery costs and delivery times can be managed in a number of different ways, most of which we have covered in this book. But one area with significant opportunity for streamlining efficiency is the document review process. As we all know, document review is the largest single cost involved in the discovery process. And it therefore must be controlled as effectively and efficiently as possible. By consciously selecting and deploying a productive review platform, companies can reduce staff workload during the review process, create a more thorough case strategy, and generally gain more control over the entire e-discovery process.

Even though the review phase of e-discovery is certainly costly and time-consuming, it has evolved significantly over the past 10 years. Historically, members of the review team typically had the following options:

- Each document was printed manually, and then reviewed, individually, with relevant material highlighted by hand. Anytime this manual process was required for a lengthy matter, the potential for error was high. Such errors were experienced as missing documents, missing relevant or critical content related to the matter, and even possibly documents that were inadvertently misplaced. Additionally, deadlines were in jeopardy and attorney review time was exorbitant, resulting in higher risk and costs.

- Each document was converted to a "true" graphics format, such as tagged image file format, or TIFF, and then reviewed using an expensive, proprietary litigation management tool. Not only was this costly in terms of the disk usage required, but also the propensity for missing material was present, as some users were not accustomed to reading printed documents on a screen. There was also a lack of context for the examiner to determine whether a certain instance of information appearing in a particular document was actually relevant to the matter at hand. Although this method is still utilized throughout the review process, it too has been drastically automated compared to the past means for reviewing TIFF images.

Neither of the preceding approaches is particularly efficient, and thus higher-end review tools were created to productively analyze and review electronically stored information (ESI). In fact, with spreadsheets and other non-textual files becoming increasingly critical in day-to-day business operations, such a manual examination of printed pages may result in overlooking important file metadata such as hidden columns, formulas, and other "under-the-covers" machinations.

NOTE

It is important to appreciate the number of documents that can be involved in a review project, especially for large litigation matters. In the Enron case, investigators seized more than 12 million documents. If those pages were printed out, the stack would be three times taller than Chicago's Sears Tower.

In another recent case an inventor brought a patent infringement suit against a large company. The inventor had to read more than 50 million pages of electronic documents and analyze them over just a few short months. A decade ago, a small army of attorneys would have required years to analyze the result set.

The Cost of Document Review

Although preserving and collecting ESI are a concern for legal and technology professionals everywhere, it is also becoming increasingly necessary to acquire talent that understands the entire e-discovery process. And, because preservation, collections, and processing are a nominal cost when compared with the document review process, it is becoming even more important to work with teams of people who have document review experience, training on multiple review platforms, and the ability to quickly understand certain document review application pitfalls or limitations. For example, companies that are considered serial litigants (those that have a need to respond to multiple legal matters annually) view the document review process as the single largest cost throughout the entire discovery process. Those industries might also be regulated and therefore could experience an even greater need to reduce their document review costs. Some of those industries include, but are not limited to, the following:

- Financial services
- Pharmaceuticals
- Energy
- Telecommunications

Often, companies end up outsourcing the review phase to outside attorneys, billing a couple to several hundred dollars an hour to analyze these vast heaps of information. Alternatively, it is also common for teams of contract attorneys to manage or assist with the document review. Some of these companies own and host a document review application, and many partner with companies that create, own, and operate a document review application. Although those rates might be more reasonable than the rates paid to law firm attorneys, it really depends on the matter at hand, your budget, and the turnaround time as to the type of team you select. It has been previously estimated that companies actually spend nearly $5 billion per year reviewing and analyzing e-mail messages for regulatory requests, investigations, and litigation.

Consider the following methods to accomplish cost savings before the document review process begins:

- Utilize early case assessment (ECA) tools to reduce data sets through analytic and first-pass culling technologies.

- Create a review workflow or adopt a review platform with seamless workflow management.

- Ensure greater visibility into the overall review process, such as productivity tracking to enable course corrections or reallocation of resources to keep the project on track.

- Automate tag conflict checking to minimize and quickly correct tagging errors, such as when attorneys have applied conflicting tags to the same document.

- Automate privilege log generation instead of manually maintaining such a log outside the review platform.

NOTE

A December 2006 Forrester Research report notes, "Tools with visual analytics built in can make these legal professionals more efficient by determining whether or not data is relevant, is privileged, or even needs to be produced in response to a discovery request."

Creating a Streamlined Document Review Workflow

As the number of documents and disparate files in an e-discovery project grows and becomes more complex to digest, a specific checklist and workflow that your organization follows for each and every discovery event becomes key to ensuring consistent, accurate results. When a new discovery project enters your business, it is easy for those members of the team to feel overwhelmed. Creating a solid support structure with predictable steps and outcomes helps the process become more manageable and reduces risk, cost, and the chance of error. Best practices are always recommended for successful outcomes; document review is no exception.

Consider the following parts of an adequate review workflow:

1. **Assign a project manager** This person should manage the project and process from start to finish and will be responsible for locating resources when necessary.

2. **Develop an "important contacts" list** As LexisNexis says, "Create a comprehensive list of all of the key players relevant to the litigation, their roles and responsibilities, and protocol for communications." Distribute this list to all stakeholders for the review process, which should seamlessly segue into the production process. Additionally and mentioned in more detail in the next chapter, it is important to determine whether your review tool will have a production management capability.

3. **Identify document reviewer assignments and roles** With the ever-changing advancement of review tools, it is critical at the onset of a case to determine your level of reviewers. Several tools available today provide you the ability to assign documents in a systematic manner. Therefore, it is important to determine whether you will have a population of first-level, second-level, and expert-level (possibly specialized within a particular field or industry) reviewers prior to beginning the review.

4. **Create a first draft of a review timeline** Write down a list of hard, non-negotiable deadlines, and work backward to determine meaningful and reachable short-term goals to ensure progress.

5. **Schedule and perform initial meetings** This is a critical step to ensuring that everyone on the team is on the same page. Specific discussion suggestions include the following:

   Meet with the litigation counsel team. It is important to collectively meet as a team to define expectations for the review and production, including what resources can be made available for the e-discovery process and what service provider, if any, should be hired for this particular project.

   For law firms involved in establishing standard review procedures, schedule meetings with your client for the purposes of establishing a single point of contact. This contact can facilitate procuring the necessary electronic data, discussing how the collection of this data must proceed to stay within the bounds of discovery code and talking about any resources that may be made available under the purview of the client.

   Set a time to talk with all stakeholders and team members on the e-discovery team, mainly to discuss policies and procedures and to obtain buy-in from all on the protocol for the review and production you are developing.

TIP

Involving all stakeholders in the initial discussions about how a project will proceed is the best way to ensure that project team members are "on the same page" and that each team member commits to specific tasks and deadlines.

6. **Define search terms** Go over key legal documents and requests to fine-tune a list of initial search strings. Document the procedure you use to develop this list for future reference.

7. **Create your search parameters** Show your proposed policies and procedures to filter and reduce the result set into a group of documents that is manageable for your review team to process and create results.

8. **Choose relevant and useful software programs** Solicit bids and guidance on all possible software programs that your team might use throughout the entire lifespan of a particular case.

9. **Create and configure internal databases** Create a procedure and guideline for determining how the result of the review will be stored in your in-house databases.

10. **Develop a notebook for attorneys to refer to during the e-discovery process**
This high-level overview can assist counsel in gaining a sense of perspective for the process as you have outlined it.

11. **Create a quick reference card or memo for the reviewer team** A quick-reference list of policies and procedures will help attorneys navigate through the waters of e-discovery and ensure best results using the e-discovery provider software.

Evaluating the Potential E-discovery Review Project

Planning and setting expectations is critical to the success of any project, but even more so when so much is at stake as it is in litigation. Before beginning a document review as part of the e-discovery process, one must get an idea of the scope and tracking mechanisms a particular project has, especially with respect to keeping the product on schedule and on budget.

Here are some things to consider, according to Richard J. Wersinger, technical trainer and consultant:

- How many documents, or document pages, are included in the overall data set?

- How many documents reside in each custodian's data?

- How many document chains, or groups of documents, does this represent?

- How many duplicates are in the data universe?

- Do certain file types, such as spreadsheets or PowerPoint presentations, occur in unexpectedly large quantities?

Wersinger says, "Having this intelligence will bring greater control to the review process and enable the review team to create effective document review assignments, evaluate potential issues or risks, more accurately forecast review completion dates, and more effectively track progress against goals."

NOTE

Because it is important to visualize the capabilities offered by different document review platforms, we have provided a number of screen captures from different companies that provide such tools. Although we do not particularly promote or prefer one product over another, each of them does offer a unique set of features useful to illustrating certain points in this chapter. It is important to point out that for the sake of brevity, only a sample of review platforms are mentioned in this chapter. This should not be interpreted as somehow suggesting these other platforms are not worthwhile tools for your consideration.

Key Points in Selecting a Review Platform

Selecting a document review platform is as important as every other aspect of the e-discovery process. Therefore, this section provides a snapshot of some of the features and questions your team should consider:

- **Speedy and accurate review using modes** How does your review platform allow for review to take place? In a linear fashion? Through grouping via threads, topics, or subject lines? Does it utilize an advanced workflow process such as parallel-style reviews, enabling simultaneous review of the same documents for different issues? What information is quickly displayed to the reviewer: headers, snippets of documents, and/or other properties of the document? Is the screen use optimized for maximum efficiency, or is a lot of it wasted with unnecessary toolbars and other user interface elements? It is important to look carefully at the features and functionality critical for your review project and not focus on which platform has more "bells and whistles" than all the others. Features you don't need can actually distract from the tasks at hand as well as add unneeded complexity to a project.

- **Workflow management** The capability to manage and automate the document review process through review platform workflow methodologies is critical to the success of this type of project. Does the platform you're considering incorporate or offer multiple user roles? As explained by OnSite Sourcing, Inc. (ONSITE[3]), Figure 9.1 provides a breakdown of potential user roles, administrators, and end-users. Additional information is outlined later in the chapter explaining user roles and responsibilities.

Figure 9.1 Sample Overview of Document Review User Roles

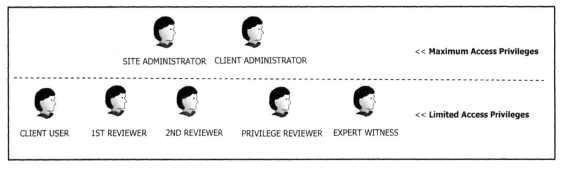

- **Easy tagging and assignment** After all, part of the rationale behind discovery is to identify key issues that may be problematic or otherwise require attention and assign them to the appropriate team members for further review. Once you find an issue with a tagged document, how easy is it to act on that information? How can you tag the issue for follow-up? Is there a simple and direct way to notify the appropriate stakeholders about a document or other item requiring further review? Once those stakeholders have reviewed the document, how is the status of those updates entered into the system so that no stone is left unturned? It is also useful to consider whether the platform utilizes automated conflict checking for tags to ensure that there are no tagging inconsistencies or errors. Automation can prevent attorneys from having to wait (potentially hours) for an administrator to assign the next batch of documents to review. Determine early in the case whether this feature is available within the tool you plan to select because it could substantially reduce the time required to manage the document review process.

■ **Identification of documents for opposing counsel review** Can you tag a set of documents as "privileged," making it easy to sort out which documents are destined for opposing counsel? Can you customize the level and amount of information given to opposing counsel? Does the review platform help you to generate a privilege log rather than requiring this to be done manually outside the platform?

■ **A variety of formats for exporting information** Can results of searches and detailed reviews be exported to non-proprietary formats, or via very accessible formats, such as PDF or XML? Can your review platform remove duplicate items during the export? Is there support for access protections such as passwords or dual authentication? Does the platform maintain the structure of the data as it was found—for instance, its folder hierarchy?

■ **Web-based applications** A review product that allows your review to be conducted through a Web-based browser is the height of convenience for the various members of your team who will be involved in the review. These people can have secure access to review the result set using software they all most likely already have in their possession. Most products with this capability also have the ability to grant access to just a single case, or a group of like cases, allowing multiple people to have access to a system that remains secure and protected. With Web-based review, there is no longer a need to print out documents for transport between teams when any sort of additional analysis is required.

■ **Simple highlighting of relevant hits** How are search results presented in the e-discovery review product? Are search terms highlighted within the context of each result set hit? Are they color-coded to reflect different kinds of issues? Are e-mail messages, documents, and attachments to messages indexed and included in this "hit-highlighting"? What formats for documents and attachments are supported? What about archiving and compression formats—will documents encoded with popular algorithms such as ZIP and RAR be able to be indexed, searched, and tagged for easy hit results? As shown in Figure 9.2, highlighting keyword hits allows the reviewer to quickly locate the hits for a more streamlined review of the document.

Figure 9.2 A Sample of Keyword Highlighting within a Document
Review Application

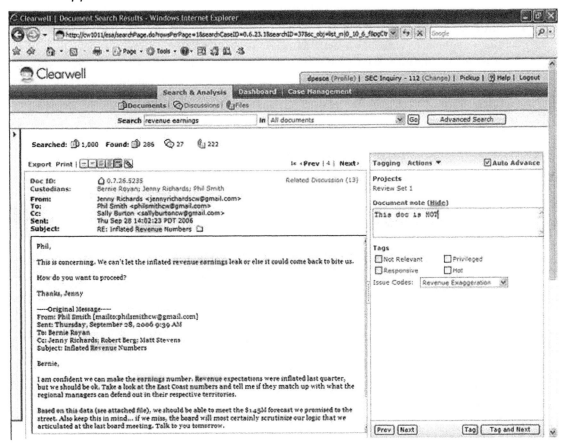

- **Risk management** Does the review application or product allow administrators to build
  in business rules that prevent (or at least limit) conflicting tags/coding from being applied
  to documents? Can access levels be customized/restricted for selective users to prevent
  them from accessing modules, tags, and so on that are not applicable to them? Does the

review application or product offer adequate checks and balances such as to prevent users from relying on complex searches/queries to ensure that all documents are reviewed, production sets are complete, and so forth?

- **Integration into overall e-discovery program** How well does the document review tool interconnect with your overall discovery program? Is the document review application or product compatible with vendor workflow/processes or does it "Plug and Play" with a variety of service providers? How easy is it to upload or produce out of the document review application or product?

NOTE

Some e-discovery companies have created applications or appliances that address the ability to integrate review platforms into the overall e-discovery process. One such application allows you to manage, process, review, and produce digital evidence without ever having to transfer data to a second application.

- **Scalability** Is the document review tool able to perform as well during both small- and large-scale projects, or does it favor one or the other? Are certain tasks (such as searching) impaired or do they slow down the database during the review process? Is database performance impacted once it reaches a certain number of records?

- **Flexibility** Is the document review tool friendly when scope, direction, or review style changes or is it difficult to change midstream?

- **Artificial intelligence and data analytics** How "intelligent: is your review platform? Sometimes the biggest hurdle for litigators is that they don't know what they don't know. Does your tool have an analytical or conceptual search engine built in? Does it integrate easily with such a tool? The ability to find otherwise "hidden" relevant data is paramount. Features, such as data analytics and artificial intelligence, can be extremely useful during the review process. One application, displayed in Figure 9.3, displays your ability to conceptually search and folder documents via "concept folders." During your review, concept folders will group information by a keyword as well as by a general concept. Depending on your case, this is extremely beneficial and could allow your team to prove or disprove allegations even more quickly.

Figure 9.3 Sample Review Application Offering Data Analytic Capabilities through the Use of Concept Clustering

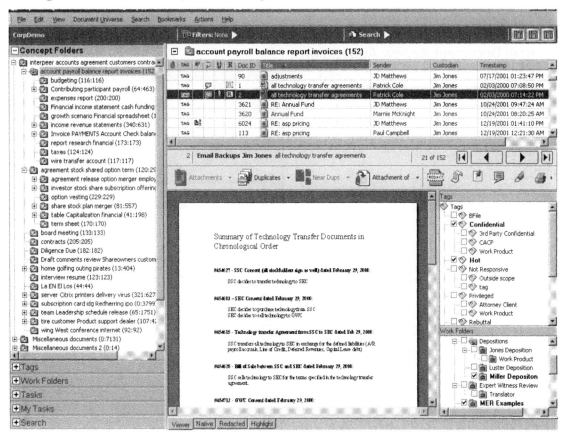

■ **Universal support** How does it handle native files? Do users launch native files locally on their machines or are native files rendered or launched within the application? If files are launched within the application, how many file types are supported? How does it handle unsupported file types? How does it handle double-byte/Unicode characters? Figure 9.4 displays FTI Consulting's Ringtail support for double-byte/Unicode characters. And following, Figure 9.5 displays its Unicode search capabilities. This particular review application provides full Unicode compliance for document review in more than 200 languages, including Mandarin, Japanese, Hebrew, Arabic, and Russian.

Figure 9.4 Sample Native Language (non-English) Support in FTI Consulting's Ringtail Document Review Application

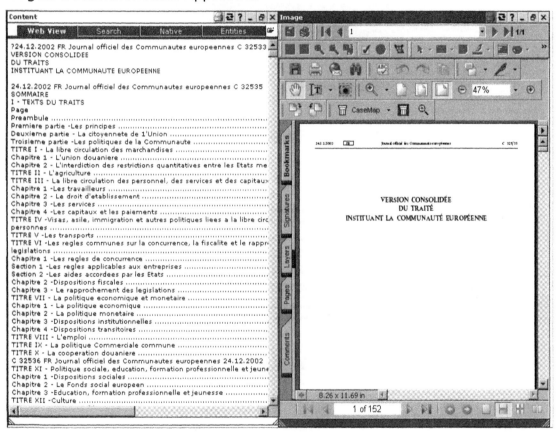

Figure 9.5 Non-English Keyword Searching within Ringtail

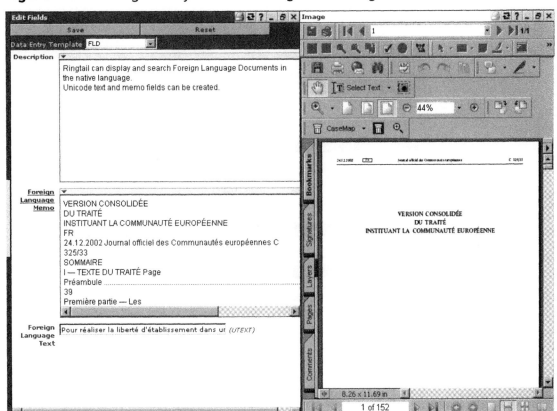

- **Administrative control** Does your internal system administrator have complete control of the process or must he or she lean on the vendor to perform basic tasks?

- **Metrics and reporting** Does your product allow you to generate summary statistics on the various status of cases integrated into the system? What about progress reporting, and metrics relating to the amount of work left to be done? Such statistics are vital to caseload management and ensuring that tight litigation deadlines are met (see Figure 9.6). Other questions might include what type of visibility does your tool offer you into the overall review process? Are "big brother" reports available to keep contract attorneys in check? Does it provide adequate metrics to allow you to make any midstream changes to your process/workflow/methodology to maximize performance/results?

Figure 9.6 Sample Reviewer Statistics within a Document Review Application

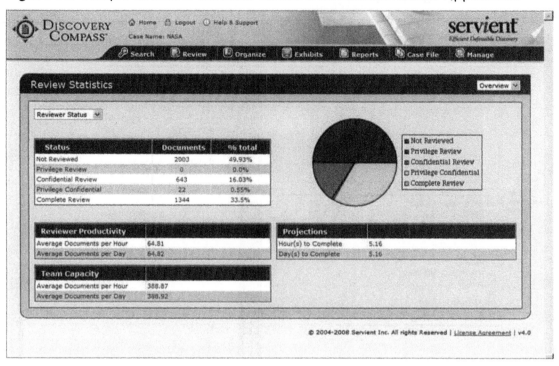

In the Real World

Document Review

A law firm used a document review product on a large manufacturing client's financial fraud investigation. In this particular case, the client hired the firm and outsourced the review of 50 Lotus Notes e-mail (NSF) files containing more than 190,000 messages. Regulators imposed a deadline to produce only the relevant, nonprivileged information in less than two months, which is an extremely aggressive schedule. The law firm was also forced to perform the document review on a shoestring budget.

The firm installed the review application and began indexing the data. The case administrator used some of the product's tagging capabilities to assign messages as equally as possible to eight attorneys, who were spread across the United States. Each attorney received secure, Web-based access to the product, and the case administrator used role-based security to ensure that each lawyer only had access to his or her assigned data set.

Continued

> The attorneys began their review. The lawyers proceeded to efficiently review and tag e-mails by discussion threads, and then by individual messages. The case administrator used the product's case analytics features to send daily reports to partners and the client that hired the firm, keeping all abreast of the progress throughout each step of the review process.
>
> Once the attorneys completed their review, the case administrator exported only the responsive messages in native format and delivered them to the government.

- **Native/image review and redaction capabilities** Does your application offer a premier viewing capability, markup, and digital mockup package through providing the ability to natively view files? If so, how many file types can the viewer support, including 2D and 3D AutoCAD drawings, EDA PCB/IC layouts and schematics, as well as scanned and raster documents from one viewer? Can you apply redactions to the native or natively rendered image? If so, are those native redactions accurately placed on a document? Are there any limitations to the types of files in which you should not natively render? One example, as shown in Figure 9.7, offers a glimpse of redaction within an image file.

Figure 9.7 Sample Scanned Image with Redaction Capabilities, by Concordance

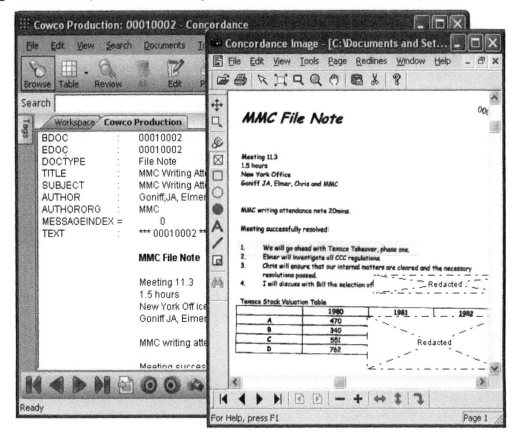

WARNING

When selecting a document review platform, ask about viewer capabilities to support the data types (file extensions) most common to your organization. If your organization creates and manages large volumes of engineering drawings or other specialized data, ask about the review platform's ability to view those types of files, as well as the ability to rotate drawings.

Understanding User Roles and Responsibilities

During the review process it is necessary for the project managers, legal team, and document reviewers to understand their roles and responsibilities. Consider the following roles and associated review platform capabilities. But remember, these are not exhaustive and the roles could vary from one platform to another.

- The **site administrator** is typically a member of the hosted review application's technical team (your vendor). Responsibilities and capabilities of the site administrator might include access to all features within the system; access to all clients and data within the system; user account creation; new case creation; new database creation; data loading; reviewer role creation; tag creation; tag rule creation; permission assignments; distribution of documents to folders; reviewer assignments; report generation, or production output and management.

- The **client administrator**, if you utilize a hosted review application or an internal system, could have very similar capabilities and responsibilities to the site administrator. However, the client administrator does not typically load data or create databases, but could do some or all of the following: add fields to the existing database structure; create new users; modify privileges; create tags and rules; create folders; manage reviewer assignments; generate reports; manage productions; and produce privilege logs.

- The **first-level reviewer** role is exactly what its name implies, the first level or initial review phase of the process. First-level reviewers, during this first pass of document review, usually have the most limited of capabilities available to them. They might be able to do the following: view the review section with documents in folders; tag documents; view the table with metadata information about the documents; view message threads; view parent/child relationships; view duplicate information; view or add comments; view files in native or image formats; or perform keyword searches. Figure 9.8 displays some of the features that might be available to a first-level reviewer.

Figure 9.8 Sample First-Level Reviewer Capabilities within a Review Platform

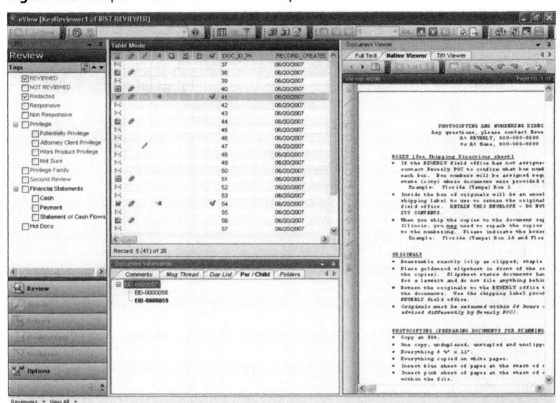

- The **second-level reviewer** performs the second review of the documents, and is therefore typically afforded the same functionality as the first-level reviewer. Again, those capabilities could include: viewing the review section with documents in folders; tagging documents; viewing the table with metadata information about the documents; viewing message threads; viewing parent/child relationships; viewing duplicate information; viewing or adding comments; viewing files in native or image formats; or performing keyword searches. The only difference is that the second-level reviewer will see previously entered tags, comments, and publicly saved searches.

- The **privilege reviewer** might have an even more defined task than the first- and second-level reviewers because the privilege reviewer is focused on reviewing the privileged set of documents. Therefore, these users typically have access to only privileged information, such as the privilege log, documents in privilege folders, redactions, and annotations. These users might be able to perform searches, but searches will be restricted to their set of privileged documents. Figure 9.9 provides a sample privilege reviewer document review screen, with privilege-only access, redactions, and previous tags.

Figure 9.9 Sample Privilege Reviewer Capabilities within a Review Platform

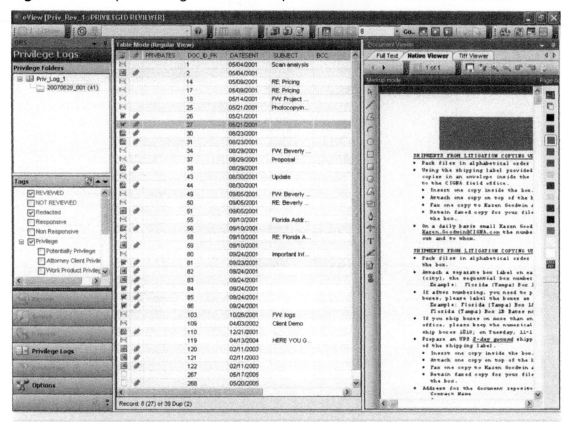

- The **expert witness reviewer** serves a specific function within the review process. The expert witness is just that, a subject matter expert having a need to review documents for possibly the purposes of a deposition, subject matter report, case strategy formulation, or testimony. Therefore, like the privilege reviewer, the expert witness typically has access to a subset of documents specific to his or her focus, but might have the same functionality within the review application as that of a first- or second-level reviewer.

NOTE

If your vendor offers a hosted review application and does not allow you to manage part of the review process, it might be time to consider other options. Client administrators reduce response times required by vendors and provide your team greater control over the actual process.

The Benefits of Using an Early Case Assessment (ECA) Strategy

Throughout this chapter, we have been discussing risks and costs associated with the document review process. But more importantly, large volumes of information have caused this proliferation in reducing the number of documents requiring review. Therefore, it is not enough to collect everything and process it through traditional e-discovery data discovery (EDD) technologies to minimize the review. More advanced methodologies and technologies have been hitting the market for the past couple of years, known as early case assessment (ECA) tools. These tools provide you with the ability to de-duplicate, identify key relationships, analyze e-mail conversations, search by keyword or phrase, and restrict data within certain date ranges. Overall, you should be able to accomplish the following with a suite of ECA tools:

- Cluster data by concepts.

- Create priority sets of data through directories or other highlighted folder features.

- Identify threads of e-mail messages which are critical to the case.

- Identify key relationships as they correspond to topics and time frames.

- Conduct traditional and advanced searches, in English and non-English documents.

- Filter corrupted content to eliminate delays in indexing.

The Essentials of an ECA

As stated by MetaLINCS, Seagate's E-discovery solutions provider and one of the pioneers of ECA, "In a perfect world, as soon as defense counsel is notified of a pending litigation, counsel performs enough analysis to create a detailed plan regarding the scope of the case, paying special attention to identifying relevant electronic documentation. This includes all locations of data and its custodians. In our imperfect, actual world counsel is buried under the current case load and has little, if any, time to plan for a case in advance. Absent a 'Rocket-Docket' scenario, or rules in certain local jurisdictions that accelerate the process, e-discovery proceeds slowly on the new case—with much rework, reprocessing and scope-creep compounding the problem. Often, significant attorney attention is applied only during the review phase. If the case settles, it does on the steps of the courthouse just prior to trial and after spending the maximum possible on e-discovery. The solution, of course, is to accomplish meaningful ECA with minimum attorney labor by leveraging scarce attorney time."[1] For more information go to www.negotiationlawblog.com/EarlyCaseAssessment.pdf.

TIP

If a custodian involved in the discovery process happens to subscribe to automated e-mail lists, which sent multiple messages to him or her over a period that can span several years (years that could be relevant to the case), these messages—which can be considered as "spam" or not—may litter your result set, numbering in the thousands and contributing no value to the case. If these messages make it into the review platform and the review team manually sorts through them, it is possible that your company could spend a significant amount of review for useless data. Another option, through the use of ECAs, is to filter data for particular domain names (e.g., website.com) to eliminate that information early in the process. Not only will you save review time, but also you will store less ESI in your review application, potentially reducing monthly hosting fees.

Per MetaLINCS, you should consider the following items for the control that ECA offers your team:

- It utilizes some of the most advanced technologies available to process the masses of ESI.

- It automates de-duplication and first-pass–culling capabilities to reduce data sets far greater than by the use of traditional e-discovery processing.

- It analyzes data for keywords, concepts, timelines, people, and threads.

- It extracts and leverages metadata to enhance searching.

- It prioritizes the data for a more efficient and effective review.

- It quickly identifies irrelevant data determined to be non-responsive.

- It verifies that your custodian and witness lists are correct.

- It uses the results to credibly argue against your adversary's overly broad discovery requests.

Early Identification of Potentially Responsive Custodians

ECA is useful in not only reducing the overall population of data before the review, but also providing you the ability to identify key and previously unidentified custodians. Utilizing tools to map the activities of potential key witnesses or suspects is critical to formulating an overall discovery strategy. Today, through the use of ECA applications, this process is more automated and user-friendly, providing the benefits of this technology to your legal team. As shown in Figure 9.10, the ability to link key custodians through e-mail communications is critical to identifying additional custodian interviews, custodians with the greatest number of communications, and relevant time frames as to when these conversations actually took place.

Figure 9.10 A Sample Custodian Chart Linking People

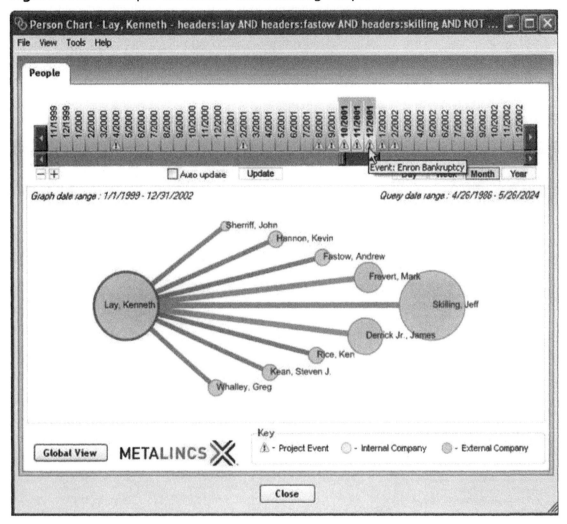

Getting to the Heart of the Matter

ECAs have become a valuable method for reducing data sets to identify the primary case contents prior to the start of the review. In many instances, through a combination of the legal team's expertise and analytical technologies, it might be possible to identify consistent patterns, isolate those patterns, and categorize them as responsive or non-responsive. Although e-discovery providers are able to provide assistance in this area through traditional processing and review applications, it might be more efficient to utilize technologies that de-duplicate, identify clusters of documents, and create a more meaningful set of ESI prior to unleashing ESI to the document review team. MetaLINCS, as shown in Figure 9.11, demonstrates the hierarchical document organization that can be used globally or within custodian sets to dramatically improve reviewer efficiency by showing documents grouped with other documents with similar content. The hierarchical organization means you can determine how focused you want to be with reviewer assignments. By collectively identifying concepts regarding a matter, the legal team is able to create theories and determine potential gaps in those theories more quickly than in the past.

Another efficiency feature in some review platforms is to score documents based on certain

Figure 9.11 A Sample of Hierarchical Concept Folder Capabilities

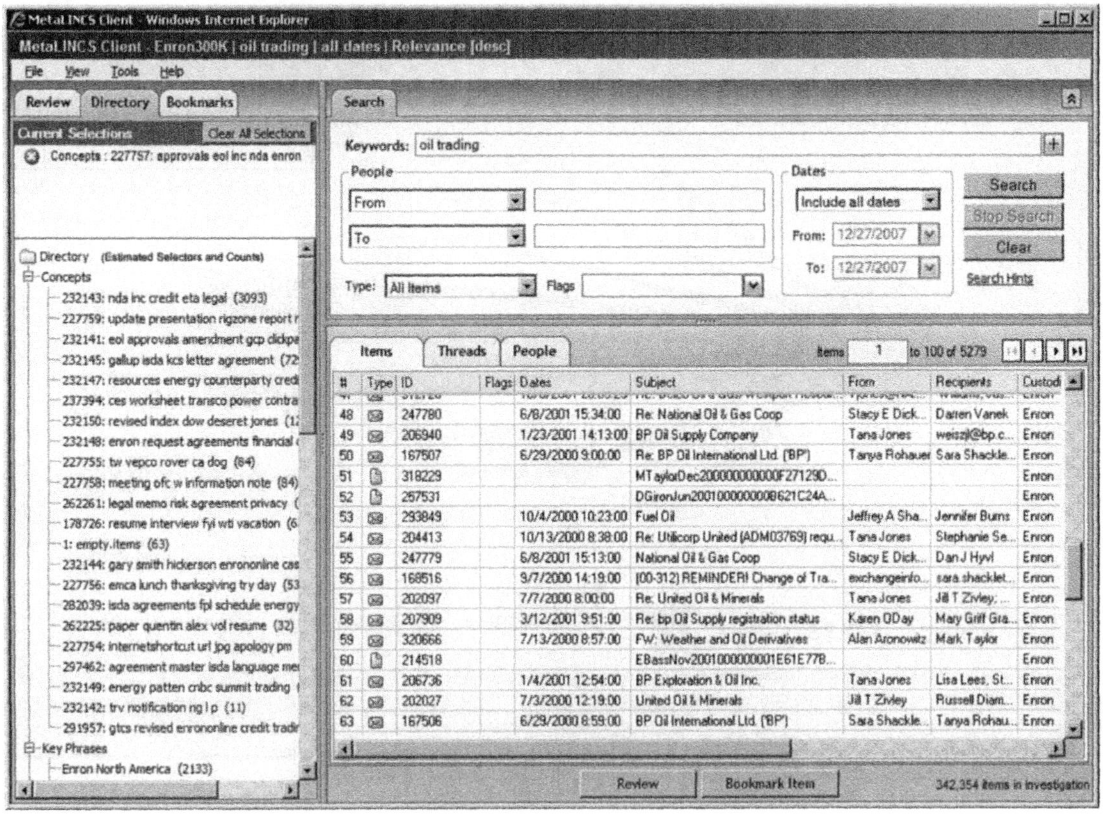

criteria (e.g., keywords, custodians). On the right side of the screen in Figure 9.12, you'll note that each document has a score. This score identifies the relevancy of it based on a keyword search, a date range, a custodian, or even the subject of the e-mail. Applications that allow you to identify relevancy early in the case limits your need to review non-responsive documents, and could even allow you to capture potentially responsive documents earlier in the process. By narrowing the population of documents to review, the overall costs and time are reduced.

Figure 9.12 Ranking Search Hits by Score: Viewing the Most Relevant Hits First

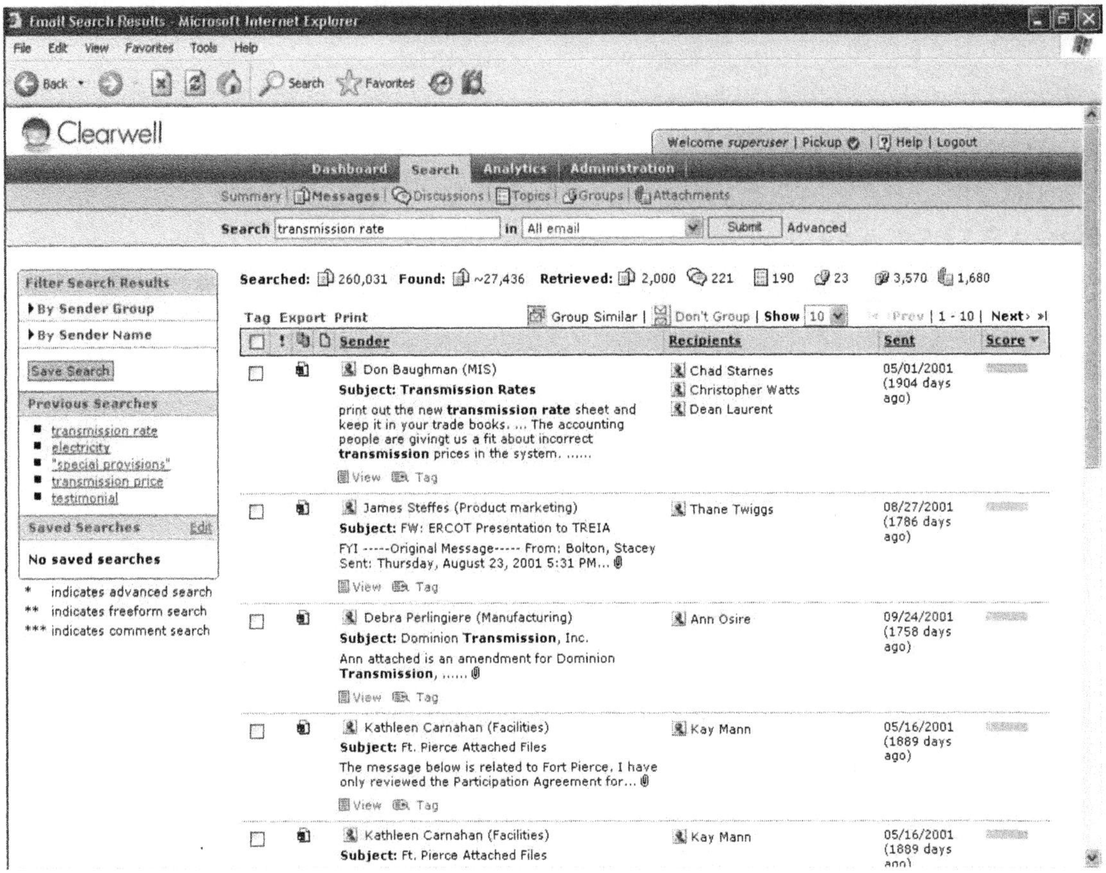

Search and pattern recognition is becoming a more widely used feature throughout e-discovery applications, and although some of the responsibility still resides with the reviewer, bulk tagging of documents eliminates the need to review non-responsive ESI. This ability is saving legal teams money and allowing them to meet their deadlines.

E-mail Thread Analysis

Although identifying potentially responsive e-mail messages and attachments is a necessary requirement during the review process, the ability to chronologically order discussion (e-mail) threads can prove to be invaluable. Even though you have a need to review documents for potentially responsive and privileged ESI, the actual discussions themselves could provide further insight enabling you to receive a settlement or dismissal from the courts.

One company, Clearwell Systems, Inc., has patent-pending technology (algorithms) that dynamically links together all related messages into a chronological thread which captures the entire discussion, including all replies, carbon copies and forwards. By viewing the thread, reviewers can identify the most important aspect of the review: who, what, where, and when. These algorithms analyze not only the contents of e-mail messages and attachments, but also the associated metadata.

Figures 9.13 and 9.14 provide a glimpse of two different review applications' ability to display e-mail message threads. Reviewers can understand individual e-mails in the context of an entire thread and review by thread, increasing review speed and accuracy. As shown in Figure 9.14, graphical and text-oriented presentation of the information shows both the structure and the content of a thread.

Figure 9.13 Sample E-mail Thread Identifying Conversations

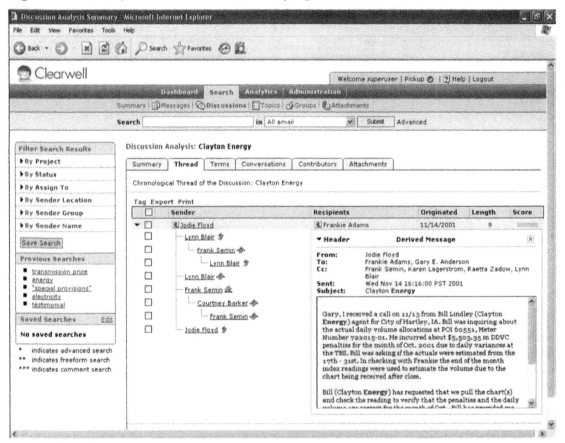

Figure 9.14 Sample E-mail Thread Analysis Identifying the Sequence
of Communications

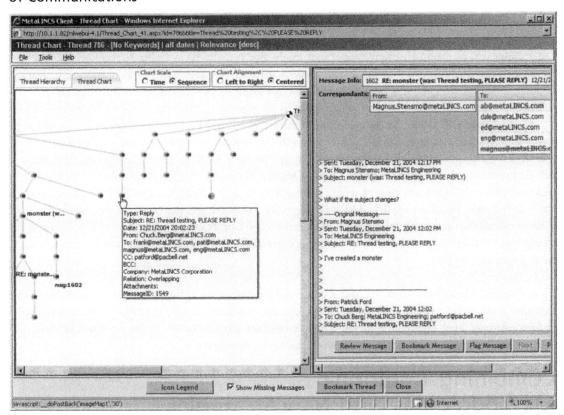

The Identification of Missing Messages

Traditionally and in the world of computer forensics, we reviewed allocated (active) files for responsive e-mail messages. Through those messages found within the active files, we were able to identify gaps in the string of the messages. Ultimately, it was a task to further investigate missing messages by searching unallocated or slack space (space that is inactive and cannot be seen by the end-user) on the media. However, this process was time-consuming and often fruitless. Today, it is possible to utilize automated technologies to identify missing messages by analyzing the active e-mail messages.

One appliance that provides the benefits of analyzing e-mail messages without utilizing forensic utilities (at least not initially) is Clearwell's Intelligent Email Platform. This appliance allows you to quickly identify missing messages within a string of e-mail messages. Through the use of Clearwell's Derived Email Processing (DEP), you can perform analyses within e-mails, extracting information that might otherwise be missed through other platforms or analysis. The analysis conducted through DEP allows you to even identify messages that might not actually be available in the e-mail file. Because of this analysis, you may be able to identify missing messages within a conversation to learn additional information about a case, ask additional questions of custodians, or even determine whether preservation was conducted accordingly.

Using Clearwell's model, we have utilized their Derived Email Processing model to dissect missing email messages. For example, when a sender forwards or replies to an email, the original message text is included within the body of the new email. Using Microsoft Outlook to further this example, the default prefix to start a message includes: "------Original Message------" or it's possible to configure each line of the included text to start with a delimiter such as ">". With Clearwell's DEP capabilities, the body of every email is parsed, included messages are extracted, and the messages are classified as derived emails. Further, and by using their advanced recognition features, you will be able to account for changes in the message prefix. DEP's advanced recognition features allow it to account for changes in message prefixes such as

"-----Original Message-----" or ">" and account for their notation as forward/reply levels change. For example, when using a prefix such as ">", it is common to add an additional prefix to notate a change in forward/reply level. The second forward/reply would use a prefix of ">>", the third would use ">>>", etc. For more information, go to www.clearwellsystems.com.

Combining Traditional Methodologies with New Strategies

Traditional EDD processing techniques are still an extremely useful mechanism for reducing the overall set of ESI requiring review. However, EDD companies cannot simply process all data any longer because of client costs. Therefore, even the most traditional EDD processing centers are creatively assessing methods and technologies to improve their clients' bottom line. In Figure 9.15, one company demonstrates an approach that could be considered in lieu of purchasing an in-house e-discovery collection, processing, and review platform. This presents a strong return on investment (ROI) for your company to entertain prior to engaging outside processing vendors. The ROI approach provides companies with a comprehensive toolkit to efficiently convert data to evidence through traditional e-discovery and review technologies.

Figure 9.15 Traditional EDD Processing Meets New Methodologies

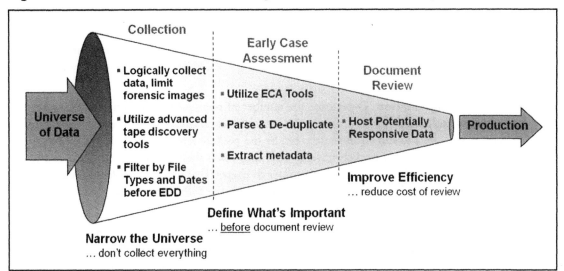

Reducing the Data Set

How can we quickly and effectively reduce the population of ESI using traditional EDD methodologies? Easy; by limiting your collections, utilizing tape discovery technologies that are flourishing, and filtering files by file types and dates before entering the EDD processing component. However, there are some technical considerations, such as the inability to filter an individual e-mail message (e.g., an MSG file) contained within an e-mail container (e.g., Microsoft Outlook's PST file). Therefore, your e-discovery processing vendor should identify pitfalls in the thinking of this strategy and combine traditional processing with possibly an ECA tool. From experience, applications such as Clearwell's Intelligent Email Processing allow you to de-duplicate.

Technical Issues Regarding Document Review

Reviews aren't done alone by attorneys. E-discovery reviews are part of a process that requires carefully orchestrated liaising with your in-house technical staff, including information technology (IT) professionals. They may request some information on how best to help you, as the attorney, better manage the review process.

Here are some items for IT professionals to look for in coordinating the e-discovery review process:

- **Internet service providers (ISPs)** Focus on two areas: reliability and performance. Reliability is most critical, especially if your review team consists of attorneys spread across a wide geographical distance. You want them to be able to conduct the review online and suffer no downtime. Bandwidth availability and overall speed are the next most important items. A good question to ask (especially in the case of vendor-hosted review platforms) is whether multiple ISPs are utilized so that if the primary ISP goes down a backup

ISP could seamlessly maintain availability of access. With large files and vast amounts of information to consume, it's important that highly priced review team members be productive in their time and not just sit waiting for items to download.

■ **The local area network (LAN)** Ensure that routers, hubs, cables, modems, and firewalls all support high-speed connections. In the case of the vendor, make sure their systems are similarly secure.

■ **Routing information** Determine the number of hops associated with traffic between locations and review. You can use the Tracert command within DOS (the disk operating system on a PC) to show the route taken by the packets across an IP network. Tracert lists all the routers that packets traverse until they reach their destination and will also tell you how long each "hop" takes from router to router. This will provide lots of relevant information that the IT professional can share with the ISP to maximize performance.

■ **Firewall operation** A firewall is necessary for almost every review process, because it plays a vital role in both the performance and security of your network. Check whether your firewall is blocking necessary ports. Does it support connections through encrypted virtual private networks (VPNs)? Perhaps there is a method of using Secure Socket Tunneling Protocol (SSTP) to avoid VPN client configuration hassles. The less overhead and configuration required the better.

Advancements in the Review Process

Traditional review is here to stay for some time, but as enterprise applications become available, the overall process will inevitably change. Although most review application companies offer streamlined and efficient hosted document review platforms, others have built enterprise applications that not only address the document review phase, but also provide a platform for collecting, processing, analyzing, reviewing, and producing potentially responsive ESI. Some of the features offered by these companies include the ability to:

■ Collect data directly from e-mail archives and e-mail servers.

■ De-duplicate and cull the ESI.

■ Perform ECAs to formulate a case strategy.

■ Identify key people, e-mail threads, or concepts.

■ Decipher code words and jargon.

■ Folder and tag ESI efficiently and effectively.

■ Identify privileged documents earlier in the process.

■ Review documents in the same application in which they were collected.

■ Produce documents in native, TIFF, or PDF format, with or without an associated load file for another litigation support application.

Document review applications providing these capabilities are powerful and enticing, and although they are somewhat newer to the marketplace, they are making headway.

Summary

The document review process incorporates more than just the review. Every aspect of the e-discovery process affects the document review phase of your project. Therefore, it is critical to understand what the market has to offer and to carefully select tools or platforms that meet your requirements. Remember to consider many of the areas we suggested when selecting a review platform. Also, sometimes one review platform fits the mold for every case. One matter might require a tool that provides very strong concept folder capabilities, whereas another matter could call for an application with well-defined workflow methodologies. Throughout this chapter, our goal was to provide you with enough options that your team is able to carefully consider multiple review tools, create a streamlined review program, and identify what is most important to your review team.

Solutions Fast Track

The Cost of Document Review

☑ Although preserving and collecting ESI are a concern for legal and technology professionals everywhere, it is also becoming increasingly necessary to acquire talent that understands the entire e-discovery process.

☑ Because preservation, collections, and processing are a nominal cost when compared with the document review process, it is becoming even more important to work with teams of people who have document review experience, training on multiple review platforms, and the ability to quickly understand certain document review application pitfalls or limitations.

☑ It is common for teams of contract attorneys to manage or assist with the document review.

Creating a Streamlined Document Review Workflow

☑ Create a sound support structure with predictable steps and outcomes.

☑ Manage risk and cost, and always attempt to reduce the risk for error.

☑ Incorporate standard project management components into the plan.

Key Points in Selecting a Review Platform

☑ Consider multiple components when selecting a document review platform.

☑ Understand the roles and responsibilities available within a review platform.

☑ Create a selection process, possibly a score card, to eliminate review tools that will not meet your needs and highlight the ones that could potentially act as your vendor.

Understanding User Roles and Responsibilities

☑ During the review process it is necessary for the project managers, legal team, and document reviewers to understand their roles and responsibilities. Responsibilities and capabilities of the site administrator might include access to all features within the system; access to all clients and data within the system; user account creation; new case creation; new database creation; data loading; reviewer role creation; tag creation; tag rule creation; permission assignments; distribution of documents to folders; reviewer assignments; report generation, or production output and management.

The Benefits of Using an Early Case Assessment (ECA) Strategy

- ☑ Strategy…strategy…strategy. Utilize ECA to create a strong case strategy.

- ☑ Identify missing e-mail messages through tools available on the market. This ensures that you are able to understand what was collected and what was not collected.

- ☑ E-mail thread analysis and relevance ranking are useful techniques available in both ECA and review tools.

Technical Issues Regarding Document Review

- ☑ Remember to ask your potential vendor about their bandwidth and ensure that your bandwidth is quick enough to support your review team.

- ☑ Check on security and the number of connections (hops) encountered to and from your review vendor, and ensure that your fault tolerance systems are properly installed.

Advancements in the Review Process

- ☑ Traditional review is here to stay, but keep an eye out for data analytics and ECA tools that could ultimately replace traditional review platforms.

- ☑ Identify the most important document review features, and don't purchase something because it offers all the bells and whistles. Sometimes that's just too much.

Frequently Asked Questions

Q: What is the single largest cost for most e-discovery project?

A: Document Review. Because of the cost and time involved in the document review process, it is the single largest cost to companies. With new technologies, this cost might be reduced in the future.

Q: What are five steps to streamline your document review?

A: Assign a project manager, develop an "important contacts" list, identify document reviewer assignments and roles, create a first draft of a review timeline, schedule and perform initial planning meetings.

Q: What is a useful technique in reducing ESI requiring review?

A: Early Case Assessment. By utilizing technologies avaialble, it is possible to reduce the overall population of ESI requiring review. However, it is important to remember that early case assessment might not be appropriate for every case.

Q: How many different roles could be assigned during the review process?

A: Five to six reviewer roles is reasonable to consider when conducting a review. Those roles could include, but are not limited to: Administrators (both vendor and client), First-level reviewers, Second-level reviewers, Privileged Reviewers, and Expert Witnesses.

Q: What type of document review platform export features should be available to you?

A: It is useful to have a document review platform that has the ability to export results to PDF or XML. XML is quickly becoming a standard throughout the discovery industry as it is transferrable into different platforms. It is also important to have a document review platform that removes duplicate items during the export, as well as the ability to maintain the structure of the data upon export.

Q: How can you manage document reviewer productivity?

A: Reporting features within a document review platform are the best manner for overseeing and determining document reviewer productivity. Typically known as "big brother" reports, they can be very useful in creating a review timeline, and possibly even a production timeline.

Q: How can you reduce the initial population of ESI?

A: Limit the ESI that is collected. By utilizing new methodologies and technologies, it is possible to reduce the set of ESI before it is ever processed or reviewed.

Note

1. "Early Case Assessment: Limit E-Discovery Expense and Improve Litigation Results." Seagate Services, 2008. www.negotiationlawblog.com/EarlyCaseAssessment.pdf.

Chapter 10

Headlines, Redlines, and Deadlines: Production Practicalities in Today's E-discovery Environment

Solutions in this chapter:

- **Production: Federal and State Rules**
- **Getting the Right Folks Involved**
- **Production Practicalities**
- **Data Conversion As It Relates to Production**

☑ **Summary**

☑ **Solutions Fast Track**

☑ **Frequently Asked Questions**

Introduction

There is no doubt that every decision made in the e-discovery process plays a critical role in the larger case as a whole, but ultimately, all of those decisions lead up to one of the most stressful times during your case: the production. Was your production in the correct format? Were all privileged documents identified and removed appropriately and/or redacted properly? Was the quality control protocol used thorough and accurate? And when do you need to produce again? At the beginning of your matter when everyone is working to establish the proper protocols for data preservation, collection, processing, and review, you also need to be thinking critically about the end of discovery and your production. Decisions made early on, during a meet-and-confer process or at the time of data processing, can dramatically affect the manner in which you need to produce, and ultimately, how long it will take.

Let's face it—there are a lot of moving parts during discovery and it takes a great deal of hard work to ensure that everything comes together so that deadlines and budgets are comfortably met or even exceeded! Successful productions are attributable not only to the teams of attorneys but also to the teams of dedicated and experienced litigation support folks. It is absolutely critical to have the right people involved in your matter to look out for the best interests of your company or the end-client and to meet or exceed those deadlines and budgets mentioned earlier.

Therefore, this chapter focuses on the practicalities of producing information in today's e-discovery environment and will touch on a number of key items when involved in matters with electronic evidence and production requirements. But first, a little bit of background…

Production: Federal and State Rules

On December 1, 2006, Amendments to the Federal Rules of Civil Procedure went into effect detailing how electronically stored information (ESI) should be handled. For the purposes of this chapter, we'll focus on the meet-and-confer process and the need to discuss forms of production and agreements for handling the inadvertent production of privileged ESI. Rule 34 allows the party requesting documents to specify the form of production of ESI. Generally, parties involved in the litigation should agree to the form of production at the Rule 26(f) meet and confer. From a practical standpoint, set this agreement up-front because you will want to ensure that the form decided upon is still an option after all processing and review have been completed. Also, because many states either have rules already in place or are looking to amend their rules to include procedures for handling ESI, it is mandatory to thoroughly review and understand any state or local rules that are applicable to your case. At the beginning of any new matter, make sure to review all pertinent rules as they relate to the discovery of electronic information, and involve the right folks to bring you up to speed as these rules are critical to the successful outcome of your matter.

NOTE

It is likely that one of the most important aspects of the Rules will be your understanding of Rule 26(b)5, which allows a party to request the return of ESI that was inadvertently produced. If you make such a request, remember to provide the basis or reason as to why you are recalling the ESI.

Planning for Production

As with all aspects of e-discovery, it is critical to properly plan for the production phase of your case. For a successful production, it is essential to initially focus on the following components:

- Identification of appropriate technical and legal resources

- Planning meetings early in the process

- Consideration of the review platform and forms of production

- Selection of vendors for hosting and conversion

- Assessment of the review workflow based on the production requirements

- Consideration of privilege issues including privilege log creation and document redactions

- Identification method for handling productions from opposing parties

Although they depend on many other factors within a case, the preceding items should be outlined, documented, and detailed individually to ensure that everyone on the team is on target with the production objectives. If a team does not have a production plan in place, it will be detrimental to the productivity of the case as a whole.

Getting the Right Folks Involved

As with any project, it is critical to compile the proper team to accomplish the results of the project or case. By this stage of the game, your team could include in-house and outside legal teams, project managers, case managers, and litigation support analysts including ESI-focused technical resources, paralegals, document reviewers, experts, consultants, and vendors. The responsibilities of these team members during production might include:

- In-house legal team:
  - Negotiating the production format
  - Reporting to regulatory agencies, if applicable
  - Communicating with regulatory agencies, if applicable
  - Communicating with outside counsel
- Outside counsel:
  - Negotiating the production format
  - Providing and training document reviewers
  - Reporting to in-house counsel or in-house legal team members
- Law firm case managers:
  - Identifying and managing vendor relationships
  - Establishing case- and production-specific timelines
  - Working to keep the project, production, and budget on track

- Litigation support analysts and project managers:
    - Running queries to identify privileged information
    - Providing reports regarding production volume
    - Identifying and managing vendor relationships
    - Reviewing the production output from the vendor to ensure quality
    - Working to identify and resolve issues with unique data types for production
    - Advising legal teams on production best practices
    - Managing and performing the production process
- Paralegals:
    - Running queries to identify privileged information
    - Managing review teams and assigning documents for review
- Document reviewers:
    - Performing responsive and subject matter review
    - Reviewing privileged documents
    - Redacting documents as required
    - Creating a privilege log
- Experts:
    - Reviewing materially relevant information
    - Assisting in the creation of case strategies based on the review of production output
- Vendors and consultants:
    - Working with litigation support analysts on production items as they relate to unique data types for proper production
    - Providing the hosting solution
    - Producing documents in TIFF, PDF, native or hard-copy format
    - Providing privilege and production reports

Production Practicalities

Planning meetings are an effective means for reducing risks and inefficiencies prior to producing ESI to opposing parties and regulatory agencies. Regardless of the matter, a planning meeting provides the ability to establish necessary quality control measures, timelines, and the ability to establish responsibilities as well as an overall game plan.

Choice of production provides your team the opportunity to negotiate the format in which you will provide ESI to outside parties. Although your options include image-based productions (TIFF or PDF), productions hosted within a document review application, hard-copy productions, or native file productions, your production should ultimately be cost-effective. With all considerations throughout the life cycle of e-discovery management, the choices of production formats come with benefits and disadvantages, some of which are noted in Table 10.1.

Table 10.1 Pros and Cons of Various E-discovery Production Formats

Production Format	Benefits	Disadvantages
Image-based production (TIFF or PDF)	Static format, metadata cannot be changed	Cost
	Format provides the ability for virtually anyone to view the images.	Limited metadata might be available to opposing parties.
	Easy to view during depositions or trials	Depending on negotiations between parties, text may not be available and performing optical character recognition (OCR) at a later time might incur additional costs.
	Ability to Bates- and confidentiality–stamp each page	Large data storage and backup server space could be required.
	Maintains integrity and authenticity	
	Might save time when producing	
	Widely accepted method of production	
	Ability to limit metadata fields available to opposing parties	
	Widely accepted method of production	
	Software requirements are limited to provide the ability for virtually anyone to view the image.	
Review database/ application	Responding party might be able to control documents reviewed by further culling the producing data set within a database	Train users

Continued

Table 10.1 Continued. Pros and Cons of Various E-discovery Production Formats

Production Format	Benefits	Disadvantages
	Responding party might be able to monitor progress of opposing party's review – usage tracking	Cost, depending on the application
	Flexibility available for querying data	Security of documents might be compromised as some review applications allow users to access the database from any location, providing the ability to download documents to local machines or servers
	Collaboration	Vendor resource conflicts
	Multiparty access	
	Parent/child relationships and conversation threads might be maintained.	
	Searchable text is available.	
	Loading the data into a review application could be done quickly.	
Native file formats	Reduced costs	Metadata is at risk for changes.
	System and application metadata is available to the requesting party.	Data can be manipulated to view aspects not available in static formats.
	Documents appear in the same view in which they were created.	Native applications are required to review the file.
	Ability to view hidden data, embedded text, and tracked changes	Software application license costs might be incurred.
	Ability to view spreadsheet formulas	Possibility of executing macros (or viruses), which could cause local computer or server issues for the reviewing party
	Shorter processing time	

Continued

Table 10.1 Continued. Pros and Cons of Various E-discovery Production Formats

Production Format	Benefits	Disadvantages
Hard copy (paper)	Ability to review without the use of a computer system	Cost and time to create multiple copies
	Ability to Bates- and confidentiality-stamp, as in TIFF or PDF productions	Scanning and OCR might be required to integrate with reviewing forms of native ESI.
	Ability to view the data at face value	No electronic tagging
		No method for searching without scanning and OCR or text data
		No metadata available for searching
		If a large production, space needed to store boxes and staff required to manage and organize

Managing Production Costs

Costs can be an issue regardless of the type of production format you choose. More importantly, you will incur costs leading up to production, an issue we discuss in other chapters. But you can at least estimate your production costs based on the format you choose. In most cases, production costs are related to the output type or format of production by volume. This means that if you choose TIFF or PDF format, the cost might be associated with a per-page, per-document, or per-gigabyte volume. If you choose native format productions, the costs could be calculated with per-hour rates to export ESI onto media. The document review application option will most likely have an associated per–gigabyte, per-month fee in addition to a licensing fee per user per month. Hard-copy productions, similar to TIFF or PDF, could have a per-page cost associated with them as well. Additionally, do not forget about the costs associated with storage media for delivering the production, as well as the shipping or delivery charges. Because the volume of production could dramatically change during the review, it is critically important to discuss the basis of production costs up-front to make sure production costs are fair for both the client and the vendor should assumptions dramatically change.

TIP

Because costs are extremely important regarding production considerations, we have included in the following scenario some calculations that might help you. Based on your review, you will need to produce a certain portion of the population of records. Remember to estimate some production costs based on the number of pages, not records. Other production costs might be related to the volume of records (typically in gigabytes). Please note that costs and/or variables may depend on the vendor or firm assisting you with this process and that these are meant to provide only a general guideline to you.

TIFF or PDF Production Costs

Here is a list of calculations for determining TIFF or PDF production costs.

TIFF/PDF creation = (# of pages) x (cost per page)

Branding on images = (# of pages) x (cost per page)

Load file creation = (per-hour rate) x (# of hours)

Hard-drive costs to store load file and images = (cost per hard drive) x (quantity of hard drives)

Delivery costs = (shipping rate) x (number of packages)

Total costs = [TIFF/PDF creation + branding + load file creation + media storage + delivery]

Review Database/Application Production Costs

Here is a list of calculations for determining review database/application production costs.

Database setup costs = (one-time setup charge or hourly rate) x (# of new databases)

Licenses = (# of licenses required) x (cost per license per month)

Host native records = (per-gigabyte hosting fee/monthly storage) x (# of gigabytes of data)

Host TIFF/PDF images = (per-image hosting fee/monthly storage) x (# of images)

Project management = (hourly rate) x (# of hours devoted to management)

Technical case management = (hourly rate) x (# of hours devoted to technical resolution)

Training = (hourly or per-session rate) x (# of sessions or hours)

One-time costs = [setup + training]

Monthly costs = [licenses + hosting (native and/or images) + project management + technical case management]

Native File Production Costs

Here is a list of calculations for determining native file production costs.

Project management = (hourly rate) x (# of hours dedicated to tasks)

Technical time = (hourly rate) x (# of hours dedicated to tasks)

Hard-drive costs to store load file and images = (cost per hard drive) x (quantity of hard drives)

Delivery costs = (shipping rate) x (number of packages)

Monthly costs = [project management + technical time + media + delivery]

Hard-Copy Production Costs

Here is a list of calculations for determining hard-copy production costs.

Project management = (hourly rate) x (# of hours dedicated to tasks)

Technical time = (hourly rate) x (# of hours dedicated to tasks)

Printing/blowbacks = (cost per page) x (# of pages)

Standard field coding = (cost per record) x (# of records)

Additional field coding = (cost per record) x (# of records)

Unitization = (cost per page) x (# of records) – usually included with coding, if coding is performed

Delivery costs = (shipping rate) x (number of packages)

Monthly costs = [project management + technical time + printing/blowbacks + coding + unitization + delivery]

Delivery Timelines and Methods

As with managing any type of project, production management is no different when it comes to creating a deliverable timeline. Therefore, you need to create a timeline that not only allows you to meet the production deadline, but also allows you to manage the production's quality and volume. One of the key decisions to account for when creating the timeline is to determine administratively exactly how you are going to produce—via a complete delivery of production data or a rolling delivery of data. With a complete delivery, the entire production will be delivered at one time, whereas rolling deliveries will provide for multiple (and generally smaller) production sets to the opposing party or government agency.

Whether delivering a complete or a rolling production, both parties should work together to load a smaller sample subset of data to confirm that all requirements from both sides are being met. This approach will reduce inevitable frustration and save time and money downstream when dealing with any potential issues or pitfalls of the production that might arise during the review of data by each side.

Although rolling productions might seem like a good idea—depending on circumstances particular to your matter—there are some considerations to take into account, such as what data to receive first, as well as what types of tracking mechanisms are required. Questions you should ask during production negotiations regarding the production delivery schedule could include the following:

- Should we consider delivery of the production on a rolling basis or a complete set?

- Should the production be de-duplicated globally or by custodian? This is a key decision to be addressed at the beginning with your vendor during processing and conversion.

- Will the deponent's questions be based on certain aspects of the production?

- Which custodians take priority, and should those be our primary concern if we select a rolling production?

- Is a rolling production even possible due to time constraints for our review?

- How will we track the receipt of one or more production sets?

- What steps can we take to ensure the integrity of each production?

With all aspects of your production, plan accordingly and do not wait until the last minute to decide which schedule is most appropriate to meet your particular deadline. If you find that your schedule is limited, consider employing technologies that could assist with the process. Also, it is absolutely critical to never assume that just because your data is electronic in format it can be produced quickly. You need to perform a number of protocols and QC procedures on productions to confirm accuracy. As you draw closer to your production deadline, make sure to address sooner rather than later production particulars with your vendor or in-house litigation support department to confirm that you are on the proper path for meeting your deadline. Later in the chapter we'll consider several types of document review applications that provide powerful tools during the production process.

TIP

If you are producing on a rolling basis, remember that the first time you produce always takes longer because many of the protocols and procedures that are used to confirm the accuracy of the production are being performed for the first time. It is very important not to push the review to the very end, leaving very little time for the technical pieces of the production to take place.

Tracking the Production

In many ways, the project management aspect of managing the e-discovery process is the most important piece. Think about it. If your project management team provides thorough and consistent tracking methodologies, your production process runs smoother and more efficiently. However, if your tracking processes are minimal, nonexistent, or inconsistent, how do you really know if your collection, processing, review, and production steps are accurate? Solid project management tactics alleviate stress and provide you with more visibility to the overall process. As it relates directly to your production, tracking will play a critical role in allowing you to defend your practices and will provide you the ability to estimate review times and costs. Tracking the production should not be a daunting task, but depending on your internal or external capabilities it can be difficult. Therefore, it is important to identify the information that should be tracked in the production log, such as filenames, dates sent, recipients, received by, or errors or issues identified by the opposing party.

TIP

Depending on the software and services available to you, you may want to establish some type of docketing request system whereby all team requests are tracked in one database. This will provide for a quick and thorough input and recall of case-specific information from one platform and will provide critical historical recall if members of your team should depart your particular project.

Choosing the Right Tool for the Job

Even though your team is well equipped to accomplish internally many of the tasks at hand, certain aspects of the production might require a more robust and efficient means so as to complete the production on time and under budget. If you need to hire a vendor to perform conversion work on your data or if you must provide a hosting environment for the review and production of your data, some of your biggest questions might be:

- Whom can I trust to do a good job?
- How do I know they're going to do the work correctly?
- How much will it cost?
- If requirements change, will my vendor work with me?
- How good (and experienced) are their project managers and staff?
- Will my data be secure?
- What types of quality controls are in place?

This section is designed to provide you an overview of questions to ask of a vendor about to perform conversions for you as well as production capabilities of hosted solutions.

Data Conversion As It Relates to Production

As critical as it is on the inside of the house to have the right management resources in place, so too is it critical to choose a vendor with the requisite project management and technical experience so as to ensure a deliverable of properly converted data for loading and review whether it is hosted internally or externally. Some items to think about during your initial design meeting with the vendor regarding data conversion might include:

- Address at the conversion design meeting the following specific items and how they will be processed: redlines, track changes, embedded comments in cells, speaker notes, hidden text, hidden worksheets and embedded objects, etc.

- For non-mail message items such as calendar and tasks, work with the vendor to detail how these are ultimately going to be reviewed and produced. For calendar items, will the vendor have the ability to process and tiff (if required) the 'Schedule' tab?

- Do the collected documents contain specialty fonts or logos? If tiffing out for review and/or production, the vendor may need these to tiff and convert properly.

Make sure to document all instructions and notes and work with the vendor to load a test batch first to confirm that all instructions are being followed accordingly.

Hosted Solutions

Hosted document review solutions are found in many flavors these days, but those with production capabilities are still somewhat limited. Although hosted solutions are a popular avenue for e-discovery service providers to pursue, some are slower to build in production capabilities. Therefore, our examples are limited to the solutions available to us at this time, and is in no way meant to detract from other solutions available on the market with possibly similar functionality.

When selecting a hosted solution, which we discussed in Chapter 9, you'll have an obligation to ask about its security, searching, and tagging capabilities. However, when considering a review solution, don't forget to ask about redaction, production, privilege screening, and reporting capabilities. Like any industry driven by technology and people, this one is no different. The same functionality is most likely displayed differently among the many alternative solutions. But in the end, you should have the same results. For the purposes of further explaining some hosted solution capabilities, we prepared examples from CaseLogistix's IndyGo, LexisNexis' Concordance FYI Reviewer, ONSITE[3]'s eView, and FTI Consulting's Ringtail. Although many hosted solutions provide useful production capabilities, the four we selected provide enough of a variety to illustrate the capabilities in the market.

Questions that you should ask of the hosting party include, but are not limited to, the following:

- What viewing options does your review application provide: images, native, native rendering, all?

- How does your review application handle redactions? Are they transparent for the review portion? Will we have the ability to create custom text for the redactions?

- Have your redaction capabilities been tested in court?

- Have there been issues with your redaction coordinates?

- Is there a mechanism in place to automatically redact the associated OCR or extracted text for those documents being redacted and produced with text?

- Can the application provide the mechanism and workflow so as to create the privilege log?

- Does the application have the ability to track productions among multiple parties?

- What production and attribute tags are available?

- How can you ensure that our data will remain secure throughout the process?

- What production "on-the-fly" capabilities does your application offer?

- Can hard-copy documents be scanned and loaded into the same system for review and production?

- Will document-specific endorsements need to be added other than Bates (e.g., confidentiality, etc.)?

NOTE

If specific document-level branding is required (e.g., confidential, highly confidential, etc.), make sure to address this in your review workflow when attributes are being applied individually so that document-level information can be automatically and efficiently burned onto images at the time of production.

CaseLogistix Production Capabilities

CaseLogistix's IndyGo production utility presents users with tabs, organized by production task (see Figure 10.1). Each production sequence begins with the expected required input: production name, export path, document numbering scheme for postback to the database, and general production output options.

Figure 10.1 IndyGo Document Publisher

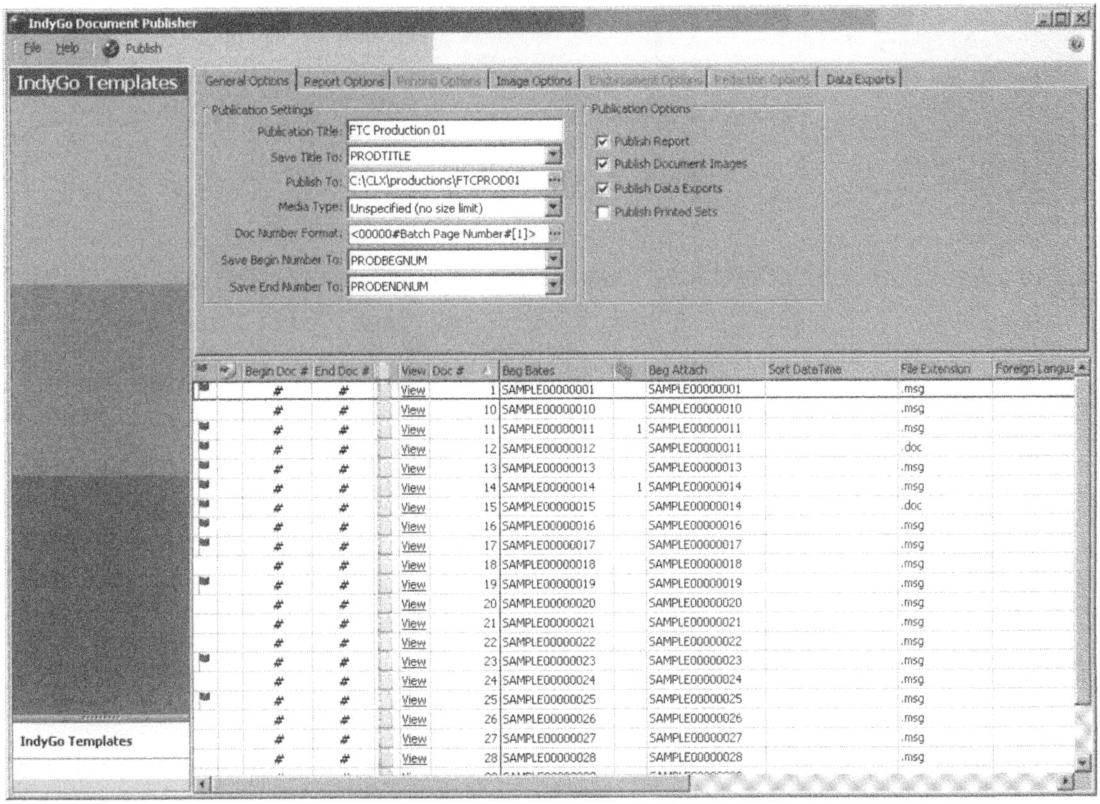

As shown in Figure 10.2, document and page-level files can be numbered differently from the Bates numbers assigned in the production setup. Any PDF or TIFF-based image format can be chosen (single or multi-page, color or black & white, with or without accompanying text).

A nice feature offered by IndyGo is the ability to brand redactions onto the exported images as shown in Figure 10.3.

Figure 10.2 IndyGo Document Publisher Image Options

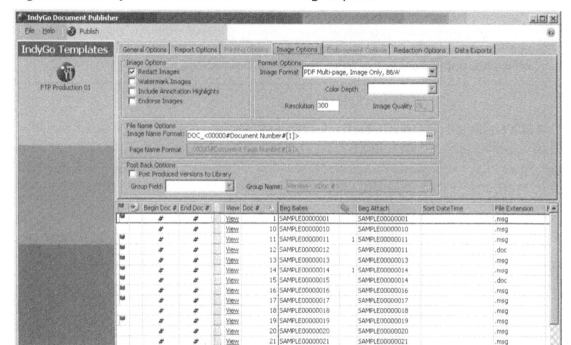

Also worth noting is that accompanying fielded data can be included in the production set. The default output format is the Electronic Discovery Reference Model's (EDRM) XML specification.

Figure 10.3 IndyGo Document Publisher Redaction Options

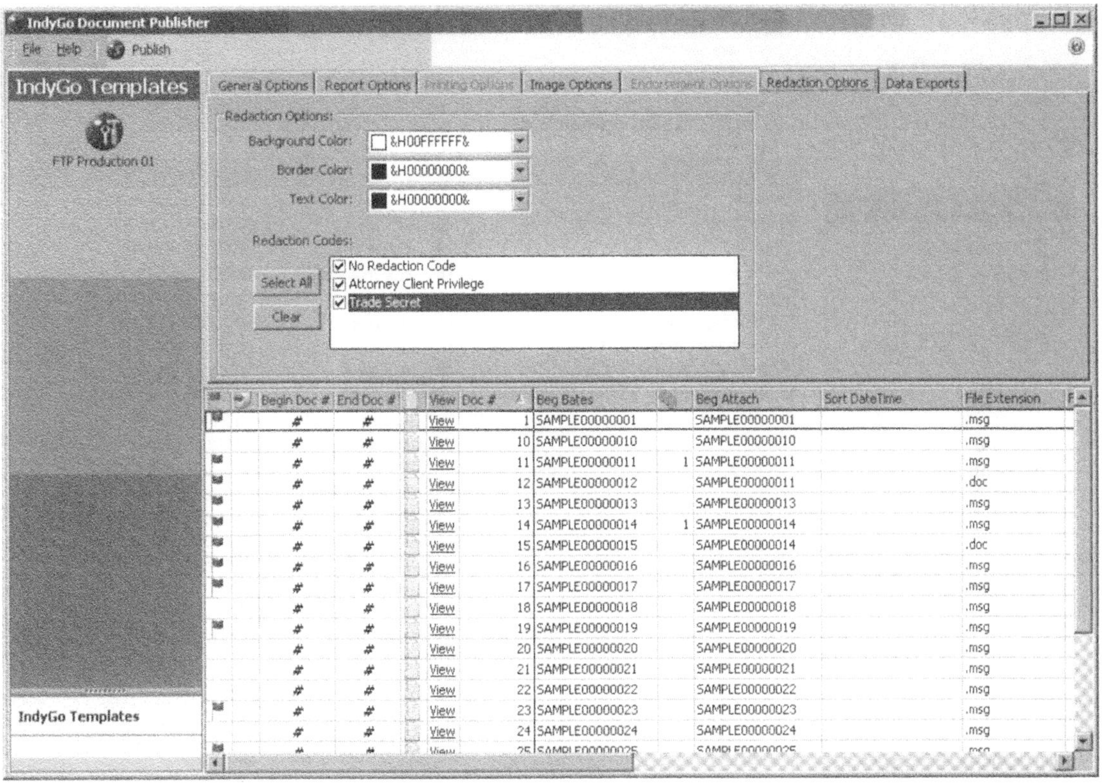

As shown in Figure 10.4, the export directory contains an Images folder, which contains all exported pages (subdivided into media-compliant units for CD, DVD, etc., if need be). If you choose the Report option, the export directory also contains the supporting files necessary for the self-contained production HTML report, which allows recipients to view the documents without any proprietary components, leveraging their system's browser and default image viewer.

Figure 10.4 IndyGo Document Publisher Data Exports

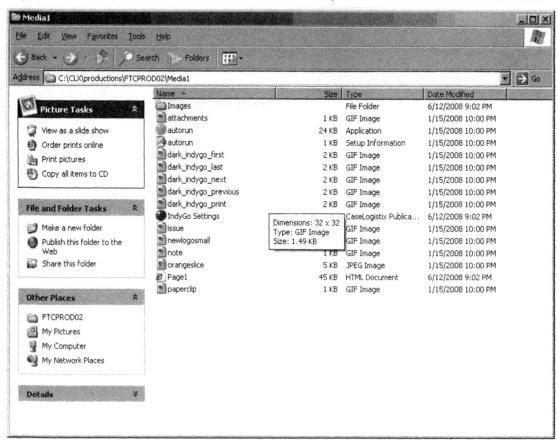

LexisNexis Concordance FYI Reviewer Production Capabilities

As Figure 10.5 shows, you can select headers and footers to permanently place on the four corners of the new images. You can place textual information on any of the four corners of the page. Concordance Image will add a header and footer section to the top and bottom of the image to accommodate any headers or footers.

Figure 10.5 LexisNexis Concordance FYI Reviewer Production – Branding

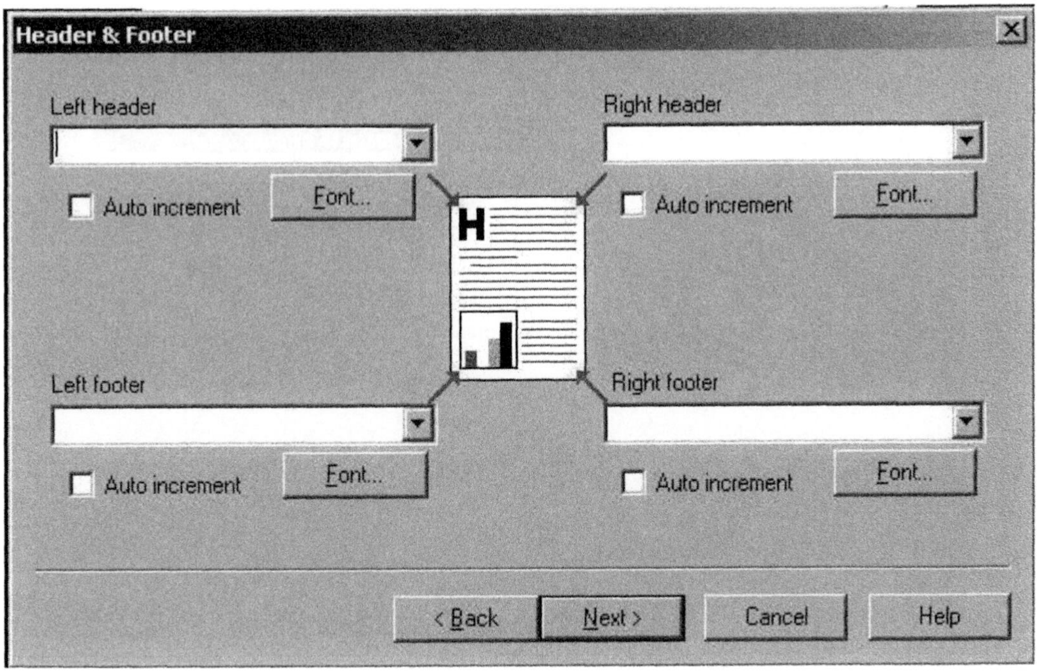

Figure 10.6 shows how a user can select what to do with redlines. There are three options to select from in the drop down list in the production wizard:

- No redlines
- Copy redlines to redlines database
- Burn redlines onto image

Figure 10.6 LexisNexis Concordance FYI Reviewer Production – Redlines

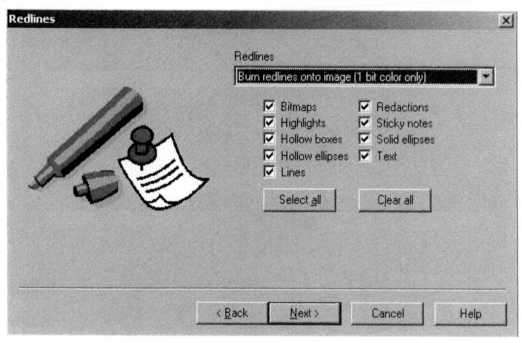

Figure 10.7 shows how you can set options such as the type of image to produce, converting multi-page TIFFs to single page TIFFs, and creating log files.

Figure 10.7 LexisNexis Concordance FYI Reviewer Production – Image Type

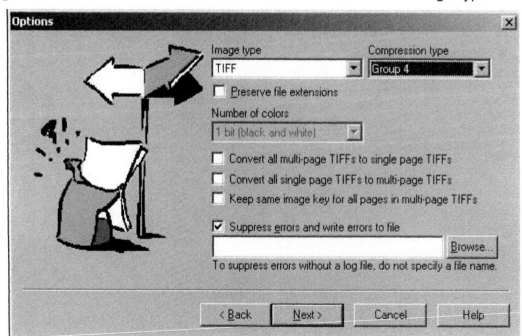

Figure 10.8 shows how you can sequentially renumber the images of a production set. To create production numbers for your images, check the Create production numbers button.

Figure 10.8 LexisNexis Concordance FYI Reviewer Production – Numbering

Figure 10.9 shows how you can create subdirectories and volume directories under the destination directory using the options located on this page. To organize the images in your production, you can have Concordance Image store the images in subdirectories.

Figure 10.9 LexisNexis Concordance FYI Reviewer Production – Volume and Directory Creation

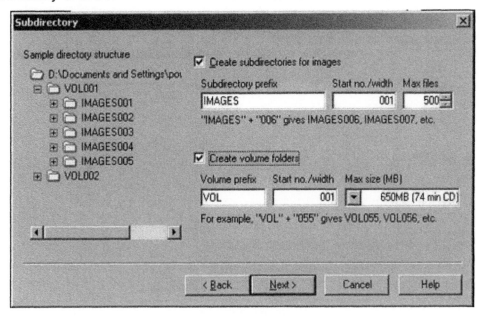

ONSITE³ eView Production Capabilities

As seen in Figure 10.10, eView can do more than provide a seamless transition into the production phase of e-discovery. With eView, you can also manage the entire production process through the same web-based interface as used during document review. eView's Production Management module provides users with the following capabilities and advantages:

- Organize production documents and production data fields from a centralized and secure document repository

- Maintain simultaneous productions for different parties, each with their own unique production rules as needed

- Automate production parameters and specifications with production control rules

- Automatically prevent the same documents from being produced twice within the same production set or across production parties

- Reduce the risk of producing privilege documents using automated error checking

- Include duplicates and parent/child documents in production sets automatically

- Track and view all of the productions for any specific document

- Quickly cycle through all produced images with a view of the original documents side by side

- Lock productions to retain the production as is

- Conduct quality control procedures before finalizing productions

- View production summaries, including production Bates numbering, CD volumes, and production dates

- Add custom production data fields for additional coding as necessary

Figure 10.10 eView Production Screenshot

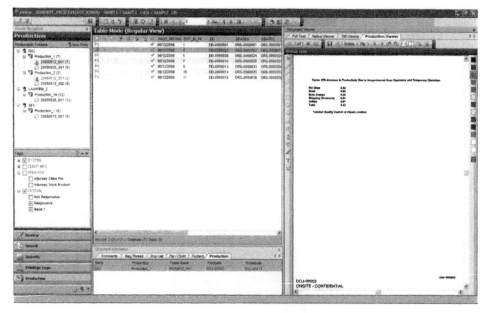

FTI Consulting's Ringtail

Productions provide a workflow within Ringtail Legal for managing the electronic review, organization and production of litigation documents as shown in Figures 10.11 and 10.12.

Once you create a production and add documents, users can add and remove documents or pages of documents from the production set, make notes on pages and code document fields. They can also assign confidentiality labels and apply redactions to the pages of the documents. These labels appear in the footer for each image. As the review progresses, users can monitor the status of the review by marking pages as checked and ready for production. Production search options enable users to view only specified subsets of the production set.

When a production review is completed, and the documents are ready for production, you can use the Production Locker to sort the documents and lock the production. You can sort a production by date, document ID or extra field and you can choose to keep attachments with their source document. The Production Locker first sorts the production into the desired order and then applies new numbers to the document pages.

Once you lock a production, it will remain intact, as produced, unless unlocked by an administrator. Any user with the appropriate passwords can then use the Production Printer to print the production or generate an electronic set of documents.

The Ringtail Production Module can:

- Identify responsive documents in image or native format

- Offers flexible regarding the re-numbering of produced documents

- Allows you to print to paper (imaged files) or rename with production numbers (native files)

- Provides a load file for other common programs

- Web-based locking and unlocking of productions for administrators

- Extended numbering options allow for use any of original (DocID, per-document numbering, per-page numbering, and alpha-numeric text) to build a customized label

- Easier document review using highlights that take advantage of the new option to convert highlights to redactions

- Export data for sharing with external parties as a Ringtail load file, or to other common load file formats

- Include native files—when a Production is exported the native file is saved as a Production Label.

Figure 10.11 FTI Consulting Production Screenshot

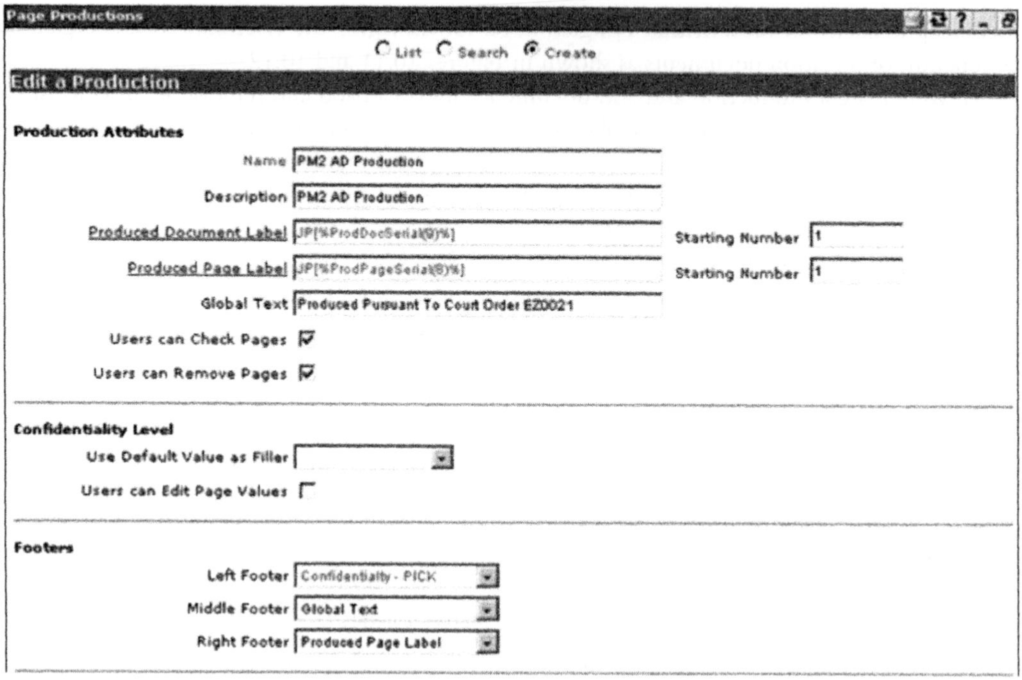

Figure 10.12 FTI Consulting Production Screenshot

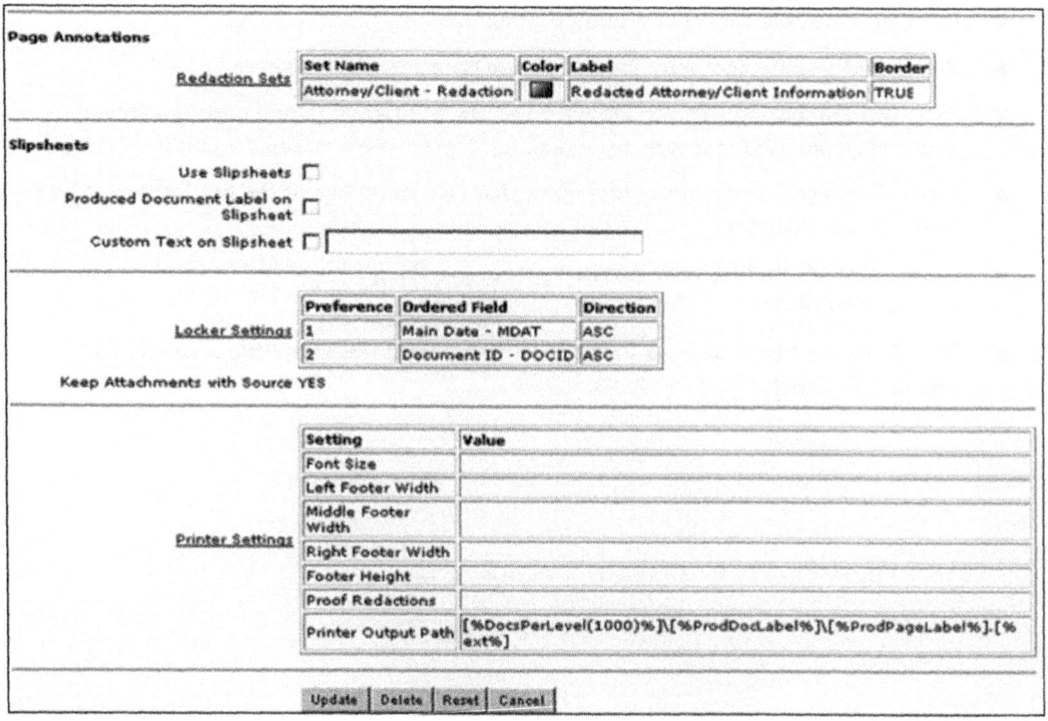

Privilege Considerations

As in any document production, it is important that the team establish a process and select the appropriate tools to ensure that "privileged" information is not produced to the opposing party. There are two primary types of privilege that must be protected: attorney-client communications and work product materials, although there are other types of privilege – e.g. doctor-patient, accountant privilege, tax advisor privilege – that may apply in particular jurisdictions and cases. Rather than provide copies of privileged documents to the opposing party, a privilege log is prepared that identifies each privileged document. In most jurisdictions, the privilege log must provide the following information for each withheld document: Bates number, author, recipient, date, description of the document that shows that it is in fact privileged, and the type or types of privilege claimed. Because privilege determinations require the use of legal judgment, attorneys will usually make final privilege determinations and draft the privilege log.

Courts and parties have expressed concern about the time and cost involved in reviewing for privilege and preparing privilege logs. In some cases, parties may enter into an agreement or the court may enter an order that protects them in the event they accidentally produce a privileged document to the other side. Under these agreements or orders, the producing party can demand the return of the inadvertently produced privileged document and the receiving party is required to return it and cannot use it. Such agreements or orders do not allow a party to conduct a haphazard or incomplete review for privilege. Some courts have found that a party that failed to conduct a careful privilege review lost the right to claim privilege for privileged documents they produced because the production was not "inadvertent."

There are search technologies and techniques that can be used to help identify potentially privileged documents, but even the best of these technologies cannot identify each and every privileged document. Human review is almost always necessary as a supplement to technological culling. Technology can also be used to facilitate the preparation of privilege logs. For instance, metadata fields can be used to populate author, recipient and date fields on the log. Once again, however, human review of the underlying documents and the draft log is necessary to make sure that the objective data is accurate so that the opposing party cannot claim that the underlying document is not – or should not be treated as – privileged. When using technological solutions to identify privileged documents, it may be useful to discuss the technology and search methodology with the other party so that there is general agreement on the processes to be used. This can be very helpful in averting time consuming and costly challenges by the opposing party.

Receiving Productions from an Opposing Party

While we've spent a lot of time in this chapter detailing how to properly staff, manage and plan for a successful production of your own documents, we also need to address what to do about data that you will be receiving.

As mentioned earlier, you should really work with the other side or government agency to test a sample set of production documents to confirm that everything is loading properly for you both and that all of the data that was negotiated to be produced is being produced. This incredibly important step will undoubtedly reduce stress and the potential for wasted time. It is also worth noting how important it is to involve the right folks to address and resolve issues if they are found. This one step will go far in reducing wasted time, effort and expense for everyone concerned.

TIP

It's a good idea to search your production set for privilege terms *before* running your final production to address and account for any questionable documents that may have been incorrectly marked during the review.

Summary

The purpose of this chapter was to create a template for you and your team to further understand production requirements. Additionally, it aimed to provide a guideline of the aforementioned practices into a standard for you. Although it does not include all of the answers, it does provide a starting point and ways to further explore and possibly improve your current production capabilities. Probably the most critical point to take away in this summary is to make sure to involve the right people immediately and to keep them involved in your project. As with any successful project, the time spent on proper planning—in the beginning and throughout—is critical to the successful outcome of not only the production, but also the matter as a whole. Also, when assigning or agreeing to deadlines, always make sure to build in enough time to perform not only the steps necessary to produce but the time to perform quality control checks as well. While all time and effort leading up to identifying the documents for production is critical, so too is the time spent on the technical and quality control aspects of preparing the production because once those documents leave your hands, the time and effort spent to recall inadvertently produced documents is something that no one wants to do.

Solutions Fast Track

Production: Federal and State Rules

- ☑ Understand the Federal Rules of Civil Procedure meet-and-confer process and how it applies to productions, specifically Rule 34 and 26(f).

- ☑ Depending on the court, federal or state, ensure that you are negotiating production formats as early as possible.

- ☑ Make sure to properly prepare for your meet and confer and cooperate accordingly as you will gain more for your client if you treat this as a collaborative, rather than an adversarial, process.

Getting the Right Folks Involved

- ☑ Ensure that your team has a senior-level stakeholder involved who is part of the decision-making process.

- ☑ Align a team that is diverse and able to provide the skill sets you desire for a positive discovery output.

- ☑ Create a project plan, work through bottlenecks, and update senior management/stakeholders as often as possible or required. Surprises are not a good thing.

Production Practicalities

- ☑ Never lose sight of the fact that productions must be useful and cost-effective.

- ☑ Build in time and setup processes to ensure that a privilege review can be completed before the production.

☑ Make sure you build in enough time for the proper QC protocols to be run on your production, especially the first time. Don't assume that just because your data exists electronically it can be produced quickly.

☑ Because the production volume could dramatically change during the review, it is very important to discuss the basis of production costs up-front to make sure that costs are fair for both the client and the vendor should assumptions dramatically change.

Data Conversion As It Relates to Production

☑ Confirm that the vendor chosen to convert and/or host data has the requisite experience to properly convert and manage all types of data.

☑ Never say, "Just do it like you did last time" to a vendor. Always have a design meeting to answer specific questions regarding the processing and conversion of data for hosting, review, and production.

☑ Design meetings are not only for technologists and staff members. Members of the legal team need to take an active role in the decision-making process with guidance from their litigation support staff.

Frequently Asked Questions

Q: I've been a paralegal for a long time and have years of experience producing documents in hard copy, but I just joined a team that is beginning a new e-discovery case and they asked me to manage it. What can I do to provide the best help?

A: Great question! First, don't panic! After that, quickly meet with your team to make sure everyone is on the same page regarding deadlines and requirements and start to learn those amended rules concerning e-discovery! Also, know that you can't do it alone, so get the proper folks involved with the requisite experience. E-discovery has its own rules and procedures and paper-based rules just won't transfer over!

Q: I'm managing a case and we are required to produce metadata. Don't I have to produce the native files to produce metadata?

A: Although producing native files for some applications might be very useful (assuming you negotiated the same for documents being produced to you), producing native files just because you negotiated metadata production does not necessarily need to take place. As an alternative, you could produce images with an associated data file containing the negotiated and agreed upon specific metadata information.

Q: Is it really important to discuss how my production is going to be sent—on CDs, DVDs or hard drive?

A: Absolutely! Depending on the format (and volume) of production, your vendor or litigation support department could spend hours and hours just copying data to the network. For example, if opposing counsel were producing 1 million TIFF images on CD, they would need roughly 40 discs to complete that production. You would then have to administratively copy 40 CDs to the network, which takes a great deal of time, whereas 1 million TIFF images delivered on a hard drive can be copied over quickly to the network in the background with very limited overview. That, and hard drives are fairly inexpensive, too!

Index

Printed and bound by CPI Group (UK) Ltd, Croydon, CR0 4YY

03/10/2024

01040341-0015